Fun with the Family™ Utah

Praise for the Fun with the Family™ series

"Enables parents to turn family travel into an exploration."
—Alexandra Kennedy, Editor, *Family Fun*

"Bound to lead you and your kids to fun-filled days,
those times that help compose the
memories of childhood."
—Dorothy Jordon, Publisher, *Family Travel Times*

Help Us Keep This Guide Up to Date

Every effort has been made by the author and editors to make this guide as accurate and useful as possible. However, many changes can occur after a guide is published—establishments close, phone numbers change, hiking trails are rerouted, facilities come under new management, etc.

We would love to hear from you concerning your experiences with this guide and how you feel it could be improved and be kept up to date. While we may not be able to respond to all comments and suggestions, we'll take them to heart, and we'll make certain to share them with the author. Please send your comments and suggestions to the following address:

The Globe Pequot Press
Reader Response/Editorial Department
P.O. Box 480
Guilford, CT 06437

Or you may e-mail us at: editorial@GlobePequot.com

Thanks for your input, and happy travels!

INSIDERS'GUIDE®

FUN WITH THE FAMILY™ SERIES

fun WITH the Family™

UTAH

HUNDREDS OF IDEAS FOR DAY TRIPS WITH THE KIDS

MICHAEL RUTTER

FOURTH EDITION

INSIDERS'GUIDE®

GUILFORD, CONNECTICUT
AN IMPRINT OF THE GLOBE PEQUOT PRESS

INSIDERS'GUIDE®

Copyright © 1997, 2000, 2002, 2004 by The Globe Pequot Press

All rights reserved. No part of this book may be reproduced or transmitted in any form by any means, electronic or mechanical, including photocopying and recording, or by any information storage and retrieval system, except as may be expressly permitted by the 1976 Copyright Act or by the publisher. Requests for permission should be made in writing to The Globe Pequot Press, P.O. Box 480, Guilford, Connecticut 06437.

Insiders' Guide is a registered trademark of The Globe Pequot Press.
Fun with the Family is a trademark of The Globe Pequot Press.

Text design by Nancy Freeborn and Linda Loiewski
Maps by Rusty Nelson © The Globe Pequot Press
Spot photography throughout © Photodisc

ISSN 1540-2150
ISBN 0-7627-2982-1

Manufactured in the United States of America
Fourth Edition/First Printing

To my good friend Marie Burt.
Thanks for your help on this project.

UTAH

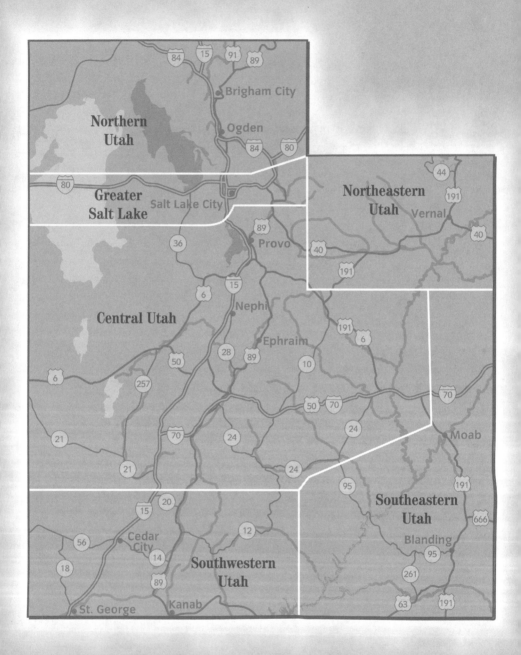

Contents

About the Author

M ichael Rutter is a freelance writer who lives in Orem, Utah, with his wife, Shari. They have two charming children and a very spoiled cat. Michael is the author of more than thirty books (including *Utah Off The Beaten Path, Fly Fishing Made Easy,* and *Camping Made Easy* with The Globe Pequot Press). Michael and crew spend three or four months a year on the road. A good deal of that time is spent exploring Utah in his Aero Cub trailer. When he's not traveling or writing, he teaches English at Brigham Young University.

Introduction

Welcome to Utah!

Utah is a land of wonder, a country of never-ending vistas, a place with every type of landscape (short of an ocean) you can imagine. It's a land of tall mountains, fruited plains, and painted deserts. Utah has the "greatest snow on earth" and the finest sunsets this side of paradise. It's a land of geologic wonders, you can be sure. But it's also a land where family life is valued above all else.

In Utah we're lucky and we know it. We have 84,990 square miles so densely filled with natural wonders that a lifetime isn't enough time to explore the mysteries. We have dozens of mountain ranges, including one that appears to float above the ground, another that beats a mysterious underground noise, and one that we like to call the steepest range in the world. We have vast deserts crowded with psychedelic twists of red and vermilion rock. We have other deserts paved with white salt that sparkles as far as the eye can see. We have a million acres of farmland and a million more where horses, sheep, and cattle graze. We have snow-fed mountain lakes that the hottest summer sun can't warm, and an inland sea that creates its own weather. We have tortoises and shrimp and cacti that are found nowhere outside our borders. No matter how many trails we hike or back roads we explore or flowers we identify, there are other wonders around the next bend, waiting for our discovery.

But it doesn't stop there. There are the people of Utah, who are just as diverse and wonderful. Don't overlook the history and wildlife museums that document our legacy—or the dance, music, and art. We support the arts with an enthusiasm not found in many larger and more urban settings. Not surprisingly, Utah's big cities offer thousands of fun and educational activities. But small towns hold some of the best secrets—Helper, Panguitch, Cedar City, Boulder, and Springdale are just a few that have excellent theaters and museums waiting to be discovered.

It should be noted that Utahns are zealous about their mid-July holiday, and an unsuspecting visitor who wanders into the state on July 24 might well wonder what is going on. The first Mormons (Latter-day Saints) entered the Salt Lake Valley on this day in 1847, and it has become the official state holiday, eclipsing statehood day. Weeks of celebration precede the actual holiday: Rodeos, pageants, parades, and craft fairs abound. The wealth of events are too numerous to mention in the text of this book, but a call to any local city office will produce specific information.

A few words of caution: Even experienced Utahns sometimes become victims of unpredictable elements in this part of the world. The hottest summer day can turn into a freezing summer night, and a beautiful winter day might be hiding a storm behind the next bend. The happiest travelers will be prepared. Summer hikers in Utah, especially in the southern part of the state, are advised to carry snacks and water—a gallon per person, per day.

As a writer, I've traveled the United States and Canada extensively with my family. However, the Rutter clan agrees that the best vacations are those close to home. We believe that the most interesting, exhilarating, fun, and yes, weird, times we've had have been in our own backyard. We wish you the happiest of travels.

For this guide considerable effort has been made to provide the most accurate information available at the time of publication, but readers are advised always to check ahead, since prices, seasonal openings and closings, and other travel-related factors do change over time. Neither the author nor the publisher can be held responsible for the experiences of readers while traveling.

Please note that where the rates for attractions do not specify adult or child, the cost is for both adults and children.

Attractions

$	up to $5.00
$$	from $6.00 to $10.00
$$$	from $11.00 to $15.00
$$$$	$16.00 and up

Lodging *(cost per room)*

$	up to $50
$$	from $51 to $75
$$$	from $76 to $99
$$$$	$100 and up

Meals

$	most selections under $10
$$	most $10 to $15
$$$	most $16 to $20
$$$$	most over $20

The prices, rates, and hours listed in this guidebook were confirmed at press time. We recommend, however, that you call establishments to obtain current information before traveling.

Attractions Key

The following is a key to the icons found throughout the text.

SWIMMING		FOOD	
BOATING / BOAT TOUR		LODGING	
HISTORIC SITE		CAMPING	
HIKING / WALKING		MUSEUMS	
FISHING		PERFORMING ARTS	
BIKING		SPORTS/ATHLETICS	
AMUSEMENT PARK		PICNICKING	
HORSEBACK RIDING		PLAYGROUND	
SKIING /WINTER SPORTS		SHOPPING	
PARK		PLANTS /GARDENS /NATURE TRAILS	
ANIMAL VIEWING		FARMS	

Northern Utah

I n this chapter, we will explore the busy urban area just north of Salt Lake City. We will continue through the less-populated farming and ranching communities that extend to Utah's northern and northeastern borders.

Some of the major recreation areas of the Great Salt Lake are here, and the wildlife-watching opportunities created by the salty lake marshes are unparalleled. Farther north, your family will find many of Utah's best-loved outdoor alpine adventure sites, including three ski resorts.

Look for Utah's premier amusement park as well as a frontier settlement that re-creates the mountain-man era. Northern Utah's dozens of museums hold collections ranging from Egyptian mummies to rocket engines. Read on to learn about other unique attractions: a park that commemorates a transcontinental railroad, the spot for famous ice cream cones, and one of the largest free-roaming buffalo herds in the world.

Bountiful

Bountiful is a quiet community just north of Salt Lake off Interstate 15. The town is nestled into the rugged Wasatch Mountains, which are to the east; the Great Salt Lake is to the west.

Skyline Drive (all ages)
The drive can be accessed near the LDS Temple at 640 South Bountiful Boulevard.

Any family will love an adventurous drive that offers one of the best bird's-eye views of the Great Salt Lake. The Skyline Drive from Bountiful to Farmington is a great example of the beautiful roads that travel through many of Utah's mountains. There are many picnic sites and nature walks along the way. The drive is not fully paved, and parts of it may require a four-wheel-drive vehicle. Even then, it is driveable only from May through October. Ask locally for road conditions before starting out. One of the neat things about the drive is that it also provides opportunities for winter recreation. In winter my family enjoys cross-country skiing and snowmobiling on this route. The grounds of the LDS **Bountiful Temple,** near the beginning of the drive, are open to the public.

NORTHERN UTAH

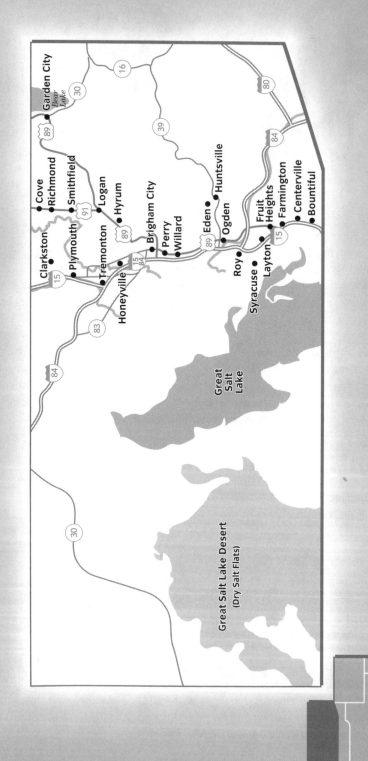

The Bountiful Davis Art Center (all ages)

745 South Main Street; (801) 292–0367; www.bdac.org. Open Monday from 5:00 to 9:00 P.M., Tuesday through Friday 10:00 A.M. to 6:00 P.M., and Saturday 2:00 to 5:00 P.M. Admission is **free.**

The Bountiful Art Center features traveling exhibits of national artists. Also of special interest, each August the Art Center hosts **Bountiful Summerfest International,** in the Bountiful City Park at 400 North 200 West. The festival features international dance, ethnic foods, crafts, and a children's art yard.

Michael's
TopPicks for fun in Northern Utah

1. Antelope Island State Park; (801) 773–2941

2. Bear River Migratory Bird Refuge; (435) 723–5887

3. Browning Firearms Museum; (801) 629–8535

4. The Logan LDS Temple; (435) 752–3611

5. Logan Canyon Scenic Byway; (435) 755–3620

6. Transcontinental Railroad National Byway; (801) 471–2209

7. The Farmington Bay Waterfowl Management Area; (801) 451–7386

8. Hardware Ranch, Hyrum; (435) 735–6206

9. The Festival of the American West, Logan; (800) 225–FEST

10. Reenactment of the Driving of the Golden Spike, Golden Spike National Historic Site; (435) 471–2209

Bountiful Recreation Center (all ages)

150 West 600 North; (801) 298–6220. Pool use or skating $.

The Bountiful Recreation Center is a popular year-round destination. A swimming pool is bubbled in winter and open to the skies in summer. Public swimming hours vary; call for times. Young skaters can also perform leaps and twirls on the huge rink here. Again, public skating times vary. Call for the rec center's hours.

Where to Eat

Casa Melinda. 3100 South Highway 89; (801) 298–1211. Mexican. $$

China Platter. 547 West 2600 South; (801) 295–0975. Chinese. $–$$

Que Pasa Mexican Grill. 512 West 750 South; (801) 298–9000. Mexican. $

Centerville

Centerville is located north of Bountiful along I–15. Somewhat smaller than its southern neighbors Salt Lake and Bountiful, Centerville offers a tranquil, rural atmosphere that can be quite relaxing.

Rodger's Memorial Theatre (all ages)
292 Pages Lane; (801) 298–1302; www.theatreutah.com. Tickets $$$.

The theater is very popular with families because of its tradition of wholesome dramas and musicals, performed live on selected weeknights and every Friday and Saturday. Special children's plays are performed on some Saturday afternoons. You definitely will not want to miss the opportunity to take in one of these productions. Ticket prices may vary. Call ahead of time for ticket information and reservations.

Farmington

Known as the home of Lagoon, Farmington has much more to offer than amusement parks. The natural wonders found in this northern Utah community may even be more enjoyable and exciting than the wild roller-coaster rides.

Lake Bonneville—an Ancient Lake

The Great Salt Lake is what is left of old Lake Bonneville.

At one time, Lake Bonneville was nearly 35,000 square miles. It was also a couple of miles deep! This lake is technically a *pluvial* lake. In the days of yore, many thousands of years ago, there was a great deal of rainfall that caused it to fill.

About 10,000 years ago, the climate changed, becoming drier. There was no longer an outlet— or as many feeder streams. Since there was no outlet for the salt, the water became salty.

Lagoon Amusement Park (all ages)

Find Lagoon by taking the Lagoon Drive exit (327) from I–15, at the junction with U.S. Highway 89. Open daily Memorial Day through Labor Day and weekends April through September. Call (800) 748–5246 or go to www.lagoonpark.com for more information. Admission $$$$.

If there is a premier "groovy kid place" in Utah, this just might be it. For more than fifty years, Lagoon has offered Utahns good times and big thrills. It ranks with the best of other big city amusement parks in terms of pleasant surroundings, beautiful gardens, and, of course, exciting rides. Featured heart stoppers include the looped Fire Dragon roller coaster, the 150-foot-drop Sky Coaster, and the new Top Eliminator Dragster, where riders can simulate a race down a four-lane strip and reach speeds of up to 75 miles per hour in 2.8 seconds. Another new ride, the Spider, is the first spinning roller coaster in North America, spinning riders in all directions as they go down a slalom track and a 360-degree turn. Three other roller coasters and dozens more rides are also part of the fun. An entire section of the park is set aside for smaller children, with pint-sized rides that move at a gentle pace. Food stands and carnival games line the walkways, along with an unending array of souvenirs to buy. Strolling singers and regularly scheduled grandstand acts provide entertainment, along with "Summer Rhythm" stage shows. An all-day pass (about $30) provides admission to the park as well as **Lagoon-A-Beach,** one of Utah's largest water parks, and **Pioneer Village,** a re-created Western town that features Wild West shoot-em-ups and other excitement. A 200-site campground is open early spring to late fall; call (800) 748–5246, ext. 3101, for reservations.

If you are in town on an October weekend, enjoy Frightmares, where all of Lagoon is Halloween themed. Rides are decked out in orange and black finery. Creatures walk around the midway, and there are various mazes and labyrinths for the whole family.

Utah Botanical Gardens (all ages)

Located just past Lagoon off I–15 in Kaysville; (435) 797–1984. Open year-round. Admission is free.

These beautiful gardens showcase the flora of northern Utah. Ongoing experiments in plant development are conducted by Utah State University students, and visitors are welcome to enjoy the fruits of their research any day of the year during daylight hours. You will enjoy the tours given each Wednesday at 10:00 A.M., May through September. The gardens are undergoing some changes, and their location may change within the next couple of years. Be sure to call for updates and more information.

Farmington Bay Waterfowl Management Area (all ages)

Follow Glover Lane to 1325 West Glover Lane; (801) 451–3395. Open daily from 8:00 A.M. to 5:00 P.M. except during the fall. Admission is free.

My children love to actively participate in wildlife activities, and the Farmington Bay Waterfowl Management Area is a perfect place to fuel their interest in nature. The area is one of the places along the Great Salt Lake shoreline set aside especially for birds. Your children will love this wonderfully tranquil place, alive with pelicans, cranes, herons, grebes, and eagles. Signs in the area explain the surrounding geology and help your children to identify the birds. Bring binoculars, and prepare to enjoy this bird-watching mecca.

Where to Eat

Pizza Place. 7 East State Street; (801) 451–6000. $

Fruit Heights

Fruit Heights may be small, but there is no shortage of amusements in this town northeast of Farmington along U.S. Highway 89. Fruit Heights is sure to win your love with its hospitality and fun-loving environment.

Cherry Hill Campground (all ages)
Just off U.S. Highway 89 at its junction with Utah Highway 273, at 1325 South Main; (801) 451–5379; www.cherry-hill.com. Open daily from early spring to late fall. Admission $–$$, camping $.

Right in the middle of this small town is a fun getaway with every type of entertainment imaginable. Cherry Hill Campground is an authentic fruit farm/destination resort. You'll find miniature "adventure golf," a wild water park, batting cages, game rooms, a swimming pool, and picnic pavilions here . . . and yes, camping, in one of 250 shaded campsites. Young children will love "hamster haven," and your whole family will enjoy the summertime outdoor theater. Call Cherry Hill for information and reservations.

Layton

Layton, north of Farmington along I–15, is quite similar to the other communities found in northern Utah. It offers various forms of entertainment while also maintaining a laid-back, small-town atmosphere.

Layton Surf N Swim (all ages)
Located at 465 North 275 East; (801) 546–8588. Admission $.

If you're in need of a summer cool-off, the Surf N Swim's Wild Wave just might fill the bill. In summer a public pool supplies calm water, while the adjacent Wild Wave provides the thrills. In winter, one of the pools is enclosed and remains open for swimmers. Call for hours and more information.

Fast
Utah Facts

- Utah has the highest literacy rate of any state in the country.
- Utah has been nicknamed the "Crossroads of the West" because of the steady flow of traffic across the state. This traffic can be explained by Utah's central location in the heavily traveled western United States.
- There are nearly 100,000 acres of mixed forest in Utah.
- Utah hosts two wild, roaming buffalo herds. One can be found in the Henry Mountains of southern Utah, the other on Antelope Island in the middle of the Great Salt Lake.
- In 1979, the Jazz moved to Utah, bringing professional basketball back to this state. The Jazz currently play in the Delta Center, in downtown Salt Lake City.

Where to Eat

Chili's Grill and Bar. 1970 North Woodland Park Drive; (801) 774–8225. $$

Syracuse

Located northwest of Layton right next to the Great Salt Lake, Syracuse serves as a gateway to your adventures on and around this natural wonder.

Antelope Island State Park (all ages)
Take exit 335 from I–15 and follow Utah Highway 108 for 7 miles. Campgrounds are open during the warm-weather months. Call (801) 773–2941 for information and reservations. Vehicles $$, per person $.

Antelope Island State Park is the only place of its kind in all the world. This 28,000-acre island lies regally in the middle of Great Salt Lake and is a refuge for millions of shorebirds on their way to and from points north and south. Other wildlife have found a home here as well, including bobcats, mule deer, coyotes, and antelope. A herd of 600 bison roam the island, offering your family a first-rate view of these rare animals in a natural setting. If your family enjoys bird-watching as well as up-close sightings of other interesting animals, this is the place for you. An annual **bison roundup** is open to the public every fall. Your family can experience real ranch action when the animals are herded by cowboys to a central area and given an assembly-line vet checkup. Wildlife watching may be the best reason to visit the island, but sun lovers also enjoy the excellent white-sand beaches here. **Bridger Beach** has cabanas, picnic tables, and showers for day visitors and a primitive campground for overnighters. White Rock Bay offers a primitive camping area for groups. Antelope Island also has hiking, biking, and horse trails. Take a drive on the island's road system and stake out your own secluded spot for stunning sunsets and sunrises over the salty water; the view from any place on the island is beautiful and unique. Part of the fun of a trip to this park is getting there. The island is connected to the shore by a 7-mile, narrow causeway, and once you leave land you will experience a flying sensation as you become entirely surrounded by water. Biking the causeway is especially fun for older children, but can be a long, hot trip in the summertime.

Antelope Island and Buffalo: **Flavor of the Old West**

Buffalo are the symbol of the Old West. Utah has two herds of wild buffalo for animal lovers to enjoy. One herd is in the southern part of the state. Another herd is a hop, skip, and a jump from Salt Lake City, on Antelope Island.

In addition to the regular roundup, there is a Children's Roundup around the first of October. The roundup is young-folk friendly and a great activity if you are in the Beehive State during the fall. You can get a buffalo-eye view as the shaggy beasts are vaccinated and weighed.

Get your kids involved and be a part of an event that, for the most part, is only in the history books. This is one of the most unique experiences you'll find. Call Antelope Island State Park (801–773–2941) for dates and details.

Roy

Roy borders Ogden on the south and, geographically, is a rural extension of that larger city. Don't confuse the two, however—Roy has its own identity and plenty of attractions suitable for your family.

Hill Aerospace Museum (all ages)

7961 Wardleigh Road, Hill Air Force Base (follow the signs from I–15, exit 341); (801) 777–6818; www.hill.af.mil/museum/info/museum.html. Open daily from 9:00 A.M. to 4:15 P.M. Admission is free.

While my children tend to prefer the outdoors, others are fascinated by science and technology. For those children, the museum is well worth a visit, and its collection of antique planes, missiles, and helicopters will captivate the entire family. The museum is devoted to the history of our national air power, and its "exhibits" are displayed in a huge indoor hangar and outdoor airfield. Self-guided walking tours will give your family a close-up view of famous war planes, including the SR-71 Blackbird, the B-17 Flying Fortress, and the P-51D Mustang. A restored World War II chapel and barracks are also on-site.

Roy Historical Museum (all ages)

Located just north of the Hill Aerospace Museum on the same frontage road, at 5550 South 1700 West; (801) 776–3626. Open Tuesday through Saturday from 10:00 A.M. to 4:30 P.M. and Sunday from 12:30 to 4:30 P.M. Admission is free.

The Roy Historical Museum is uniquely housed in a log cabin designed after those of the early Utah pioneers. The museum's large collection of pioneer artifacts is designed to both impress and amuse your children as they learn about the first residents of the area.

Where to Eat

5 Star Restaurant. 5676 South 1900 West; (801) 776–9366. $$–$$$

Ogden

This is one of Utah's "big three" cities. Along with Salt Lake City and Provo, Ogden is a strong anchor for the Wasatch Front population. However, Ogden still retains a portion of the small-town atmosphere that makes it a very pleasant and inviting place to visit. Located in the shadow of the Wasatch Mountains, Ogden's earliest recorded events were gatherings of mountain men—the rugged, pelt-covered hunters who trapped and traded fur animals. In wintertime, it seems, mountain men grouped together, "took Indian wives," and settled down in makeshift housing for several months of tanning hides, playing games of skill, and generally resting up. Ogden is named after one of these men, Peter Skene Ogden, and this valley, now called Weber County, was once called Ogden's Hole.

Fort Buenaventura State Park (all ages)

2450 A Avenue. Open daily from 8:00 A.M. to 8:00 P.M. April through September; 8:00 A.M. to 5:00 P.M. March, October, and November. Call (801) 399–8099 for information; (800) 322–3770 for day use and group camp reservations. Group campsites are $100 minimum. Admission $.

Ogden's first Anglo settler was Miles Goodyear, who in 1846 planted a garden, built a cabin and shelter for his animals, and constructed some outbuildings to house his mountain-men compatriots. His settlement has been re-created on its original site, and set aside as a landmark—Fort Buenaventura State Park. The settlement has been carefully and accurately reconstructed from archaeological research. You'll find no modern shortcuts to construction here—wooden pegs serve as nails, and tenons lash together wooden joints. The actual number and placement of cabins and outbuildings is just as Goodyear planned it. Expect to be greeted by guides dressed in 1840s garb. Mountain men will explain what life was like back when this spot was surrounded by wilderness. Artifacts from the era are displayed and interpreted. Timing your visit around a "rendezvous" celebration will double your family's fun. During the rendezvous, modern-day mountain men gather here, setting up tents, spinning yarns, playing games, and showing off the skills that were vital to "real" mountain men.

Fast Utah Facts

- Utah's nickname is the Beehive State.
- Utah's motto is "Industry."
- Utah's state bird is the seagull.
- Utah's state flower is the sego lily.
- Utah's state tree is the blue spruce.

Daughters of the Utah Pioneers Museum (all ages)

1066 East 5600 South; (801) 393–4460. Open Monday through Saturday during the summer months from 9:00 A.M. to 5:00 P.M. Admission is free.

Miles Goodyear's actual cabin has been moved from its original site to Ogden's **LDS Temple Square.** The cabin is part of the Daughters of the Utah Pioneers Museum, which is also home to numerous historical items and other memorabilia from the days of the pioneers.

Union Station (all ages)

This building houses a number of museums. Located in the center of town at 2501 Wall Avenue; (801) 629–8535; www.theunionstation.org. Open Monday through Saturday from 10:00 A.M. to 5:00 P.M.; during summer additional hours Sunday from 11:00 A.M. to 3:00 P.M. Admission $.

The growth of the railroad played a large part in the development of northern Utah. Ogden's population grew dramatically both in size and diversity after the railroad was completed. The valley proved an ideal junction as a connector for western cities in all directions. The railroad brought stockyards and industry as well as jobs and money to the area. An architectural tribute to the railroad era remains at Union Station, an imposing building found in downtown Ogden. Until late 1996, Union Station operated as a train depot. Now it is home to a wonderfully diverse mix of museums and shops chronicling Ogden's past. Several of these are dedicated to railroading: The **Utah State Railroad Museum** is here as well as the **Wattis-Dumke Model Railroad Museum** and the **Eccles Railroad Center.** In these collections you will see an exact model replica of the 1,776-mile transcontinental route, and the largest historic railroad display in the world, featuring an outdoor pavilion that covers a Centennial locomotive, a diesel locomotive, several cabooses, and more. John M. Browning, an Ogden native, made a fortune in the firearms business, and his legacy is exhibited in the **Browning Firearms Museum** here. You and your family will learn all about the evolution of the firearms industry as you look at both original and reproduction models of the world-famous firearms. The **Browning-Kimball Classic Car Museum,** also located in Union Station, is a collection of classic and antique automobiles from the 1930s. The **Myra Powell Art Gallery,** the **Natural History Museum,** and a reproduction of an authentic Japanese tea room round out the family of museums at Union Station.

Browning Firearms Museum

There are few museums like this one. It's a once-in-a-lifetime experience, so plan on taking your time. If you like guns or are interested in the development of firearms, this is an interesting place in which to get lost. Plan on spending some time wandering back and forth between the exhibits. Mr. Browning was certainly one of the great inventors in our history.

Young children will likely be ready to leave before you are. If you're not finished, take a break and come back for another look. We usually figure a little less than half a day.

Historic Twenty-fifth Street (all ages) 🏛
In downtown Ogden, east of the museums at Union Station.

A few steps east of Union Station is yet another celebration of Ogden's past, the shops and restaurants of Twenty-fifth Street. A hundred years ago this street was notorious for its bars and brothels, but today it is home to a much calmer scene. Restored buildings house antiques stores and boutiques. The restaurants will delight the shoppers in your family. If your children enjoy renovated architecture, take time to visit **Peery's Egyptian Theater** at 2415 Washington Boulevard. The ceiling here is "atmospheric," and during performances the sun "rises" and "sets" across its width. To arrange a tour, call (801) 395–3227 or see www.peerysegyptiantheater.com.

How Utah Streets Are **Organized**

While traveling through Utah, I'm sure you've noticed that our streets are quite commonplace. Organized in blocks with all the roads running almost exactly north-south or east-west, the roads probably don't appear to be too special. In fact, here in Utah, we usually don't think much about them. That is, until we need to find an address.

You see, the streets have been laid out in a systematic fashion that makes finding any address a breeze. When the Mormon pioneers, under the direction of Brigham Young, organized their cities, they usually did so around a central point, such as a church, city hall, or park. The streets in the city radiate from this point in increments of 100.

Now when you find Utah addresses like 100 East 400 South to be odd or boring, you will also know that they were made like this just to make things easier for you.

Ice Sheet (all ages)

4390 Harrison Boulevard, on the campus of Weber State University; (801) 399–8750; www.co.weber.ut.us/icesheet/. Open Monday through Saturday noon to 2:00 P.M. (Wednesday until 3:00 P.M.), and Friday and Saturday evenings from 6:00 to 8:00 P.M. Admission $.

Summer or winter, the indoor ice rink, located at Weber State University, offers open skating to visitors on its Olympic-size ice arena. This arena was one of the skating venues for the 2002 Winter Olympics, which were hosted by Utah. Skate rentals are available. Call for hours and rates.

Ott Planetarium (all ages)

Located on Weber State University campus, at 2508 University Circle; (801) 626–6855; physics.weber.edu/planet/ott.html. Open Wednesday evening September through May. Shows at 6:30 and 7:30 P.M.; star party at 8:00 P.M. Admission $.

The university campus has several other family-friendly attractions. We particularly enjoy stargazing, and the planetarium offers a program guaranteed to inform and entertain. Located in the Lind Lecture Hall, the planetarium opens to the public every Wednesday night, with star shows on a variety of subjects starting at 6:30 and 7:30 P.M. Weather permitting, there is a star party at 8:00 P.M. Just a few steps away in the same building is the **Museum of Natural Science,** with exhibits ranging from prehistoric animals to a display on open-heart surgery. Call (801) 626–6653 or log on to community.weber.edu/museum/ for more information.

Collett Art Gallery (all ages)

3750 Harrison Boulevard, on the campus of Weber State University; (801) 626–6000. Open Monday through Thursday from 8:30 A.M. to 9:00 P.M., Friday and Saturday from 8:00 A.M. to 4:00 P.M. Admission is free.

The gallery, also on the WSU campus, features traveling exhibitions of contemporary art. The museum offers a wide variety of displays, depending on the time of year, so call ahead for more information. There are also other visual arts activities on campus that you may enjoy. For information, call the number listed above.

Treehouse Children's Museum (all ages—especially younger children)

455 Twenty-third Street; (801) 394–9663; www.treehousemuseum.org. Open Tuesday through Saturday from 10:00 A.M. to 6:00 P.M. (until 8:00 P.M. on Friday) and 10:00 A.M. to noon on Monday. Admission $.

This museum is dedicated to the art of learning to read. The Treehouse features an Alphabet Area, a giant mechanical "Grandma" who never tires of reading stories, a Pen and Ink Studio where books and stationery are waiting to be created, and a Computer Garden. A giant treehouse forms the hub of the museum and is the stage for a regularly scheduled "partici-play," where children read all of the parts. Ongoing craft activities are based on children's books. Treehouse is a very popular place for families, especially on the weekends, so expect to wait in line for a few minutes.

Christmas Village (all ages)

Municipal Park at Twenty-fifth and Washington Streets; (801) 393–3611. Open November 29 to January 2.

Each November Ogden begins its Christmas celebration with the lighting of the Christmas Village. The city's Municipal Park transforms into a special animated town, made merry with music and thousands of tiny lights. Dozens of different attractions are open to the public and will satisfy the Christmas cravings of each member of the family. Call for more information.

Ogden-Hof Winter Carnival (all ages)

Call (801) 629–8253 for dates and special event information.

If you visit Ogden during January you are in luck. One of the larger German festivals in the state is held at Union Station during the winter carnival. The festival is a celebration of Ogden's sister city, Hof, Germany. You'll experience German music, food, costumes, and a "ski hill" in the middle of town, perfect for small children.

Ogden Nature Center (all ages)

966 West Twelfth Street; (801) 621–7595; www.ogdennaturecenter.org. The center is found between a major Internal Revenue Service processing center and the Ogden Defense Depot. Open 9:00 A.M. to 5:00 P.M. Monday through Friday and 10:00 A.M. to 4:00 P.M. Saturday. Admission $, children under 4 free.

Ogden may be one of the few industrial cities anywhere with a wildlife sanctuary set aside in its midst. The 127-acre park is found in the middle of a large industrial park. For the last twenty years, the goal here has been to restore this land to its natural condition. Your family will surely marvel at this home for wildlife complete with ponds, marshes, and thousands of trees. It features a petting farm, nature trails, picnic areas, and a museum. A "treehouse" tethered from a series of rope swings is great fun for older children. Getting out and walking the 1½ miles of nature trails is the best way to view the wildlife. Expect to see a plentitude of birds, including great blue herons and flocks of regal snowy egrets. These are also wonderful trails for cross-country skiing during the winter months. Tours of the Ogden Nature Center are available for a small additional fee. Call for information and picnic reservations.

George S. Eccles Dinosaur Park (all ages)

Located at 1544 East Park Boulevard; (801) 393–3466; www.dinosaurpark.org. The park is open March through November at 10:00 A.M. Monday through Saturday and at noon on Sunday. Closing time changes with the season. Admission $.

Is your family interested in wildlife of a more ancient sort? Don't miss this fabulous dinosaur museum. More than one hundred life-size, anatomically correct dinosaur models lurk along the leafy pathways here, perched in trees and hiding behind foliage. These models reflect the very latest in dinosaur theories, and many of them are brightly colored in neon, illustrating new skin and hide discoveries. Kids will delight in the 165 million years of evolution on display here, from crawling creatures to marine life and flying reptiles. Dinosaur lovers will relish the gorier exhibits, including a baryonyx gnashing its teeth on a bloodied ancient fish. A welcome center has interpretive exhibits and a gift shop, including a sandpit where kids can "excavate" bones.

Ogden River Parkway (all ages)

The parkway extends from Washington Boulevard in Ogden to Ogden Canyon; (801) 629–8284. Use of the parkway is free.

The Ogden River Parkway consists of 3 miles of paved paths set aside for walking, biking, picnicking, and fishing. The paths stretch through the heart of Ogden, from Washington Boulevard to the mouth of Ogden Canyon, connecting parks, gardens, and sports facilities. My family enjoyed a quiet, leisurely Sunday afternoon in the parkway, but it is not always so tranquil along the river. The last weekend of August brings families to the **Ogden River Parkway Festival** for games, crafts, music, food, and fun. Call for event information.

Ogden Canyon (all ages)

Follow Twelfth Street until it ends, then take the Scenic Byway (Utah Highway 39). For campsite information call the ranger station at (801) 625–5112.

The canyon follows the path of the Ogden River and squeezes out just barely enough room for a two-lane road. It is an exceptionally rugged and beautiful surround and can be a hair-raising drive for the uninitiated. Many summer homes are located here, as well as dozens of national forest campsites. A favorite canyon outing for enthusiastic hikers is called **Indian Trail.** Consider taking two cars for this trip, parking one at the Twenty-second Street terminus and then driving up the canyon to the Smokey Bear sign, where the eastern end of the trail originates. Indian Trail is 5 miles long, and if you picnic along the way it will take three to four hours to complete. The hike is excellent for older children, but may prove to be a little too difficult for the younger ones. You will climb up and down about 1,500 feet in elevation and experience several thrilling views, some narrow-squeeze spots, low overhangs, and rock stairs along the way.

Pack a **Tasty Lunch**

"Good food makes landscape lots lovelier," my six-year-old, Abbey, says.

She's right. When you're wandering the Utah wilds, a wonderful picnic in nature is a lovely experience. Utah is a big state with a lot to look at.

Kids get hungry, though, and there isn't a restaurant on every corner (nor a handy grocery store) when you're out in nature. It's a good idea to pack a tasty lunch and forget about finding a place to eat.

A packed lunch is a lot cheaper, of course. But the real benefit is the convenience. You aren't tied to a town or a schedule.

Pineview Reservoir (all ages)
Follow Utah Highway 39 to the top of Ogden Canyon.

At Ogden Canyon's summit, you can't miss the reservoir, a favorite summer recreation area. Anchored by Pineview Dam, the reservoir reaches back in tentacle formation, about 4 miles in several directions. Fishing, boating, windsurfing, and waterskiing are popular here, and the Wasatch-Cache National Forest has supplied the reservoir with boat ramps and camping and picnicking facilities. The **Ogden Bay Waterfowl Management Area's North Arm Viewing Site** is located just adjacent to the reservoir, with excellent bird-watching from its own nature trail.

Snowbasin (children old enough to ski)
Take I–15 north to Ogden (Twelfth Street exit). Travel east through Ogden Canyon to Utah Highway 226. Open from mid-November through April, depending on snow levels. For ticket prices and other information, call (888) 437–5488; write to 3925 East Snowbasin Road, Huntsville 84317; or go to www.snowbasin.com.

Ogden Canyon leads to three ski resorts. Snowbasin is one of the oldest resorts in the nation, with a chairlift in operation since 1946. Its steeper slopes were selected as the site for the downhill and super G races of the 2002 Olympic games. There are plenty of tamer runs as well inside the resort's 1,800 acres of trails. A ski school is open seven days a week during the winter, as well as a full-service ski shop and day lodge.

Powder Mountain (children old enough to ski)

Take I–15 north to the Twelfth Street exit in Ogden. Turn east and follow the signs through Ogden Canyon. Open from mid-November through April, depending on snow levels. For lift ticket prices and more information, call (801) 745–3772; write to P.O. Box 450, Eden 84310; or go to www.powdermountain.net.

This is another fine ski resort, with four mountain lodges, an overnight facility called Columbine Inn, and two full-service ski shops. Sixteen hundred acres of packed and powder skiing can be reached from chairlifts, and another 1,200 acres are available through snow cat skiing. Snow cat skiing involves riding a specially designed machine up the side of a mountain. Snowboarding, especially popular with teenagers, is encouraged on Powder Mountain's "half pipe" run.

Nordic Valley (children old enough to ski)

Fifteen miles northeast of Ogden. Take Twelfth Street exit from I–15 north and head east up the canyon. Follow the signs to Nordic Valley. Open daily for day skiing and Monday through Saturday for night skiing, from mid-November through April, depending on snow levels. Call (801) 392–0900 or write to 3567 Nordic Valley Way, Eden 84310 for information and ski conditions.

A favorite choice for beginner skiers, Nordic Valley offers gentler slopes and lower lift prices.

Where to Eat

Farr Better Ice Cream. 286 Twenty-first Street; (801) 393–8629. Ice cream. $

Prairie Schooner. 445 Park; (801) 392–2712. American. $$

Cajun Skillet. 2550 Washington; (801) 393–7702. American, Cajun. $

Union Grill. 2501 Wall; (801) 621–2830. American. $$

Where to Stay

Western Inn. 1155 South 1700 West; (801) 731–6500. $$

Best Western High Country Inn. 1335 West Twelfth Street; (801) 394–9474. $$

Huntsville

East of Ogden on Utah Highway 39, Huntsville is a smaller, more agrarian community. Be sure to take advantage of the unique sights around this friendly town.

Huntsville Trappist Monastery (all ages)
1250 South 9500 East; (801) 745–3784; www.xmission.com/~hta/.

It's not often in Mormon country that you run across a Trappist Monastery—so if you pass by here, be sure to stop in for a visit. Local people frequent the monastery for the fabulous honey collected and sold by the monks. The raspberry honey is a family favorite, but there are many flavors from which to choose. Aside from the flavored creamed honey, you can also pick up natural peanut butter and two-grain cereal at the monastery. These monks belong to the Order of the Cistercians of the Strict Observance, also known as Trappists. They dress in plain, hooded robes, and they observe a quiet and meditative life. Although it may seem strange to come across a monastery in northern Utah, you will find it to be a peaceful, interesting place. The reception room and church are open to the public, and visitors are invited to attend services. For more information, call the number listed above.

Where to Eat

Chris'. 7345 East 900 South; (801) 745–3542. $$

Eden

Located to the west of Huntsville on Utah Highway 39, Eden is another small farming community similar to others found in rural northern Utah.

Carvers Cove (all ages)
Call (801) 745–3018 for rates, directions, and reservations. Open Memorial Day through August.

Your family will enjoy the solitude of the surrounding hills and valleys on a guided trail ride in this beautiful area.

Willard

Willard, north of Ogden on U.S. Highway 89, is well known for the popular Willard Bay State Park, which is inviting to both recreation seekers and bird watchers alike.

Willard Bay State Park (all ages)

There are two points of entry to this 10,000-acre reservoir and marina: The northern one (I–15, exit 360) has the best swimming beaches; the southern one (I–15, exit 354) is used mostly by day boaters. For park information (including information on day-use fees), call (435) 734–9494.

The park's easy access from the freeway makes it an extremely popular spot for boaters, anglers, and water-skiers. Here you'll find a picnic area, camping sites, rest rooms, hot showers, and dump stations for RVs. If you look at a map, you might think that Willard Bay is part of the Great Salt Lake, but it is actually a river-fed freshwater reservoir, separated from the lake by a dam. Part of the park has been set aside as a waterfowl management area, and in the spring and fall it is an excellent place to watch migrating birds.

Easy Travel Tips: **Curbing Car Sickness**

Nothing is more fun than discovering new places with your kids. Nothing is more troublesome than having a carsick child. Let me give you a few Rutter family tips that have made life on the road easier.

1. If your kid is prone to feeling queasy, feed him or her cereal for breakfast—not greasy foods like bacon. Go for bland.

2. A half hour before you start, give your child a motion sickness pill (you might want to check with your doctor first). There are a number of good brands that can be purchased in the grocery store—and they work! Some won't make your kid drowsy. (We carry both—sometimes letting them sleep is a good thing if we have to drive a ways to get to the fun stuff.)

3. Let your kids munch on crackers and bread and nonfat snacks as you travel. If a kid is easily carsick, don't let him or her read while the car is moving.

4. Each child should have a handy barf bag—a plastic grocery bag works well.

5. Train your kids to tell you if they are getting sick—that way you can stop the car in time.

6. Carry diaper wipes for cleaning up messes.

Fruitway (all ages)

For seasonal information call the Ogden Convention and Visitors Bureau at (866) 867–8824, or go to www.ogdencvb.org.

A very satisfying afternoon's outing is a drive through Northern Utah's Fruitway. This is actually U.S. Highway 89/91, a back road between the towns of Willard and Brigham City that is nicknamed for the fruit stands that line its path. Starting with the first harvest of summer, several dozen local growers set up shop and sell cherries, peaches, corn, peppers, tomatoes, and other fresh goods. In autumn, your children will love the weird gourds and squashes they'll find in huge supply here, including pumpkins that range in size from half-pounders to barely-fits-in-the-back-of-the-car. For about $10 you can amass a sizeable pile of great stuff to eat.

Perry

Perry is the ultimate small town. Enjoy dinner at a traditional Western steakhouse, or take in a play at the community theater. Whatever the case, you can't miss the entertainment in this great little town.

Heritage Community Theatre (all ages)

2505 South Highway 89; (435) 723–8392; www.heritagetheatreutah.com. Admission $$.

One of Utah's most loved restaurants, Maddox is located along the rural roadside in Perry. For fifty years Westerners have trekked here for the house specialty—burgers and steaks. A favorite local outing is dinner at Maddox and then a short trip down the road to the Heritage Community Theater, which offers family-oriented plays. Call for a schedule and ticket prices.

Where to Eat

Maddox. 1900 South Highway 89; (435) 723–8545. $–$$

Brigham City

Golden Spike National Historic Site (all ages)

Thirty-two miles west of Brigham City; follow the signs on Utah Highway 83; (435) 471–2209. Open daily from 8:00 A.M. to 6:00 P.M. Memorial Day to Labor Day and 8:00 A.M. to 5:30 P.M. the rest of the year. Vehicles $$, adults $, children 17 and under free.

About 130 years ago the United States was in the midst of railroad fever, with Congress paying huge subsidies for those who would help connect the rails between the East and West Coasts. Two companies, the Union Pacific and the Central Pacific, became the main contenders for that money, with one working its way west and the other east, and each laying rail as fast as it could. The railroads finally met on May 10, 1869, and the entire nation celebrated its first transcontinental railroad. The unlikely spot for this joining was an isolated town called **Promontory,** and a golden spike was driven into the last tie to mark the celebration.

Promontory is now a National Historic Site, and the visitor center's exhibits and films interpret the area's railroad history. This attraction will be both entertaining and educational for children of all ages. The site features two working replicas of 1869 steam trains, which operate during the warm-weather months. Each May 10, your family can watch the **reenactment of the driving of the golden spike,** complete with actors in period costume. An annual **Railroader's Festival** is held the second Saturday in August.

Thiokol Rocket Display (all ages)
Two miles (and one hundred years, as they say locally) north of Golden Spike. Admission is free.

An outdoor park of sorts, the rocket display houses real examples of the solid rocket motors that propel our astronauts into space. Part of the high-tech Thiokol plant (located on Utah Highway 83), where these rockets are made, can be seen from the display area. Occasionally the rockets are tested here, and their flights can be viewed from the road.

Marble Park (all ages)
On Faust Valley Road. Call the Box Elder County Chamber of Commerce at (435) 723–5761 for more information. Admission is free.

Horse-drawn wagons and equipment from the 1800s are displayed here in truly original style. The park offers a quiet break during a busy day and is an excellent spot for a picnic.

Union Pacific Museum (all ages)
833 West Forest Street; (435) 723–2989. Hours are 1:00 to 5:00 P.M. Monday, Tuesday, Thursday, Friday, and Saturday, or anytime by appointment. Admission is free.

If your trip to Golden Spike didn't quench your thirst for railroad knowledge, visit the old museum in the middle of town. Here your family will find an educational center and gift shop documenting the history of this former major shipping center.

Tabernacle (all ages)
251 South Main Street; (435) 723–5376. Free tours of the tabernacle are available from May through October from 9:00 A.M. to 6:00 P.M., or by appointment the rest of the year. Call for information.

By now you have probably noticed the city's landmark, the Mormon Tabernacle. Brigham City is justifiably proud of this structure, with its sixteen buttresses and towers. Original construction of the tabernacle was completed in 1890, but within a decade it had burnt down and been rebuilt.

Going to the Birds **at Bear River Bird Refuge**

We're a family of bird watchers. One of our favorite places to get "birdy" is the Bear River Bird Refuge, where over 140 different species have been spotted. There is a 12-mile loop that is perfect for seeing marsh wildlife. This one-way drive takes you around dikes and refuge impoundments, so you get a bird's-eye view of our feathered friends in their natural world.

You'll enjoy mudflats, marshes, open water—and lots of birds. Early mornings and late evenings are the best. Take a field guide so you can identify different species. We have our kids keep a list of the different birds and frequency of species.

You'll need a pair of field glasses. We have a pair for each child—watching wildlife is, after all, a serious business in our family. I also take a spotting scope, a camera with a variety of lenses, rubber boots so I can get off the road, a good lunch, and an ice chest of chilled Coke.

Bear River Migratory Bird Refuge (all ages)
From U.S. Highway 89 north, exit 368, travel 15 miles west of Brigham City; (435) 723–5887. Call for more information.

One of the best wildlife watching areas in the state, and one of our family's favorite spots, is the Bear River Migratory Bird Refuge. This is the largest of the eight wildlife refuges maintained on the Great Salt Lake. The Bear River enters the Great Salt Lake here, and the resulting 65,000 acres of delta, marshes, and wetlands support an incredible variety of birds. About sixty species nest here, and many more visit on their way to and from seasonal homes. Migrating birds by the millions stop here in late summer and tank up on brine flies before heading on to their destinations. Your family can enjoy endless hours of bird-watching, identifying numerous rare species of birds. Be sure to bring your binoculars and bird guide, and drive or bike the 12-mile dike road for the best views of white-faced ibis, whistling swans, great blue herons, bald and golden eagles, hawks, and many species of ducks. The weather is usually the best in the fall, but the refuge is open year-round during daylight hours.

Peach Days (all ages)
For more information call (435) 723–3931.

If you are in town in September, you may be in luck. The weekend after Labor Day, Brigham City honors its most famous crop with Peach Days. This is the oldest continuing harvest festival in Utah and is celebrated with a parade, antique car show, Dutch oven cook-off, and carnival.

Where to Eat

Calls Drive In. 1650 South Highway 89; (435) 723–2345. $

Peach City Ice Cream Co. 306 North Main; (435) 723–3923. $–$$

Idle Isle Cafe. 24 South Main; (435) 734–2468. $$

Honeyville

Crystal Hot Springs Resort (all ages)
8215 North State Route 38. Open every day except Thanksgiving and Christmas. Call (435) 279–8104 for more information. Pools $, pools and slide $$.

Naturally warm mineral waters make the hot springs a favorite family place to relax and enjoy the beauty of the surrounding mountains.

Hot and cold springs supply water for six pools and three saunas, all outdoors, which are enjoyed year-round. There is a campground here, and snacks are sold at the concession stand.

Tremonton

Eli Anderson's Wagons (all ages)
8790 West Highway 102; (435) 854–3760. Showings are by appointment only: Call ahead.

If anyone in your family is interested in antique modes of transportation, it is worth your while to travel to this small town. Here you will find Eli Anderson's Wagons, one man's collection of horse-drawn vehicles—reported to be the largest private grouping in the West.

Where to Eat

George's Crossroads Restaurant. 1640 West Main; (435) 257–3726. $–$$

Plymouth

Belmont Hot Springs (all ages)

Two miles south of Plymouth on Utah Highway 13, at 5600 West 19200 North; (435) 458–3200. Call for more information.

Another resort blessed with natural springs of warm mineral water is Belmont Hot Springs. The Springs offers any number of relaxing activities; here your family can swim, golf, picnic, camp, and, reportedly, even scuba dive in the middle of winter. Tropical fish and lobsters are raised here in ninety-five-degree water.

Hyrum

Hardware Ranch (all ages)

Follow Utah Highway 101 east of Hyrum for 17 miles; (435) 753–6206. Admission $, children under 4 free.

If your family simply can't satisfy its hunger for knowledge about elk, you'll want to visit this lovely farming community. The ranch exists as a year-round refuge for these beautiful beasts, and visitors here can learn about elk management and view up to 700 elk in their natural surroundings. In winter, a horse-drawn sleigh conveys passengers through the areas where the elk are fed winter wheat; the sight of these animals close up is awe-inspiring. The sleigh rides take about twenty minutes, and they are scheduled throughout the day, seven days a week, from mid-December to mid-March, generally between 10:00 A.M. and 5:00 P.M. A rugged back road continues on from Hardware Ranch for 25 miles to meet up with Logan Canyon just before its summit. This is a beautiful ride for the adventurous and informed traveler. In winter it is passable by snowmobile only, and in warm weather it should be attempted only in a high-clearance vehicle. Ask locally for directions and road conditions. Snowmobile rentals, fuel, and hot meals are available near the Hardware Ranch visitor center.

Hyrum State Park (all ages)

405 West 300 South; (435) 245–6866. Camping, day-use, and entrance fees are charged year-round. Call for more information.

A small reservoir right in the middle of town is a popular local hangout for water recreation enthusiasts, especially during the warm summer months. The park has a boat dock, camping facilities, and a swimming area. The reservoir is fishable all year long.

Hyrum City Museum (all ages)

83 West Main; (435) 245–6033. Open Tuesday, Thursday, and Saturday from 2:00 to 5:00 P.M. Admission is free.

If you want to visit a museum but feel that it is too difficult to find something to interest everyone in the family, the Hyrum City Museum is absolutely perfect. The museum is home to an eclectic collection of old stuff. Egyptian mummy masks are displayed near an 1872 schoolroom, and 180-million-year-old dinosaur bones from central Utah share museum space with a classic doll collection. This odd museum offers something to please even the strangest visitor. The museum shares building space with the city library. For more information call the library at the number listed above.

Fast Utah Facts

- Utah has a population of nearly 2.5 million.
- Utah gained statehood on January 4, 1896.
- Utah's capital and largest city is Salt Lake City.
- Utah is known for large families.

Logan

Cache Valley is located in the far northern reaches of Utah, where it enjoys one of the most spectacular settings of any region in the state. Surrounded on all sides by steep, forested mountains, its flat valley is crisscrossed by abundant water, large farms, and a number of small industries. Notable is the mountain range that rims the western edge of the valley. **The Wellsvilles** are said to be the steepest mountain range in the world rising from such a narrow base. Box Elder Peak is the highest point in this range, measuring 9,372 feet in elevation. Logan is Cache Valley's largest city and an educational and cultural magnet for surrounding communities.

You might want to start your visit here with a trip to the **Chamber of Commerce Building and Information Center** at 160 North Main. Dozens of brochures are available, explaining everything from historic home tours to area snowmobile trails.

Daughters of the Utah Pioneers Museum (all ages)
160 North Main; (435) 752–2161 or (435) 752–1635. Open 10:00 A.M. to 4:00 P.M. Tuesday through Friday, June through September, and by appointment during the rest of the year. Admission is free.

Be sure to walk down the hall from the Chamber of Commerce to this small museum. It features demonstrations of old crafts, such as spinning and tatting, and also displays pioneer artifacts.

Center Street (all ages)
Logan's entire Center Street has been designated a National Historic District. As you walk past the carefully restored exteriors of these downtown buildings, it is not hard to imagine

life in a bustling 1890s Western town. One of these restorations is the **Ellen Eccles Theater** (435–750–0300), where musicals, theater, and ballet are performed throughout the year.

Summerfest (all ages)

Logan Fairgrounds, 400 South 500 West; (435) 716–9250; www.loganutah.org/parksrec /summerfest. The festival is held in June. Call for specific dates and more information.

Each June the beautiful Logan Fairgrounds is the setting for the three-day Summerfest, a festival devoted to music and art. The **Children's Fair and Art Yard** at Summerfest features hands-on giant sculpture projects, a puppet theater, face painting, and special design classes. Your children will also enjoy the carnival rides and carriage trips around the tabernacle grounds as well as the food and art booths and continuous live music.

Sherwood Hills Resort (all ages)

Twelve miles southwest of Logan in Sardine Canyon, Highway 89/91, Wellsville; (435) 245–5054. Call for more information.

If you think some cultural events might fit nicely with your recreational activities, be sure to visit this resort. Located just outside of town, Sherwood Hills is a full-service getaway. It produces outdoor theatricals in the summer, which are especially popular with children. Guided one- or two-hour horseback rides and hayrides are also available here.

Willow Park (all ages)

400 West 700 South; (435) 750–9893. Open 9:00 A.M. to dusk year-round. There is no entrance fee, but visitors are encouraged to donate 25 cents.

Take a picnic along to this beautiful area, which is dwarfed by huge trees and surrounded by burbling streams. For younger children, there is a child-sized zoo.

Utah State University (all ages)

(435) 797–1129. Free tours given weekdays at 10:30 A.M. and 2:30 P.M. during the school year, 1:00 P.M. during the summer.

The campus of Utah State University sits directly below the mouth of Logan Canyon, on Logan's eastern border. The school was established in 1888 as Utah's land grant college, and it has become one of the premier research universities in the United States. Free, informal tours of the campus are given weekdays at designated times. To take a tour, just show up in the lobby of the University Inn at the appropriate time, or call the number listed above for details.

Discovery Center (all ages)

Utah State University campus. Open Monday, Wednesday, and Saturday. Hours vary, so call (435) 797–0723 for specific information. Admission is free.

In your travels around campus, look for the Science and Engineering Research Building (called SER on campus) and find Room 132 for the center, a hands-on science exploration center for children and their parents. The center is not open very often, but if your children are lovers of science this is a place worth investigating.

Nora Eccles Harrison Museum (all ages)

Utah State University campus, 650 North 1100 East; (435) 797–0163. Open Tuesday through Saturday. Call for hours and information on traveling exhibits. Admission is free.

This fine art museum on campus has six exhibition spaces with rotating exhibits featuring photographs, ceramics, and Native American artifacts. After visiting the museum, throw any thoughts of a fat-free afternoon away, and take your family to the **Food Science Building** at the eastern end of campus. The extraordinary ice cream sold here is made on campus by students, and it is revered for its extra creaminess.

Ronald V. Jensen Living Historical Farm (all ages)

U.S. Highway 89, south of Logan, at 4025 South Highway 89/91, Wellsville; (435) 245–6050. Open Monday through Saturday from 10:00 A.M. to 5:00 P.M. during the summer. Call for an events schedule. Admission $.

The university operates an historical farm, just south of town, that makes for a fun and educational afternoon. Visitors can wander freely all over the acreage at this authentic 1917 dairy farm, and see draft horses, cows, pigs, chickens, and a flock of sheep "at work." Antique farm equipment surrounds the country farmhouse, barn, and smokehouse. Most weekends bring special events to the farm, including threshing, quilting, sheep shearing, taffy making, and apple harvesting. An old-fashioned Christmas is celebrated each December.

The Festival of the American West (all ages)

On the Utah State University campus; (800) 225–FEST; www.americanwestcenter.org. Call for more information. Adults $$$, children $$.

If you can only be in Logan for a short time, try to plan your trip around this festival. Summertime on campus brings this major event to Logan, and you definitely don't want to miss out. For nine days a massive 1870s-era **Great West Fair** encamps on the lawns, complete with mountain-man tepees, a frontier military barracks, an Indian village, a pioneer Main Street, and more. Visitors are invited to experience this history lesson up close and watch contests of skill, quilt making, Dutch oven cook-offs, medicine shows, and old-fashioned artisans at work. A nightly mega-pageant, "The West: America's Odyssey," celebrates the settlement of the West through dance, drama, music, and multimedia effects.

A Rutter Family Adventure: **Autumn in Logan Canyon**

We have a number of family rituals. One is to enjoy the Utah fall.

Utah doesn't take a backseat to New England when it comes to glorious autumn colors. The canyons are lovely when the leaves change. You can't find a better place to celebrate the fall than Logan Canyon.

This 40-mile drive (Logan Canyon Scenic Byway, U.S. Highway 89) takes you from Logan to Bear Lake. You start at the rushing Logan River and climb upward into heaven.

When the weather gets crisp, the aspen trees turn several shades of golden yellow and the maples turn a dozen shades of fiery red. We stop at the numerous turnouts and breathe the mountain air—taking in the visual feast. We also have a contest to see who can find the reddest maple and the most golden aspen leaf. It's a great celebration.

No trip is complete without hiking through the forest and collecting a bouquet of leaves for our kitchen table.

Logan Canyon (all ages)

U.S. Highway 89, east of Logan. Call the Logan Ranger District at (435) 755–3620 for conditions and reservation information.

The canyon can be accessed directly from the eastern edge of town on U.S. Highway 89, often named in national publications as one of the most beautiful scenic drives anywhere. The canyon's forested walls are especially stunning in the fall, when the aspens and maples are at their height of color. The twisting, steep-sided canyon hides dozens of **Wasatch-Cache National Forest** campgrounds.

There are many terrific family hikes in this 40-mile-long canyon. A level 1½-mile hike that even very small people will enjoy is the **Riverside Nature Trail** to Spring Hollow, reached from a marked trailhead about 5⅓ miles up the canyon from Logan at Guinavah-Malibu Campground. This is a beautiful, much-photographed area, and you will see fossils of sea plants and animals along the way. A more difficult hike is found close by: A 1½-mile steep climb will take your family 1,000 feet up to the **Wind Caves,** an exciting place that shows off rock arches and rooms formed by wind and ice. The Wind Cave trailhead is found across from the Guinavah-Malibu Campground.

Adventurous older children will be rewarded with the sight of a 3,000-year-old tree if they tackle the **Jardine Juniper Trail,** 9 miles round-trip. Though it's steep in places, most children can hike the trail; its length, however, may be prohibitive. The Jardine Juniper is 44 feet high and has a 26-foot circumference. Photographers love this tree, both for its age and its beautiful shape.

A much easier hike to see another old tree is **Limber Pine Nature Trail,** an outstanding trail. A 1-mile loop trail takes you up through wooded paths to a huge limber pine tree, once thought to be 2,000 years old, but which actually consists of several old limber pines that creatively intertwined to look like one ancient tree. The hike features plentiful wildflowers and wonderful viewpoints. A perfect place for a picnic is found 20 miles up the canyon at **Tony Grove Lake,** which is reached from a well-marked, paved road. A boardwalk leads to picnic tables near the parking lot, or take the ½-mile walk around to the Beach Area for more picnic sites.

Old Ephraim's **Grave**

Few things interest my kids like a good story, and right outside of Logan a great story waits to be told.

In the 1920s, grizzly bears frequently roamed the forests of northern Utah. One bear in particular was a great enemy to nearly every rancher and shepherd in the area. Frank Clark crusaded to rid the area of bears and tracked "Old Eph" for several years.

In 1923, Clark finally met up with his nemesis. Old Eph, with bear traps clamped to his arm and foot, went after Clark. Clark had just awakened and was only partly dressed when Old Ephraim raised up and was about to take a bite out of him. Luckily, Clark was able to fire a fatal shot at the bear and killed him.

Today there is a monument at **Old Ephraim's grave,** located about 15 miles from the mouth of Logan Canyon. Travel up the canyon about 8 miles, then leave the highway and drive 7 miles on Forest Road 056. The monument tells the complete story and also serves as a sad reminder that grizzly bears no longer tromp through the Bear River Mountains.

You can also see Old Eph's skull at the Bridgerland Travel Region office at 160 North Main Street in Logan.

Beaver Mountain Ski Area (children old enough to ski)
Twenty-seven miles east of Logan, at 40000 East Highway 89, Garden City; (435) 753–0921; www.skithebeav.com. Three chairlifts and a day lodge operate from late November through the second week of April (except Christmas) 9:00 A.M. to 4:00 P.M. $$$$

Beaver Mountain is a wonderful place for children to learn to ski. The flat, open area at the entrance of Beaver Mountain is called **Sink Hollow,** and a groomed, beginner cross-country ski trail is maintained here. The surrounding area is also popular for sledding.

Beaver Creek Lodge (all ages)
Just east of Beaver Mountain Resort; P.O. Box 139, Millville 84326; (435) 946–3400. Call for more information.

The lodge offers full overnight accommodations as well as guided horseback riding in summer and snowmobile rentals in winter.

Fast
Utah Facts

- The highest point in Utah is King's Peak, which is 13,528 feet above sea level.
- The lowest point in Utah is Beaver Creek Dam, which is 2,000 feet above sea level.

Where to Eat

Caffe Ibis. 52 Federal Avenue; (435) 753–4777. Deli/cafe. $$

Copper Mill. 55 North Main Street, #301; (435) 752–0647. American. $$

Gia's Restaurant & Deli. 119 Main Street; (435) 752–8384. Italian. $$

Zanavoo. 4880 East Highway 89; (435) 752–0085. American. $$

Where to Stay

Best Western Baugh Motel. 153 South Main; (435) 752–5220. $$

Best Western Weston Inn. 250 North Main; (435) 752–5700. $–$$

Anniversary Inn. 169 East Center Street; (435) 752–3443. $$$$

Best Western Sherwood Hills Resort. Highway 89/91, Wellsville; (435) 245–5054. $–$$$

Providence Inn Bed and Breakfast. 10 South Main Street, P.O. Box 99, Providence 84332; (435) 752–3432. $$$$

Garden City

This tiny town is located at the spot where Logan Canyon empties onto the shores of Bear Lake. Most people who live here operate farms in the area, and their friendliness and rural pace is a welcome change from city life. Garden City's high elevation encourages cool nights year-round, providing a serendipitous climate for raspberries. You can't help but notice Garden City's pride in its star crop because **fruit stands and raspberry shake outlets** line the roads. Raspberries are further honored with a three-day celebration the first weekend of August. **Raspberry Days** features a parade, rodeo, craft fair, and dance.

Bear Lake (all ages) 🔺🅐🌳🏕

Along U.S. Highway 89, about 20 miles east of Logan. Call the park at (435) 946–3343 for a calendar of events. Reservations for state park campsites are advised; call (800) 322–3770 from 8:00 A.M. to 5:00 P.M. Monday through Friday. Vehicles $$.

Garden City also supports a water recreation business for Bear Lake, known for its unique turquoise color. Boating and waterskiing are popular on the lake during the short summer season. Water recreation and bicycle rentals as well as guided adventures are available at a number of businesses that line Garden City's main drag, Bear Lake Boulevard. Call the Bear Lake Convention and Visitors Bureau for more information at (800) 448–BEAR. **Bear Lake State Park** hosts three campgrounds on the lakeshore: **Bear Lake Marina** has fifteen sites and harbor and docking facilities; **Rendezvous Beach** has great sand and 138 sites; and **Eastside** has primitive camping in an isolated setting.

Rendezvous Beach also hosts **Mountain Man Rendezvous,** an old-time mountainman gathering the second weekend of September. This festival celebrates the rendezvous held annually on this spot from 1825 to 1840. Eat, drink, and test your frontier skills with costumed mountain men. Day-use and camping fees are charged. A dozen other private campgrounds and overnight facilities operate on the lake as well. Camping is allowed only in specified areas on the shores of Bear Lake.

Bear Lake—**It's the Water**

Bear Lake is charming!

The fishing isn't bad, but not great. It's a bit cold for waterskiing, unless you are a duck. Bear Lake simply makes you feel good—the same way that Yellowstone Lake makes you feel good. The water is wide and deep and shallow. There are mountains and winds, and the water is very blue. It's a moody lake, changing whimsically. At times it's flat as glass; seconds later a squall blows in and the whitecaps are pounding with a tropical fury.

We love to drive along the shores and look at the ever-changing water, which has a relaxing effect, like looking at the ocean. Bear Lake is a great stress reliever. If you're in the area, take the time to wander the miles of shoreline. Eat a picnic lunch, roll up your pants, and wade.

This is an area rich in Western history, but most important, you'll take back a mental slide show that will play for a lifetime.

If your family desires a unique-in-the-world fishing opportunity, come to Bear Lake in winter for the **Bonneville cisco run.** Cisco are a tiny fish, similar to smelt, that are found only in Bear Lake. The fish come to shallow water to spawn in late January and early February, and during this time it is possible to cut a hole in the ice and scoop them up with nets.

If your family enjoys snowmobiling, there are over 200 miles of groomed trails in the hills surrounding Garden City. Several full-service rental outlets are found here.

Pickleville Playhouse (all ages) ♪

Call (435) 755–0961 or write to 2049 South Bear Lake Boulevard, Garden City 84028 for rates and a playlist.

Looking for a little true Western entertainment? You've come to the right place. A local theater group takes up residence in town during the summer months. The playhouse offers Western cook-out dinners along with melodrama-style plays, on Thursday, Friday, and Saturday as well as Monday in July.

The road north from Garden City leads to Idaho. If you continue on this way, a good choice for a summertime family outing is Minnetonka Cave near the town of Paris.

Where to Stay

Beaver Creek Lodge. P.O. Box 139, Millville 84326; (435) 946–3400. $$$

Smithfield

Stage Stop Theatre (all ages) ♪

141 North Main; (800) 248–2530. Tickets $–$$, depending on the night you attend and the age of each family member.

This popular theater offers family-oriented comedies and musicals throughout the year. Open Monday through Saturday in summer, with reduced hours in winter. Call the number listed above for a schedule.

Richmond

Black and White Days (all ages)

Second weekend in May. For information call (435) 258–2092.

For a behind-the-scenes view of "real" ranch life in the West, visit this community during the second weekend in May. Holstein cows have been thriving on the green pastures here since 1904, and the town celebrates its prize stock each year with Black and White Days. Much of the activity centers around cattle competition; your family, however, will enjoy the fun town parade and food stands.

Fast Utah Facts

- Utah is the home of many important inventors, including television pioneer Philo T. Farnsworth. Two of the men responsible for the development of the artificial heart, Robert Jarvik and Willem Kolff, and the inventor of the traffic light, Lester Wire, have also called Utah their home.

- On Antelope Island, you will find not only antelope, but also wild buffalo, range cattle, and rattlesnakes.

- Within fifty years after entering the Salt Lake Valley, the Mormons who settled Utah had founded nearly 500 settlements throughout Utah and the surrounding states.

- Approximately 60 percent of Utah's population are members of the Church of Jesus Christ of Latter-day Saints, also known as Mormons.

Clarkston

Martin Harris Pageant (all ages)
For pageant dates and directions, call (435) 563–0059. The pageant runs for two weeks in August and begins at 8:15 P.M. in the outdoor Martin Harris Memorial Theater. Admission is free, but reserved tickets are required. Tickets are available only by writing to Martin Harris Pageant, P.O. Box 151, Clarkston 84305.

For two weeks in August, this quiet farming community greets thousands of visitors to this pageant, a tribute to one of Utah's more colorful Mormon pioneer leaders. Harris spent the last years of his life here and is buried in the town cemetery. Before the show, dinner can be purchased in the nearby Mormon Church for $5.00.

Pony Express Days (all ages)
Late June; (435) 563–6884.

In late June Clarkston hosts this festival with a reenactment of the thrilling horse and rider system that once moved the mail in this part of the country. Ask locally for specific dates or call the number listed above for information.

Cove

Hummingbird Hill Trail Rides (all ages)
(435) 258–2025. $$$ an hour per person for a family of four.

If any of your family are dedicated horse people, check out Hummingbird Hill, in this remote farming community. This outfit offers all sorts of customized rides, including sunrise, campfire and dinner, and lunch outings in the surrounding canyons and hills. This is not an easy place to find, and it's recommended that you call ahead for availability and directions.

Top Annual Events in Northern Utah

JANUARY
Ogden-Hof Winter Carnival, Ogden; (801) 629–8242

MAY
Black and White Days, Richmond; (435) 258–2092

Reenactment of the driving of the golden spike, Golden Spike National Historic Site; (435) 471–2209

JUNE
Pony Express Days, Clarkston; (435) 563–9646

AUGUST
Festival of the American West, Logan; (800) 225–FEST

Martin Harris Pageant, Clarkston; (435) 563–0059

Raspberry Days, Garden City; (800) 448–BEAR

Cache County Fair, Logan; (435) 716–7150

Weber County Fair, Ogden; (801) 399–8711 or (800) 44–ARENA

Country Fair Days, South Weber City; (801) 479–3177

Davis County Fair, Farmington; (801) 451–4080

Rich County Fair and Rodeo, Randolph; (435) 793–5155

Box Elder County Fair, Tremonton; (435) 230–0207

SEPTEMBER
Mountain Man Rendezvous, Bear Lake State Park; (435) 946–3343

Peach Days, Brigham City; (435) 723–3931

NOVEMBER
Annual bison roundup, Antelope Island State Park; (801) 773–2941

Christmas parade and lighting of Christmas Village, Ogden; (801) 393–3611

Hof Oktoberfest, Ogden; (801) 629–8242

Greater Salt Lake

The city of Salt Lake is actually a small urban corner of a much larger area known as the Salt Lake Valley. This outlying valley houses a dozen or so suburbs that have turned into one of the fastest-growing population centers in the country. Cities with names like Sandy and West Jordan boast clean, safe, and rural lifestyles and a citizenry of large, young families. This chapter also describes the canyons immediately surrounding the valley as well as the vast area west of Salt Lake City known as the Great Basin.

The Greater Salt Lake area sports resorts famous for world-class skiing, a treasure trove of Mormon history, a multitude of fine arts entertainment, and, of course, its namesake, the Great Salt Lake. There are two major indoor malls in the heart of downtown Salt Lake City, about one hundred boutiques and specialty shops, and many fine restaurants representing almost every ethnic derivation.

Salt Lake City was the world's chosen site for the 2002 Winter Olympics, confirming the area's claim of "The Greatest Snow on Earth." This honor boosted both the city's name recognition and visitation, and by the next decade the quiet, western town that used to be Salt Lake will most likely be changed forever.

Salt Lake City

"This is the right place," said LDS Church Leader Brigham Young when he first saw Salt Lake Valley. The date was July 24, 1847, and Young was the leader of a band of road-weary church faithful who had wagon-trained from Illinois, determined to find a home for themselves. Brigham Young and his followers were wildly successful in establishing an oasis in this desert country, and today Salt Lake City remains, perhaps, most famous as headquarters of the Church of Jesus Christ of Latter-day Saints, also known as the Mormon Church or the LDS Church. Young's legacy provides a well-planned city for those who live here and a fascinating glimpse of history for those who visit. Throughout the month of December, Temple Square is transformed into fairyland, when more than 500,000 tiny colored lights are draped over trees and bushes and arranged in patterns in the flower beds. A larger-than-life nativity scene depicts the birth of Christ, and special performances are given

GREATER SALT LAKE

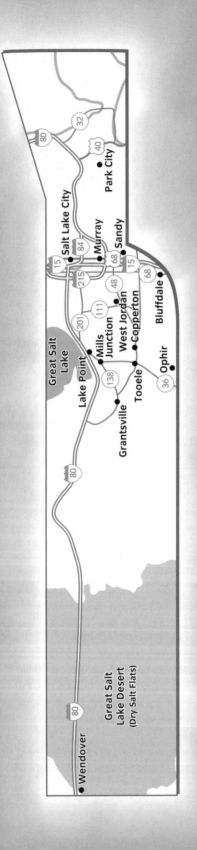

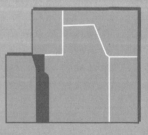

each night in the Tabernacle. All tours and events are **free** to the public. For more information on Temple Square, call the visitor center (801–240–2534).

Most of the central area of downtown Salt Lake City is owned by the LDS Church, including world-famous **Temple Square,** located in the heart of downtown, and its surrounding museums, which are visited annually by more than four million people. The ten-acre square is located, literally, in the center of the city, and three surrounding roads bear its name—North, West, and South Temple Streets. An original church surveyor's marker can be seen on the southeast corner of Temple Square, designating that site as the exact center of the city. This square block is the most visited space in Utah, revered for its beauty and beloved for its spiritual significance. The very first LDS temple started in Utah is here, built from granite quarried in local canyons. The first day after the Mormons' arrival in the valley, this square was measured by Brigham Young's walking step and set aside as sacred ground. Work on the temple was begun in 1853, and its completion took almost forty years. Today, only church faithful are allowed inside, but anyone can admire its lovely architecture. Note the golden angel sounding his horn on top of the temple—this is Moroni, honored here for his major role in church history.

Michael's
TopPicks for fun in Greater Salt Lake

1. The Salt Lake LDS Temple, Salt Lake City; (801) 240–4872

2. Temple Square Visitor Centers, Salt Lake City; (801) 240–4872

3. Joseph Smith Memorial Building, Salt Lake City; (801) 240–1266

4. The Museum of Church History and Art, Salt Lake City; (801) 240–4615

5. Clark Planetarium, Salt Lake City; (801) 456–7827

6. Utah Museum of Natural History; (801) 581–6927

7. The Bonneville Salt Flats, Wendover

8. Park City; (435) 615–5000

9. This is the Place State Park, Salt Lake City; (801) 582–1847

10. Hogle Zoological Gardens, Salt Lake City; (801) 582–1631

Seagull Monument (all ages)
On Temple Square. Tours begin at the flagpole nearby every few minutes from 9:00 A.M. to 9:00 P.M. Tours are free.

There are several other places to visit within the square, and tourists are welcome at all of them. If you would like a guided tour of the square, walk inside the gates and find the monument, a stone spire topped by stone seagulls and surrounded by a pond. Not only did the Mormons choose to honor the seagull in a monument, but it is also the official state bird. This stems from the bird's early role in church history, when seagulls stopped a nasty invasion of crickets.

Seagulls in Utah?

While visiting downtown Salt Lake City, you may have noticed that Utahns have a special relationship with their state bird, the California gull. This relationship can be traced back to an extraordinary event that took place more than 150 years ago.

In 1849, Utah's early settlers were having quite a bit of trouble with some annoying insects. It appears that crickets were destroying the crops and leaving little in their path. The farmers feared that their fields were doomed. That is, until they were rescued by some unlikely heroes.

California gulls descended from the heavens and gobbled up the crickets in massive numbers until they were all devoured. The crops were saved, and the Utahns were and will always be grateful to their feathered saviors.

Assembly Hall (children ages 8 and up)

On Temple Square; (801) 240–3318. Performances Friday and Saturday at 7:30 P.M. During the Christmas season, performances are given Tuesday through Saturday. Call for a concert schedule. Admission is free.

Just west of Seagull Monument is Assembly Hall, built in 1880. A classical concert series is held here year-round. Tickets are not required, and there is no admission fee. However, children under eight are not invited.

Mormon Tabernacle (all ages)

On Temple Square. Free performances Thursday at 8:00 P.M. and Sunday mornings at 9:30. These Sunday performances are broadcast live around the world and require the audience to be seated by 9:15 A.M. Half-hour organ recitals, sans choir, are given Monday through Saturday at noon and Sunday at 2:00 P.M. Call (801) 240–4872 for more information.

Across from Assembly Hall is the famed Mormon Tabernacle, home to the even more famous **Mormon Tabernacle Choir.** This domed building is known for having perfect acoustics, as well as a 12,000-pipe organ. When your family is inside the tabernacle, note the pillars that line the aisles. When this building was constructed in 1863, the prized hardwoods of the time were not to be found in this area. What you see is actually the lowly pine, painted to look like oak. When your family visits other LDS buildings built around this time, look for other replications of materials—such as sandstone painted to look like marble. The Tabernacle seats 6,500 people for Mormon Tabernacle Choir rehearsals.

Temple Square Visitor Centers (all ages)

On Temple Square; (801) 240–4872. Open daily from 9:00 A.M. to 9:00 P.M. Admission is free.

Two visitor centers are located within Temple Square, offering pamphlets, short lectures, and movies that describe the LDS Church's teachings and history. Additional exhibits describe the building of the Salt Lake temple, humanitarian efforts, and the family. A replica of Thorvaldsen's Christus is also there.

LDS Conference Center (all ages)

Located north of Temple Square, at 60 West North Temple. Free tours are available. For theater information call (801) 240–0080. For more information on tours, call (801) 240–0075.

The Conference Center is one of the largest capacity religious buildings in the world. It can hold up to 21,000 people and occupies an entire city block. Free tours are offered between 9:00 A.M. and 9:00 P.M. daily. If the roof is open, wander among the field, trees, and fountains that you'll find up there. Or attend a play or concert in the 850-seat theater located downstairs.

Joseph Smith Memorial Building (all ages)

Located at the corner of South Temple and Main Streets at 15 East South Temple. Note: Tickets are available for specific times only. You might consider obtaining your tickets at the beginning of your tour, to assure a showing that fits your schedule. You can also get tickets in advance by calling (801) 240–4383. Admission and film tickets are free.

Immediately surrounding Temple Square are several other important LDS Church buildings that your family will enjoy visiting. Do take time to visit this attraction found just east of Temple Square. This grand old structure operated as the Hotel Utah from 1911 to 1987, and in its time was one of the most famous hotels in the West. The building has undergone a $45-million renovation and now serves as an office building for Mormon leaders and a showcase for church history. If you are interested, you may obtain free tickets to see *The Testaments,* a film about Christ in Jerusalem and the New World. Free tickets are also available for *Legacy,* a film about the Mormon pioneers and their trek to Utah. Both films are shown on the second floor of this building.

While you are waiting to watch the film, walk through the lobby and around the northeast corner, and you will find the **Family Search Center** (801–240–4085). This wonderfully educational place is a "Genealogy 101" for dabblers in family history. The LDS Church is a world leader in tracing family lineage, and your personal history is most likely contained in the massive memory system here. Find an empty desk and sit at a computer. Within three or four minutes, your children should experience the thrill of calling up at least one of your forebears and from there finding the names, birthplaces, and birthdates of six generations of your ancestors. For a nickel a copy, you can take this information home. Top off your visit to the Joseph Smith Building with an elevator ride to the tenth floor, where magnificent views of Salt Lake City are revealed from the east and west windows, and two restaurants serve lunch and dinner.

The Beehive House (all ages)

67 East South Temple; (801) 240–2671. Open Monday through Saturday from 9:30 A.M. to 6:30 P.M. June through August and until 4:30 P.M. the rest of the year; Sunday and holidays 10:00 A.M. to 1:00 P.M. Free tours start every ten minutes. Admission is free.

Don't lag behind. There is plenty more Mormon history to be viewed within a block's walk. A few doors east of the Joseph Smith Memorial Building, the Beehive House is a favorite visiting place for children. The house was built in 1854 as a home for the second president of the LDS Church, Brigham Young, and his family. Dozens of pioneer children grew up in this home, and their way of life is charmingly displayed through the furnishing and artifacts that remain. The house has been restored as a museum, and with a guide you can view the bedrooms, books, toys, in-home school, and eating areas that were used by a Mormon family more than 150 years ago. Original to the house, and part of the museum, is a dry goods store, where old-fashioned horehound candy can be purchased.

As you make your way around the state of Utah, you might notice that the bee and the beehive are repeated themes in many areas' architecture. In fact, the beehive is the state symbol, stemming from Brigham Young's admiration for the industrious way bees live and work together. As you leave the Beehive House, notice the carved beehive that sits on top of the roof's cupola.

We Call This Part of the World **the Great Basin**

It won't be long before you hear the term the "Great Basin." It was coined by a famous mountain man named John Freemont. He spent a lot of time wandering over what we lovingly call Utah and was an expert on the terrain. He cleverly noticed that streams ran into several large lakes. However, there was no outlet for the water to run into the ocean (this lack of drainage, by the way, is why the Great Salt Lake is salty).

Thus he called the land a "Great Basin." The name stuck— and rightly so. The basin is about a mile high at its lowest elevation. It covers a good part of western Utah. It is composed of forests, plains, deserts, and rugged mountains (which are very steep).

The Lion House (all ages)
Next door to the Beehive House; 63 East South Temple; (801) 363–5466.

Just next door to the Beehive House is a building with a carved lion crouched above the main entrance. This, indeed, is the Lion House, originally built to house Brigham Young's extended family. It is not open to visitors, although they may dine inside at the Pantry Restaurant.

Eagle Gate (all ages) 🏛
At the intersection of State and South Temple.

Outside the Lion House, head a few steps east and view the span of the Eagle Gate that decorates the intersection at State and South Temple Streets. A 6,000-pound eagle with a wingspan of 20 feet guards what was once the entrance to Brigham Young's property. This is the third incarnation of the original. It has been expanded over the years to accommodate wagon traffic, trolley cars, and finally, the automobile. The original wooden eagle can be seen at the Pioneer Memorial Museum, which is described later in this chapter.

LDS Church Office Building (all ages)
50 East North Temple. If you would like a free tour of this building, one can be arranged by calling (801) 240–2190. Tours are available from 9:00 A.M. to 5:00 P.M. April through September and until 4:30 P.M. the rest of the year.

From Eagle Gate, you can head due north for a block's walk to the Church Office Building. You can also take a more scenic route by heading half a block west, cutting through the gorgeous gardens and fountains that announce the building's formal entrance. This is where official church business takes place, and tourist traffic is not routine. This is also the city's tallest building, and the two observation decks on the twenty-sixth floor offer incredible views of the entire valley. Find the elevator bank in the middle of the downstairs lobby and take the express car to the top floor.

In addition, free garden tours of Temple Square and the surrounding areas meet in the Church Office Building from May to September. Monday through Saturday tours leave at 10:00 A.M., noon, 2:00 P.M., and 4:00 P.M.; additional tours are given Tuesday through Thursday at 7:00 P.M. and Sunday at 10:15 A.M. For more information call (801) 240–2331.

Family History Library (all ages)
35 North West Temple; (801) 240–2331. Opens every morning except Sunday at 8:00, and closes at 5:00 P.M. on Monday, 9:00 P.M. Tuesday through Saturday. Admission is free.

For the final two stops on this tour of Temple Square and its environs, head west, back through the grounds of Temple Square, and emerge on West Temple. Cross the street to the library. Remember your family history experience on the computers at the Joseph Smith Building? That was only an introduction to genealogy. What goes on here is much more complex. Housed inside this building is the world's largest collection of genealogical records, and people come from all over the world to compile their family histories. If you decide to delve deeper into your family tree, consult the trained staff and volunteers who are on duty here. There is no fee for this service. Tours of the building are available.

Museum of Church History and Art (all ages)

45 West North Temple; (801) 240–3310. Open Monday through Friday 9:00 A.M. to 9:00 P.M. Open weekends and holidays 10:00 A.M. to 7:00 P.M. Call for tours or information. Admission is free.

Displayed here are all sorts of interesting artifacts and memorabilia from the pioneer past. One second-floor exhibit honors each of the LDS Church presidents, and another shows a permanent collection of paintings by Mormon artists. A permanent exhibit on pioneers includes ship bunks for kids to play in and a life-size replica of a hand cart.

ZCMI Center (all ages)

Main and South Temple, at 36 South Main; (801) 321–8745. Open Monday through Friday 10:00 A.M. to 9:00 P.M., Saturday 10:00 A.M. to 7:00 P.M. Closed Sunday.

There is plenty to do and see in downtown Salt Lake City of a less ecclesiastical nature. Two huge indoor malls are located across the street from each other, facing Main Street at its intersection with South Temple. ZCMI Center is named after the original mercantile, Zions Cooperative Mercantile Institution, which sat on this corner in pioneer days. It is now the home to mall anchor Meier and Frank, as well as two floors of specialty stores, a food court, and an expansive parking structure. The mall's central courtyard is often the site of traveling exhibitions and seasonal displays, which are of interest to children.

Crossroads Plaza (all ages)

Main and South Temple, at 50 South Main; (801) 531–1799. Open Monday through Saturday 10:00 A.M. to 9:00 P.M., and Sunday noon to 6:00 P.M.

The plaza houses four floors of specialty stores and restaurants, as well as movie theaters and covered parking. An arcade popular with teenagers is located on the lower level.

The Gateway

90 South 400 West; (801) 456–0000; www.boyercompany.com/gateway. Open Monday through Saturday 10:00 A.M. to 9:00 P.M., and Sunday noon to 6:00 P.M.

This mall, located across the street from the Delta Center, was built in the old Union Pacific building. The 1908 French Renaissance architecture has been restored in the grand hall. The mall is host to numerous shops and restaurants, and the new Clark Planetarium will soon be the site of the new Children's Museum. The centerpiece of the outdoor mall is the Olympic Legacy Plaza, complete with fountains that dance to music; you and your children may also enjoy running through them on a hot day.

Clark Planetarium (all ages)

110 South 400 West; (801) 456–7827; www.hansenplanetarium.net. Adults $$, children $.

A first-rate planetarium awaits the star buffs in your family right in downtown Salt Lake. Clark Planetarium's spectacular star shows take place in a domed theater filled with comfortable chairs. Individual electronics in each armrest allow the audience to interact with the action above. Two floors of exhibits, including a twenty-four-hour pendulum clock and a moon rock, as well as an innovative gift shop and a 3–D IMAX theater, are also here. Late-night weekend shows feature rock music and corresponding light shows.

Indoor **Stargazing**

My family and I love to look at the stars, but when the weather turns cold, it kind of puts a damper on our interest. That's why we always make it a point to visit the Clark Planetarium. Located in the heart of Salt Lake City, the planetarium is a great activity any time of year, but especially on a chilly winter night.

We like to stop by Temple Square and see the Christmas lights, then head over to the planetarium for one of their amazing laser light shows. The kids love the wild special effects and cool laser animation, and I must admit that I find it quite impressive, too. One of the best things about these shows is that they are set to music.

The shows vary, but I recommend Laser Pink Floyd for you reformed (and not-so-reformed) rockers of the '70s. The kids will dig Laser U2 and some of the other more current groups, but you can't go wrong with any of the shows. Top the night off with a cup of hot cocoa, and you've got entertainment that is truly heavenly.

Capitol Theatre (recommended for children 8 and up) 🎵
50 West 200 South; (801) 355–2787. Prices vary, depending on the performance.

Utah's opera and ballet companies call the Capitol Theatre home. This Rococo-style building also hosts touring companies of Broadway plays. For information, call the number listed.

Salt Palace Convention Center (all ages)
100 South West Temple; (801) 534–4777; www.saltpalace.com.

Salt Lake City is very proud of its new convention center. This is a busy site for conventions and festivals, and it also houses an excellent visitor information center. The staff here can supply maps and brochures as well as give you advice about lodging, dining, transportation, and special events.

Salt Lake Art Center (all ages)

20 South West Temple; (801) 328–4201; www.slartcenter.org. Open from 10:00 A.M. to 5:00 P.M. Tuesday through Thursday and Saturday, 10:00 A.M. to 9:00 P.M. Friday, and 1:00 to 5:00 P.M. Sunday. Admission is **free,** but a small donation is greatly appreciated.

The art center has traveling exhibits that emphasize contemporary art in its galleries and a permanent learning space for children on the main level. Kidspace is full of child-sized stations where hands-on activities amplify the main exhibits. Kidspace is open during art center hours. For a schedule of events, call the number listed above.

Delta Center (all ages)

301 West South Temple. For event tickets call (801) 325–SEAT or go to www.deltacenter .com. For information on Days of '47, call (801) 325–7328 or go to www.daysof47.com.

The Delta Center is perhaps best known as home to the **Utah Jazz** NBA basketball team. In addition, one of the largest rodeos in the world is held annually at the Delta Center in conjunction with **Days of '47,** a statewide celebration of the Mormon pioneers' 1847 arrival in the Salt Lake Valley. The rodeo is one of the highlights of the celebration, with world-champion cowboys and cowgirls competing for $140,000 in prize money.

Salt Lake Stingers (all ages)

Franklin Quest Field at 77 West 1300 South; (801) 485–3800; www.stingersbaseball.com. The season extends from April through mid-September.

The Salt Lake Stingers, the city's AAA baseball team, plays at the beautiful Franklin Quest Field. Don't miss out on the chance to watch an exciting baseball game in a wonderful new park. Call the number listed above for tickets and information.

Utah Arts Festival (all ages)

Library Square, 400 South 200 East. Call (801) 322–2428 or go to www.uaf.org for dates and information.

The Utah Arts Festival, held each June, offers wonderful activities for kids, including inter-active science exhibits, face painting, and many arts and crafts projects. Artists from all over the country display their wares, and food booths feature a variety of ethnic meals.

Rio Grande Railroad Depot (all ages)

300 South Rio Grande Street; (801) 533–3500. Call for current exhibit information and oper-ating hours (generally weekdays 8:00 A.M. to 5:00 P.M.). Admission is **free.**

Exhibits that interpret Utah's past are displayed year-round at the depot, home to the Utah State Historical Society. Rotating collections include artifacts of Utah's Indian culture, a display of early dental and medical offices, and pioneer relics. An excellent bookstore is here as well, specializing in Utah history. Also located in the depot is the Rio Grande Cafe (801–364–3302), a Mexican restaurant popular with families.

John W. Gallivan Utah Center (all ages)

239 South Main; (801) 535–6110. Call for music schedules and skate rental information.

When your family is in the mood for a quirky park full of fun things to do, find the Gallivan Center. This plaza space in the middle of downtown features a pond that turns into a skating rink in the winter, a huge outdoor chess board, large-scale art projects, and an aviary. Live music at the amphitheater is enjoyed by many brown-baggers at lunchtime and by visitors on many weekend nights as well, weather permitting. Every holiday is a major theme event at this park.

Washington Square (all ages)

Between 400 and 500 South on State Street; (801) 533–0858. Free tours are given every Tuesday at noon and 1:00 P.M. and Saturday by appointment.

This historic ten-acre public area is the site of the City and County Building, a sandstone structure built in 1894. For its hundredth birthday, the building was given a major restoration, and it is now returned to its ornate Romanesque origins. Fifty years before the City and County Building was constructed, the square served as a campsite for Mormon pioneers who had just arrived in the valley. It became a major social center and was the scene of carnivals, cattle drives, and circuses. The first peace treaty between the Ute and Shoshone Indians was signed here.

Kearns Mansion (all ages)

603 East South Temple; (801) 538–1005. Free tours are offered April through December on Tuesday and Thursday from 2:00 to 4:00 P.M.

This exquisite home was built by a mining magnate in 1900 and was the most elegant Western residence of its time. Now the governor of Utah calls this elaborate structure home. Guided fifteen-minute tours of the mansion are available. Call for more information.

Salt Lake City Public Library (all ages)

210 East 400 South; (801) 524–8200; www.slcpl.lib.ut.us. Open Monday through Thursday 9:00 A.M. to 9:00 P.M., Friday and Saturday 9:00 A.M. to 6:00 P.M., and Sunday 1:00 to 5:00 P.M.

This new library was designed to resemble a roller coaster outside and Utah inside. The glass ceiling and windows stretching five stories allow light to flood in. The lobby is paved with limestone and lined with shops that sell everything from flowers to puppets to jewelry. The library hosts a myriad of events at its collection of galleries and grottos, including poetry readings, book signings, concerts, and lectures.

Council Hall (all ages)

Located at the northernmost end of State Street, at 300 North State; (801) 538–1900. Open Monday through Friday 8:00 A.M. to 5:00 P.M. and weekends 10:00 A.M. to 5:00 P.M.

Salt Lake's Capitol Hill area is home to a lovely old residential area as well as the state's center of government. You will want to start your tour of the hill with a visit to Council Hall. This 130-plus-year-old building saw a lot of Utah's history as the seat of Salt Lake government and the meeting place of the Territorial Legislature. Today it serves another important role as home to Utah's tourism offices. The visitor center here is staffed with professionals armed with directions and maps and brochures to help you on your way. A bookstore in the building sells area-specific maps and guidebooks as well as posters and trinkets. By calling the toll-free number above you can leave your vacation information requests on a recording and receive mailed information.

Utah State Capitol (all ages)

Next to Council Hall, at 350 North Main. Free tours are given Monday through Friday between 9:00 A.M. and 4:00 P.M. every half hour. Meet your tour leader on the lower level by the big map. Call (801) 538–3000 for details.

Across the street from Council Hall is the impressive State Capitol, completed in 1915 and patterned after the nation's capitol in Washington, D.C. The main entrance hall is rimmed with commissioned murals that illustrate the settlement of the Salt Lake Valley. Notice the domed ceiling, which rises 165 feet from the floor. If you look closely, you'll see that sea gulls are painted inside the dome—it is hard to believe, but their seemingly tiny wingspan is 6 feet wide. Statues and busts of Utah's favorite sons and daughters populate the marbled hall. The lower floor of the capitol is lined with Utah history–inspired exhibits. At the eastern end of this level is an exhibit honoring Utah Senator Jake Garn, who orbited the earth aboard the space shuttle *Discovery.*

Memory Grove (all ages)

East of the State Capitol, at 135 East North Temple.

If you look east of the capitol grounds, you will notice that the ground drops off steeply just across the street. But if you walk to this hilltop, find a paved path and a set of stairs that lead to the bottom of the hill, and you will find yourself in the heart of Memory Grove, a park dedicated to Utah's war veterans. City Creek flows through the middle of this area, surrounded by marble and granite pavilions and a replica of the Liberty Bell. This is a popular picnicking, biking, and jogging area, which extends up the road and into the mountains.

Pioneer Memorial Museum (all ages)

300 North Main; (801) 538–1050. Open year-round, Monday through Saturday from 9:00 A.M. to 5:00 P.M. and Sunday, June through August, from 1:00 to 5:00 P.M. Free guided tours, which take about one hour, are available.

Directly west of the State Capitol grounds and tucked away behind a triangle of traffic is the Pioneer Memorial Museum, a favorite place of children, where all sorts of neat old stuff is found. Four floors of this museum house "the West's most complete collection of authentic nineteenth-century memorabilia," including quilts, furniture, and handmade clothing. Displays interpret early Mormon artifacts, the history of Utah's mining and railroad industries, and Indian artifacts from the period 1847 to 1900. The **Carriage House** that adjoins the museum displays early transportation vehicles, including the wagon in which Mormon Leader Brigham Young was riding when he first entered the Salt Lake Valley.

Marmalade Hill (all ages)
Residential area located on Capitol Hill.

You might have noticed that many of the streets on Capitol Hill take their names from fruit—Quince, Apricot, and so forth. Because of these appellations, this area of town is known as Marmalade Hill. The homes here were built by the early tradesmen of the pioneer era, and their many distinctive styles and ornaments make this an interesting area in which to take a walk.

Historic Trolley Square (all ages)
602 East 500 South; (801) 521–9877. Open Monday through Saturday 10:00 A.M. to 9:00 P.M. and Sunday noon to 7:00 P.M.

The square is now a shopping center, but its brick walkways and eccentric architecture give clues to its original purpose—a barn for trolley cars. Its huge water tower once held 50,000 gallons of water for fire protection. The square is filled with specialty shops and restaurants and is a fun place to spend an afternoon.

Liberty Park (all ages)
589 East 1300 South. Open year-round. Free concerts featuring local artists are held in the park each Monday in August at 7:00 P.M. Call (801) 972–7800 for more information. Call (801) 322–BIRD or go to www.tracyaviary.org for show times at the Tracy Aviary. Admission to aviary $.

Liberty Park is to Salt Lake what Central Park is to New York, albeit a lot smaller. This park is the largest green space in the city center and is filled with all sorts of attractions for children. Dozens of acres of open area are filled with landscaped grounds, tennis courts, and several large playgrounds. In summer an inventive fountain in the middle of the park mimics the mountain canyons to the east of Salt Lake Valley (on a small scale), and shows the path their rivers take to the valley lakes below. Seasonal amusement rides, including a merry-go-round and Ferris wheel, will delight the small children in your family. Older kids will enjoy the walled creative playground, with its two-story slides, sinking ball room, and roped climbing areas. Paddle boats can be rented on the small lake in the park, and a swimming pool is open to everybody. Many special events are held in the park throughout the year, including the largest **Belly Dance Festival** in the United States each August. In the wooded sixteen acres in the midst of Liberty Park is **Tracy Aviary.** This is America's only public bird park and home to more than one thousand birds from around the world. Even if your children aren't especially interested in birds, they will love the excellent **Free Flying Bird Show** here, where eagles, hawks, and a variety of other birds perform amazing feats for their trainer in an open-air setting. The show is presented Wednesday through Sunday during the summer and weekends only in the spring and fall. The **Chase**

Home Museum of Folk Art is the largest building in the park and is open every day in the summer and weekends in spring and fall. Your family will enjoy the collections of quilts, ranch equipment, woodcarvings, and ethnic arts here. **Free** admission.

Utah Museum of Natural History (all ages)

At the University of Utah on President's Circle, a one-way loop reached via University Street and 200 South. Call (801) 581–6927 or go to www.umnh.utah.edu for information on traveling exhibits. Open Monday through Saturday 9:30 A.M. to 5:30 P.M., Sunday and holidays noon to 5:00 P.M. Admission $.

The 1,400-acre campus of the **University of Utah** is located at the easternmost boundary of Salt Lake City. Twenty-four thousand students ensure that the campus and its perimeters are a beehive of constant activity. Of special interest to children is the Natural History Museum, with its world-class dinosaur and fossil collections. Your children will love the simulated mine, extensive rock display, biology and anthropology exhibits, and child-centered gift shop here.

When the Utah Museum of Natural History
Opens the Basement Doors

Utah is the right place for a family that loves dinosaurs, and the Utah Museum of Natural History is a great family activity anytime. However, there's one drawback. Unfortunately, only 10 percent of the museum's magnificent collection (dinosaurs, geology, and more) is displayed.

Once a year in the fall, a day we never miss, the museum "opens the basement doors" and lets the public view the entire collection. There are stands of drawers and racks of "stuff" from floor to ceiling. There are bones, fossils, minerals, and Native American baskets and pots—to name a few things.

Your family can see scientists working on dinosaur bones, as well as botanists and archaeologists, among other professionals, and you can ask questions. There are also a number of activities for kids, including a sand pit with "artifacts," so the kids can hunt for dino bones. My daughter, Abbey, can spend hours in the sand pit with a paintbrush searching for dinosaur remains. My son, Jon-Michael, focuses on the Native American collections. Shari, my wife, hones in on the rock collections. I love it all!

Fort Douglas Military Museum (all ages)

32 Potter Street; (801) 581–1251; www.fortdouglas.org. Find the museum by following South Campus Drive to Fort Douglas. Open Tuesday through Saturday from noon to 4:00 P.M. Admission is **free.**

Army buffs in your family will enjoy the military displays at the Fort Douglas Military Museum. The museum traces the history of this former army fort, founded in 1862 by President Abraham Lincoln. The surrounding grounds contain cannons, former officers' quarters, and a 130-year-old cemetery.

Easy Travel Tips: **The Learning Log**

Have your kids keep a learning log of their travel adventures.

Before you leave home, buy each child a notebook. As you travel, have your kids record what they learn and what they've seen. Then, at the end of each day, they can add to their notes—a few sentences, a paragraph, a page may be appropriate—whatever feels right.

Let me give a few examples. At a bird refuge, have your children list the name of each bird they see. At a museum, have your child take notes on a few of his or her favorite exhibits. At an Indian ruin, have your kids write a creative story. We also encourage sketching and drawing in the learning log.

Red Butte Garden and Arboretum (all ages)
At the far eastern end of Wakara Way, which is reached via Foothill Boulevard at about 400 South; 300 Wakara Way; (801) 581–4747; www.redbuttegarden.org. Open Monday through Saturday 9:00 A.M. to 8:00 P.M., Sunday 9:00 A.M. to 5:00 P.M. Admission $.

A five-minute drive from the museums is Red Butte Garden and Arboretum, a wonderful place for children to explore nature. Miles of paved walkways here are surrounded by water, native trees, shrubs, and floral displays. A late-afternoon concert series during the summer draws hundreds of families for picnics on the spacious lawns.

This Is the Place State Park (all ages)
2601 East Sunnyside Avenue; (801) 582–1847. The park visitor center is open daily from 9:00 A.M. to 7:00 P.M. year-round. Old Deseret Village is open Monday through Saturday 10:00 A.M. to 5:00 P.M., Memorial Day to Labor Day. Admission to the village: adults $$, children $. Admission to the park is free.

Close by Red Butte is one of Utah's premier parks. If you remember Brigham Young's words when he first viewed this valley, you will know how the park got its name. This place marks the end of the Mormon Trail, which reaches back 1,300 miles east, all the way to Illinois. It was here that the Mormon pioneers first glimpsed their new home and where Young's prophecy was fulfilled. He had dreamed of this valley, and when he first glimpsed it, he said, "This is the right place. Drive on." A large monument honors the pioneers, and a visitor center nearby has three floors of exhibits and information. A well-worth-it fee is required to pass through the visitor center and on into **Old Deseret Village,** a living history village that shows everyday life as it was lived in the pioneer era of Utah from 1847 through 1869, when thousands of Mormon faithful made their way to Utah. Farming and domestic chores are performed by costumed docents, and your family can wander freely through the village, spending time where they choose. Activities include adobe brick making, wool carding, and riding in a horse-drawn wagon. You'll see a livery stable, a drug store, a bank, a barbershop, a blacksmith shop, and much, much more.

Utah's Hogle Zoo (all ages)

Located across the street from "This is the Place State Park," at 2600 East Sunnyside Avenue; (801) 582–1631; www.hoglezoo.org. Open in summer from 9:00 A.M. to 5:00 P.M. and in winter from 9:00 A.M. to 4:30 P.M.; the grounds stay open until 6:30 P.M. Admission $$.

Directly across from This Is the Place is the home of 1,200 animals from around the world. Utah's Hogle Zoo is Utah's largest zoo. It features a giraffe complex, a house for giant apes and another one for smaller monkeys, a circular house for lions and tigers, an elephant building, and hundreds of other exhibits. Discovery Land is a hands-on learning area with arts and crafts, a petting zoo, and a mini-train ride. Children will enjoy feeding one or two of the 350 freeflight Australian birds in the Outback Adventure.

Rockreation Sport Climbing Center (recommended for older children)

2074 East 3900 South; (801) 278–7473.

Rock climbing is a popular sport in the canyons surrounding Salt Lake. The climbing center is a good place to test your skills indoors. Instruction is available for all climbing levels. Call the number above for hours and rates.

International Peace Gardens (all ages)

Located inside Jordan Park, at 1000 South and 900 West. Open May through October from 8:00 A.M. to dusk. Admission is free.

A unique set of outdoor floral displays make up the International Peace Gardens. The idea here is to represent, in separate bordered areas, flowers from different countries around the world.

Raging Waters (all ages—adult supervision recommended)

1200 West and 1700 South; (801) 972–3300; www.ragingwatersutah.com. Open from Memorial Day weekend until Labor Day. Call for rates and pool hours.

A hot summer afternoon is well spent at Raging Waters, an outdoor collection of eleven pools that features a giant wild wave, a watery roller coaster, and numerous ways to slide into a swimming pool. Smaller children will enjoy a tamer area set aside just for them.

Hale Centre Theatre (all ages)

3333 South Decker Lake Drive, West Valley City; (801) 984–9000; www.halecentretheatre .org. Reservations are suggested. Prices vary with showtimes and sections. Call for details.

A long tradition of family entertainment continues year-round, Monday through Saturday, at Hale Centre Theatre. The comedies and musicals presented here delight audiences of all ages. *A Christmas Carol* plays each December to packed houses, and a special production for children is presented most Saturday mornings.

A Rutter Family Adventure: **More Than a Day at the Zoo**

Several times a year we have a zoo day . . . a Hogle Zoo day. We love animals.

To get into the spirit of the thing, we sometimes dress up like our favorite beast (okay, Shari and I have some dignity—we just pretend). We always have breakfast at Midvale Coal and Mining (off 72nd South), so we're filled to the gills. Zoo food, no matter where you go, is expensive and tasteless.

Hogle Zoo is nicely arranged and has a wonderful selection of animal friends. Each of us has our favorite— we often fight each other over which to see first. I want to see the bears; Shari, the penguins; Abbey, the leopards; Jon-Michael, the pit vipers.

After a lively discussion in the parking lot, we work out some sort of family compromise. We see the bears first (I'm the biggest). Then we see the penguins. Next could be either the leopards or pit vipers—depending on which kid was the most polite on the drive up.

After seeing our favorite creatures, we start at the beginning and admire each beast in turn. By afternoon, we're starved. Animal watching is hard work. We grab our picnic lunch, find a shady table, and relax.

By early afternoon, after seeing our favorites again, we head home, beating the traffic. A perfect day with the animal kingdom.

Wheeler Historic Farm (all ages)

6351 South 900 East; (801) 264–2241; www.wheelerfarm.com. Open Monday through Saturday 9:30 A.M. to 5:00 P.M.; however, peak season for farming activity is during the warm-weather months. Special events celebrate the holidays. Admission is free.

If your children are interested in the goings-on at a working dairy farm, they can join in the daily chores at Wheeler Historic Farm. Turn-of-the-century life has been re-created here, and horses and humans provide the work power. Your children can help milk cows, feed chickens, and gather eggs each afternoon. An original Victorian farmhouse is centered on this seventy-five-acre property, complete with a large kitchen garden. Fishing and nature walks are popular, as well as horse-drawn wagon rides. Admission includes a tour.

Festival of Trees (all ages)
For more information call (801) 588–3684.

During the first weekend in December, Salt Lake City hosts the Festival of Trees. For a minimal fee (which is donated to the local children's hospital), the whole family can view elaborately decorated Christmas trees and gingerbread mansions. For kids there's an area to make Christmas crafts. There are also performances by local artists throughout the day.

Where to Eat

Lamb's Grill Cafe. 169 South Main; (801) 364–7166. Greek, American. $$

Lion House. 63 East South Temple; (801) 363–5466. American. $

Ruby River Steak House. 435 South 700 East; (801) 359–3355. American, Steak. $$

Rio Grande Café. 270 South Rio Grande; (801) 364–3302. Mexican. $

Where to Stay

Travelodge Hotel Airport Inn. 2333 West North Temple; (801) 539–0438. $$

Econo Lodge. 715 West North Temple; (801) 363–0062. $$

Super 8 Motel. 616 South 200 West; (801) 534–0808. $$

Anton Boxrud Bed-and-Breakfast Inn. 57 South 600 East; (801) 363–8035 or (800) 524–5511. $$$–$$$$

Saltair Bed and Breakfast. 164 South 900 East; (801) 533–8184 or (800) 733–8184. $$$

Peery Hotel. 110 West Broadway (Third South); (801) 521–4300. $$$$

Murray

Known primarily as one of the many suburban communities surrounding Salt Lake, Murray also has its own identity. An attitude of fun and excitement distinguishes this town, just south of the city on I–15, from its neighbors. You won't want to miss out on its freewheeling entertainment and friendly atmosphere.

Utah Fun Dome (all ages)
4998 Galleria Drive; (801) 293–0800; www.fundome.com. Take I–15 to the Fifty-third South exit, go west to the traffic signal at 700 West, turn north, and 700 West will lead you there. Admission is free, but attractions vary in price.

A popular hangout for young teens is the Fun Dome. This indoor cornucopia of mini-golf, bowling, mini carnival rides, batting cages, arcade games, and food courts is known as

America's entertainment mall. Special events are regularly scheduled, and party rooms may be rented. Be sure to try the challenging Laser Tag game; children and adults alike will love it!

The Desert Star Playhouse (all ages)
4861 South State Street; (801) 266–7600. Tickets $$. Call for a play schedule and show times.

The Playhouse offers fun evenings of entertainment for families. Comedies and melodramas include much booing and clapping, sing-alongs, and more. You can purchase pizza, soft drinks, and ice cream to eat and drink while you watch the show.

Fast Utah Facts

- In the months of December and January Snowbird averages more than 200 inches of snow.
- One third of Utah is considered desert.
- Utah is a leading producer of prosthetic body parts.
- Hikers along Utah's Wasatch Front can still find fossilized shoreline evidence of the Great Lake Bonneville that once covered most of Utah and portions of Idaho and Nevada.
- Utah's birth rate is the second highest in the nation; its death rate is the second lowest.
- The state's population is younger than the national average—25.7 years compared to 32.7.

Sandy

South of Salt Lake on I–15, Sandy has the good fortune of serving as the gateway to a number of Utah's premier ski resorts. It also offers a variety of entertainment opportunities, including great outdoor fun in the summertime.

Salt Lakers are proud of their quick access to the alpine canyons that rim their valley. Within minutes your family can travel from the midst of urban clutter to the wild surround of the mountains. To the east is the Wasatch Range, the westernmost range of the Rocky Mountains, with peaks rising to 12,000 feet. One destination is 15-mile-long **Big Cottonwood Canyon,** famous for **Brighton** (801–532–4731) and **Solitude** (801–534–1400), two ski resorts located near the canyon terminus. Both resorts have plenty of steep terrain for experts, but are beloved by children and cautious parents because of their kinder, gentler beginner hills. Both offer special ski packages and lessons for children, restaurants, lodging, and year-round planned activities.

Just to the south of Big Cottonwood is **Little Cottonwood Canyon,** an equally glorious outdoor playground. On your drive up this canyon you will notice the rugged granite walls that rise on either side. This rock was quarried for the exteriors of both the Salt Lake Temple and the State Capitol. Little Cottonwood boasts Alta and Snowbird ski resorts. Utah's first ski resort, **Alta** (801–742–3333), is located in Albion Basin, one of the most beautiful mountain surrounds in the world. **Snowbird**'s (801–742–2222 or 800–453–3000) tram carries 125 skiers on a thrilling ride, straight up 2,900 feet to the top of Hidden Peak. The stunning view here takes in Salt Lake Valley, Heber Valley, and the Uinta and Oquirrh Mountains, and, fortunately for non-skiers, the tram also carries passengers back down the mountain. Both Alta and Snowbird offer plenty of beginner runs and special ski packages for kids as well as lodging and restaurants.

During the summer, Big and Little Cottonwood Canyons are much visited by city dwellers seeking relief from the heat. Excellent stream fishing abounds, as well as picnicking, biking, rock climbing, and camping in Forest Service campgrounds. Call (801) 943–1794 or (801) 466–6411 for camping information. Hiking in these mountains is a wonderful family activity. The lakes near Brighton are all good destinations and good fishing holes as well. Snowbird's tram runs year-round and eliminates the uphill part of Hidden Peak's hiking trail. However, be aware that the gorgeous downhill route can be challenging for children. The Plaza at Snowbird hosts a summer concert series and during the fall months is the scene for **Oktoberfest.** Albion Basin is world-famous for its wildflower season in late spring and early fall. Trail maps are available in local stores; call the resorts for more information.

Jordan Commons (all ages) 🎵 🍽
9400 South State; (801) 304–4636. Admission $–$$.

Jordan Commons is a large entertainment complex containing seventeen theaters and an IMAX screen, an arcade, and a number of restaurants, including China Lily, Ruby River, Tucci's, Joe's Crab Shack, and a food court. The restaurant that garners the most attention is the Mayan, a Mexican restaurant that tries to capture the feel of southern Mexico with a kid-friendly menu, a tree-top atmosphere, animatronic animals, and cliff divers who perform twice an hour.

Where to Stay

Comfort Inn. 8955 South 255 West; (801) 255–4919. $$

Park City

This resort community is located in Summit County, home to the highest mountains in the state. Park City was settled by prospectors in 1868, and it grew in size and stature as a mining community for more than fifty years.

Snowmobile tours are a popular activity in the hills and meadows surrounding Park City. Sleigh rides can be combined with a Western cookout dinner for an all-evening outing. In warm weather, hiking, biking, and horseback riding in the aspen and pine surroundings are the featured sports. Enjoyed year-round in these parts is hot-air ballooning, for a bird's-eye view of northern Utah. Call the **Park City Chamber/Bureau** (435–649–6100 or 800–453–1360; www.parkcityinfo.com) for a list of outfitters who offer rentals and guides for these activities.

Tips on **Day Trippin'**

The best way to see Utah is on foot and from your car. From my perspective, the best things in Utah aren't that expensive. Most of the time, the major expense is driving to and from the adventure, food, and perhaps a modest entrance fee. Day trips are a great way to go.

Let me give you a few tips on successful day traveling. Utah is a big state; some counties are bigger than many eastern states. This is the West! They don't say we have wide-open spaces for nothing. There isn't always a gas station or a burger joint on every corner.

1. Buy a good map and refer to it so that you know where you are—getting lost is a drag.

2. Always keep your gas tank at least half full.

3. Even in the summer, everyone should have a jacket. Your car should have a couple of blankets, too.

4. Have an emergency kit tucked away: Have a few gallons of extra water and some food. (We carry peanut butter, crackers, jerky, peanuts, dried fruit, and canned fruit.)

5. Pack a generous lunch, and don't count on fast food. Rural fast food, most of the time, is very predictable, and usually bad.

Historic Main Street (all ages)
Main Street.

The town's Main Street retains the spirit of that frontier mining community, with original storefronts that have been carefully restored. Today these buildings hold specialty shops, restaurants, and night spots. A window-shopping walk up or down this busy street is fun any time of day or night. On summer Saturday afternoons, your stroll will be accompanied by outdoor musicians, who play from 1:00 to 4:00 P.M. The largest arts festival in the state takes place on Main Street during the first weekend in August. More than 200 visual artists display their wares during the **Park City Arts Festival.**

The Visitors Center and Museum (all ages)

528 Main Street; (435) 649–6104. Open Monday through Saturday 10:00 A.M. to 7:00 P.M. and Sunday noon to 6:00 P.M. Admission is free.

The Visitors Center and Museum chronicles the city's past and is found at the old territorial jail. Stop in for information and directions before you begin exploring this resort town.

Egyptian Theatre (all ages)

328 Main Street. Call (435) 649–9371 or go to www.egyptiantheatrecompany.com for performance information.

Another noteworthy building on this street is the Egyptian Theatre, constructed in 1926. Its stage is now used for musicals, dramas, and comedies.

Kimball Art Center (all ages)

638 Park Avenue; (435) 649–8882; www.kimball-art.org. Park City has a Cultural Arts Hotline with information on films, concerts, events, and exhibits: Call (435) 647–9747 for updated information. Admission is free.

More than a dozen art galleries do a booming business in this area, selling handcrafted jewelry, photographs, watercolors, and sculptures. Kimball Art Center, one of the largest, is just off Main Street. Artists in your family will enjoy the traveling exhibits, the gift shop, and the scheduled arts and crafts classes here.

Factory Stores at Park City (all ages)

Just off the I–80 turnoff to Park City, at 6699 North Landmark Drive; (435) 645–7078. Open from 10:00 A.M. to 9:00 P.M. Monday through Saturday and 11:00 A.M. to 6:00 P.M. on Sunday.

The forty-eight stores here service the bargain hunter looking for savings on clothes, kitchenware, linens, books, and more. A children's playground and two restaurants are part of the outdoor mall.

Park City Resort Center (all ages)

Thirty-seven miles east of Salt Lake City on I–80, at 1310 Lowell Avenue. The Alpine Slide is open in summer from 2:00 to 9:00 P.M. Monday through Friday and 11:00 A.M. to 9:00 P.M. on weekends. One slide $$, five-ride coupon $$$$. Children ages 2 to 6, $. Silver Putt Mini Golf, single round $, foursome $$$. Call (435) 649–8111 for more information. Little Miner's Park Rides $; booklet good for ten rides $$$.

A sure summertime favorite for children is the thrilling **Alpine Slide,** located at the Park City Resort Center. This requires a chairlift ride halfway up the Payday ski run to the top of the slide and a breathless, speedy trip down 3,000 feet of winding concrete track. After your slide, play a round at Silver Putt Mini Golf, also located at the resort center.

Adjacent to the golf course is Little Miner's Park, built especially for the very small children in your group. The array of gentle rides and activities here includes a mini-Ferris wheel, train cars, and a set of gliding airplanes. Guided horseback rides are also available in the area.

Park City Mountain Resort (ages 3 and up)

Thirty-seven miles east of Salt Lake City on I-80, at 1310 Lowell Avenue. For general information call (435) 649-8111. For accommodations call (800) 222-7275 or go to www.park citymountain.com. Adult Full-Day rate varies. Adults $$$$, kids 6 and under ski free with paying adult.

In winter, the Park City Mountain Resort becomes the largest ski resort in Utah as well as the official training site for the U.S. ski team. Its promoters say you can "ski an entire weekend and never cover the same run twice." On a cold day your children will appreciate the enclosed (and heated) gondolas that carry skiers to the top of the mountain. Thirteen other lifts operate at the same time, carrying up to 23,000 skiers an hour over the resort's 2,200 acres. Group and private lessons are available for all ages. The Kinderschule program takes advantage of the 3-mile beginner run and teaches children ages three through six.

Deer Valley Resort (children who ski)

Take I-80 east toward Cheyenne. Take exit 145 (Park City) and travel about 6 miles until you reach the intersection of Park Avenue and Deer Valley Drive. Turn left and continue on Deer Valley Drive until you reach the Snow Park Lodge at 2250 Deer Valley Drive South. For general information about Deer Valley, call (435) 649-1000 or go to www.deervalley.com. For lodging reservations call (800) 424-3337.

The recreation resorts surrounding Park City played a major role in the 2002 Winter Olympics, with venues for seven events, including slalom, giant slalom, Nordic combined, bobsled, and luge. Deer Valley's architecture and atmosphere is modeled after European resorts, and it is known for its luxurious restaurants and accommodations. More than 33 percent of Deer Valley's sixty-seven runs are groomed daily. Its ski school accepts students four years old and up, with group and private classes each day. Child care is offered for younger children. During the summer months a concert series takes place on the lower grassy hills here, and the Sterling Chairlift takes hikers and bikers (along with their bikes) up to a network of trails.

Utah Winter Sports Park (all ages)

3000 Bear Hollow Drive. Call (435) 658-4200 for more information.

The Utah Winter Sports Park at Bear Hollow is one of the few western resorts devoted to ski jumping. Novices and experts alike can practice flying on the four downhill ski jumps here, as well as enjoy a summer and winter aerial freestyle jump, a half pipe for snowboarding, and a bobsled/luge course. Lessons are available (beginners start out on snow bumps in the park's play area), and scheduled competitions showcase the pros. A day lodge offers a snack bar and rest rooms. A two-hour ski jumping session is available in winter only. The session also includes an introductory lesson.

Olympic **Parks**

Now that the 2002 Winter Olympics have come and gone, the Olympic venues are now Utah playgrounds. **Soldier Hollow** (435–654–2002), near Midway, offers cross-country skiing, tubing, and snowshoeing. Those who would like to try their marksmanship skills can receive instruction on the biathalon course year-round. Summer activities include horseback riding, hiking, biking, ATVs, and golf. If speed is your addiction, try the **Utah Olympic Park** in Park City (435–658–4200), which offers ski jumping instruction and bobsled rides year-round. Or you can skate on "The Fastest Ice on Earth" at the **Utah Olympic Oval** (801–963–7109) off 5400 South in Salt Lake City. They offer year-round skating, drop-in hockey, and instruction on everything from speed and figure skating to hockey and curling. For more information about any of these sites, go to www.olyparks.com.

White Pine Touring Center (all ages) 🚫
201 Heber Avenue; (435) 649–8710. Open daily from 9:00 A.M. to 7:00 P.M. Adults $$, children 12 and under free. For more information call or write to P.O. Box 680068, Park City 84068.

Park City's golf course doubles in the winter as the White Pine Touring Center, an 18-kilometer groomed track for cross-country skiers. Choose between flat or rolling terrain or try both.

Dolly's Book Store (all ages) 🔒
510 Main Street; (435) 649–8062. Open daily 10:00 A.M. to 10:00 P.M.

This bookstore is a fun place to relax with the family after a hard day of skiing or window shopping. The children's section is full of colorful selections that are sure to grab the kids' attention. Everyone can choose a book and then curl up in a cozy chair (maybe with the resident cat). The staff is friendly and eager to offer recommendations for young and old alike. After reading for a little while, step through the door into the little candy shop and have a sample of fudge.

Where to Eat

Chimayo. 368 Main Street; (435) 649–6222. American. $$$$

Grub Steak Restaurant. 2200 Sidewinder Drive; (435) 649–8060. American. $$$

Main Street Pizza & Noodle. 530 Main Street; (435) 645–8878. Italian. $–$$

Park City Pizza Company. 1612 Ute Boulevard; (435) 649–1591. Pizza. $–$$

Rocky Mountain Chocolate Factory. 1385 Lowell Avenue, #2; (435) 649–2235. Ice cream. $

Zoom. 660 Main Street; (435) 649–9108. American. $$

Where to Stay

Chateau Apres. 1299 Norfolk Avenue; (435) 649–9372. $$

Gables Hotel. 1435 Lowell Avenue; (435) 658–1417. $$–$$$$

Park City Marriott. 1895 Sidewinder Drive; (435) 649–2900. $$$

Stein Eriksen Lodge. 7700 Stein Way; (435) 649–3700. $$$$

Bluffdale

While Bluffdale is only about fifteen minutes south of Salt Lake on I–15, it is quite different from its neighbor. Bluffdale, located at "the point of the mountain" (on I–15 between Provo and Salt Lake City), offers a more rural atmosphere for those who need a break from hectic city life.

Bluffdale's **Ball Mountain** is a jump site for a number of adventurous hang gliders. Those with four-wheel drive can drive to the top of the mountain and watch people soar like the birds. Or you can enjoy the view from below.

Copperton

This small town is home to the massive Kennecott copper mines, the largest open-pit mines in the world.

Kennecott Utah Copper Bingham Canyon Mine (all ages)

Located on Utah Highway 48 West at Midvale; P.O. Box 6001, Magna 84044. The visitor center is open from April through October from 8:00 A.M. until 8:00 P.M. Call (801) 252–3234 or go to www.kennecott.com for more information. Vehicles $.

Kennecott is said to be one of the few manmade constructions that can be seen from space. Two Empire State Buildings could be stacked on top of each other inside this crater. Five billion tons of rock have been removed since 1906, yielding copper, gold, silver, and molybdenum. The visitor center has fascinating indoor exhibits, a film that explains the history of mining, and outdoor exhibits that display mining equipment. By looking down into the ½-mile-deep, 2½-mile-wide excavation, you will see "tiny" trucks moving their loads inside the mine. The parts of these trucks are displayed here; the tires alone are about 8 feet high!

House of Copper (all ages)
Call (801) 569–2822 for information.

Leave time for a stop at House of Copper, a truly unique store that sells exclusively copper items. Your children will be amazed at some of the oddments found here—everything from copper chandeliers to rolling pins.

West Jordan

West Jordan, like the majority of the communities in the Salt Lake Valley, has a strong pioneer heritage. You will surely enjoy the historical attractions of this town, just west of Salt Lake, while taking in the beautiful natural surroundings.

Gardner Historic Village (all ages)
1100 West 7800 South; (801) 566–8903.

In 1877 Archibald Gardner was asked by Brigham Young to build a mill in the south end of Salt Lake Valley. His business prospered and for many years provided flour for the surrounding community. His mill has been made over into Gardner Historic Village, a countrified emporium brimming with three floors of old-fashioned furniture, accessories, gifts, and restaurants. The surrounding grounds carry on the country theme, where transplanted historic homes have been made over into quaint shops.

Fast Utah Facts

- It took almost fifty years for lawmakers to admit Utah to the Union.
- There were nearly 140,000 marriages and 13,000 divorces in Utah in 1994.
- The word Utah comes directly from "Ute," the name of a resident Indian tribe.
- Most of Utah is more than 4,000 feet above sea level.
- The California gull has been the state bird since 1849.
- Utahns rank number four in the longest lifetime category at almost 76 years.

Lake Point

This junction 17 miles west of Salt Lake City, on I–80, offers access to the main recreation center for the south shore of the **Great Salt Lake.** But long before you reach Lake Point, you will notice the lake from your car window, stretching endlessly to the north. This is the world-famous inland sea, the largest lake west of the Mississippi, a 2,000-square-mile body of water with a salt content up to twelve times as high as the ocean's. The Great Salt Lake is the water collection point for the vast geographical area called the Great Basin, which encompasses northwestern Utah and much of northern Nevada. The Great Basin has many inflowing water sources, but no exits for that water. This circumstance allows minerals and salts to collect in the relatively shallow water and results in many oddities, including Great Salt Lake, the **Bonneville Salt Flats,** wetlands, springs, and barren deserts. Today the lake supports several industries. Salt, potash, and magnesium are mined from the lake, via evaporative ponds, and used for a variety of purposes. Perhaps the most interesting lake-dependent business is the brine shrimp industry. Brine shrimp are unique to the ecology of the Great Salt Lake, requiring the lake's high salinity to thrive, and, in fact, are the only creatures to survive in the salty water. The tiny shrimp lay eggs twice a year—in the warm weather a soft-shelled egg and in the cold season an extremely hard-shelled egg. These smaller-than-a-pinhead winter eggs can wash up on the shore, be left stranded for years, be recaptured by the lake, and still manage to hatch. In winter you will see small planes swooping over the lake looking for the blood-red, winter egg deposits—hundreds of millions of eggs floating together, looking almost like an oil slick. Once they sight the eggs, boats and nets scoop them up by the ton, package them, and send them off to the Far East, where they are rehydrated, hatched, and used for prawn food. The tiny brine shrimp add about $30 million to Utah's economy each year. They are also responsible for the . . . ahem, unique smell that sometimes emanates from the lakeshore.

Great Salt Lake State Park (all ages)

Take exit 104 off I–80, near Lake Point Junction; P.O. Box 16658, Salt Lake City 84116; (801) 250–1898. Saltair is open daily 9:00 A.M. to 6:00 P.M. from Memorial Day through Labor Day, with seasonal hours during the rest of the year. Admission to the state park free; camping $$.

On the south shore of the lake is Great Salt Lake State Park. From the park's sandy beaches you will view a panorama of salty water, mudflats, and islands. If you time your visit at dusk, you will most likely be rewarded with a spectacular sunset. The park is dominated by a turreted building called **Saltair.** The original Saltair building was an extremely popular meeting place in the late 1800s, when trolley cars used to deposit city dwellers for Sunday picnics and nighttime entertainment. That building was destroyed by fire, and the current building is meant to be a re-creation. Concerts are held here, there are food stands open seasonally (usually April through October), and an orientation video for the lake can be viewed here. Nearby, weather permitting, there are also camel rides, bumper boats, mini-car racing, and gift shops galore. A 300-slip sailboat marina provides year-round activity on this lake that never freezes. Seasonal overnight camping is available here, with open showers, rest rooms, and picnic tables. Another popular access to the Great Salt Lake is Antelope Island State Park, described in the "Northern Utah" chapter.

Mills Junction

As you enter Mills Junction, you will pass Adobe Rock, a landmark honoring the Mormon scouts who first viewed this valley in 1847. A spring nearby was a valuable water source for long-ago travelers. Continue south for 1 mile to find the renovated Historic Benson Grist Mill.

Historic Benson Grist Mill (all ages)

One mile south of town, at 325 State Road 138, Stansbury Park; (435) 882–7678. Open from May through October, Monday through Saturday from 10:00 A.M. to 4:00 P.M. Special events commemorating the history of the area are held throughout the season here. Call for more information. Admission $.

This mill was at one time known as "Brigham Young's Mill" and was a primary source of flour for the early pioneers. In operation from 1860 to 1940, it is one of the oldest standing buildings in western Utah. The mill has been renovated for tourists, and much of its original equipment can still be seen.

Grantsville

Just west of Salt Lake City, on Utah Highway 138, you will find this small town with an important place in Utah history.

The Donner-Reed Museum (all ages)

On the corner of Cooley and Clark Streets, at 90 North Cooley. Museum tours can be arranged by calling in advance. Admission is free.

This museum tells the tale of the ill-fated Donner-Reed party—a group of emigrants who in 1846 formed one of the first wagon trains to attempt crossing the salt desert that surrounds this area. After weeks of thirst and exhaustion, the group did make it across the desert, only to be caught in the Sierra Nevada Mountains by an early winter storm. They were forced to winter in the mountains, digging holes in the snow for shelter. They subsisted on the leather from their shoes and harnesses, and finally, desperately, by eating the flesh of their dead comrades. When spring came, only forty-four of the original eighty-seven members of the group had survived. During their trek across the desert, they abandoned many of their wagons and supplies, and the museum here has collected many of these artifacts. A log cabin and blacksmith shop are also on the premises.

Tooele

The name of this western Utah community is pronounced "two-ILL-uh," and while its origin is not clear, it may be named after a Goshute Indian chief named Tuilla. For information about special events in Tooele, visit the Tooele County Chamber of Commerce at 201 North Main Street (upstairs) or call (435) 882–0690.

Railroad Museum (all ages)
Vine and Broadway Streets, in the old Tooele Valley Railroad Depot, at 35 North Broadway; (435) 882–2836. Open during the summer months only, Tuesday through Saturday from 10:00 A.M. to 4:00 P.M. Admission is free.

The Railroad Museum is especially fun for children, with its simulated mine and locomotive displays, including an outdoor steam engine, several cabooses, and a dining car.

Pioneer Hall (all ages)
35 East Vine; (435) 843–5436. Open for visitors on Saturday between Memorial Day and Labor Day from 11:00 A.M. to 3:00 P.M. Admission is free.

The hall was built in 1867 as a courthouse, and the cabin next door was one of the first constructed in the Tooele Valley. Both are now operated by the Daughters of the Utah Pioneers as a museum and offer displays of artifacts and pictures. To arrange a tour call the number listed above.

South Willow Canyon (all ages)
Located west of town on Utah Highway 112. For information on camping and fishing, call the Wasatch-Cache National Forest Service office at (801) 466–6411.

An easy drive west of town takes your family to South Willow Canyon in the Stansbury Mountain Range, open for car and horse traffic during the nonsnow months. South Willow is dotted with campgrounds, and the higher elevation here makes this a favorite getaway spot from the summer heat. South Willow Creek makes a pleasant meander through the canyon and is stocked with trout for your fishing pleasure. The canyon borders the **Deseret Wilderness Area,** which is set aside for nonmotorized traffic. If your children are older and feeling especially hardy, you might attempt the hike to **Deseret Peak,** the highest in the Stansbury Range. This is a lovely, 4-mile trek up a well-marked trail, but the grade is relentless, and near the end the trail becomes quite steep. Those who reach the summit are rewarded with marvelous views in all directions; on a clear day you will see the islands in the Great Salt Lake to the north, Skull Valley and the Deep Creek Mountains to the west, and all of Tooele Valley to the east.

Festival of the Old West (all ages)
Tooele County Fairgrounds at 400 West 400 North, (435) 882–0690.

The fourth weekend of each September brings the Festival of the Old West at Tooele. The festival has three parts: a rendezvous, a powwow, and a gem and mineral show. For three days mountain men, Native Americans, and other lovers of history converge on Tooele to show off their skills, perform native dances, and sell their wares. Ceremonies of particular interest to children, such as a tomahawk throwing and children's dances, are scheduled throughout the festival, so it's wise to call Tooele County Chamber of Commerce for specific days and times.

Ophir/Mercur

If you have a four-wheel-drive vehicle, consider exploring Ophir. This small town was founded in 1865 when soldiers of the U.S. Army noticed Indians making bullets out of silver. The soldiers quickly settled, and the find became public. In 1870 the town's name was changed from St. Louis to Ophir after King Solomon's mines. Ophir eventually emptied after the silver ran out.

Located just off Highway 73 west of Tooele, Ophir still contains a number of buildings from its silver-mining heyday. Many of the buildings are private property (please respect the NO TRESPASSING signs), but there is a general store that is open on occasion and numerous examples of ornamental mining architecture.

Mercur, a few miles south, is more difficult to find. This town went through several mining booms, but it died for the last time in 1951. In the eighties, the whole area was demolished and strip mined. All that remains is the cemetery. For more information about either of these towns, visit www.ghosttowns.com/states/ut/.

Oquirrh Mountain Mining Museum (all ages)
Deseret Peak Recreation Complex, 2930 West Highway 112, Tooele; (435) 843–4000. Guided tours by appointment only. Admission is free; donations accepted.

If you are interested in the mining or history of this area, head to this museum, located between Tooele and Grantsville on Highway 112. Exhibits feature old mines, current mines, and reclamation practices, and an educational mining video is shown during the tour.

Wendover

As you drive on I–80 toward Wendover and the Nevada border, you will travel through **Great Salt Lake Desert,** known as one of the most barren stretches of land in the country. The road here is dead-on straight; 100 miles of asphalt with a 1,000-mile view circling your window. You are looking at the remains of Lake Bonneville, now shrunk to the parameters of the Great Salt Lake, and the ancient and exceedingly flat lakebed provides an unusual outlook. Optical illusions are common, with mountains seeming to float above the earth and nonexistent pools of water hovering in the distance. If you happen to pass this way during a rainstorm, or in the middle of the sunset hour, the visuals are astounding. In the midst of all this flatness, you will come across one of the more peculiar artistic statements in the world. This desert inspired Swedish artist Karl Momen to weld large metal balls to a gargantuan vertical structure and name it the *Tree of Life.* The town of Wendover straddles the Utah/Nevada border, and its Nevada side is a gaming mecca that lures hundreds of thousands of Westerners each year to try their luck at the slot machines and tables.

The **Salt Flats**

If you want to get specific, the salt flats are called "playas." There are a number of playas in this part of the world. The largest are the Bonneville Salt Flats in the northwestern part of Utah. (I–80 cuts through it.) As Lake Bonneville started to dry up (about 10,000 years ago), it left these magnificent plains, one of the flattest places on earth.

This alkaline geological wonder is nearly 4,000 square miles of, well, salt. It's no wonder the early pioneers would travel days out of their way to avoid crossing this old lakebed. Travel, at best, was difficult and dangerous. Bonneville was referred to as the "dreaded" flat.

Speed Week (all ages)

Bonneville Salt Flats; (801) 485–2662; www.saltflats.com. Races are held in August. Call for schedules and information.

The Utah portion of Wendover is the gateway to the Bonneville Salt Flats, the rock-hard salt beds that provide a perfect venue for car racing. The salt flats are the legacy of the above-mentioned Lake Bonneville, a huge ancient lake that once covered most of Utah and parts of several surrounding states. A combination of weather and human meddling have eroded these flats in the last decade, and during the 1990s they were closed from time to time for reclamation purposes. But most years, in August, this 26,000-acre salt bed attracts the latest in race car technology for seven days of races and events called Speed Week. Three additional racing events are scheduled each year during the late-summer months.

Wendover Air Base (all ages)

Take exit 2 from I–80 and then a left turn at the airport sign onto Main Street; (435) 571–2907 for a free self-guided tour pamphlet; www.wendoverairbase.com.

The old Wendover Air Base played a prominent role in World War II, providing the training ground for bomb crews who went on to participate in the first nuclear bombardment in history, which dropped atomic bombs on Hiroshima and Nagasaki. In 1943 this was the world's largest military reserve, with more than 17,000 troops stationed here. A small museum honoring the military people who worked here is housed in the operations building of Icarus Aviation (located on the air base). A self-guided driving tour will take your family to historic places around the base. The **Enola Gay Monument,** named after the plane from which the first atomic bomb was dropped, is found on Main Street, across from the Peppermill Resort. In September you can enjoy a vintage air show.

Top Annual Events in Greater Salt Lake

JUNE
Utah Arts Festival, Salt Lake City; (801) 322–2428

JULY
Days of '47 Rodeo, Delta Center; (801) 325–7328

SEPTEMBER
Festival of the Old West, Tooele; (435) 882–0690

SEPTEMBER AND OCTOBER
Oktoberfest, Snowbird; (800) 232–9542

DECEMBER
Festival of Trees, Salt Lake City; (801) 588–3688

Winterfest, Snowbird; (801) 742–2222

The Nutcracker, Ballet West, Salt Lake City; (888) 451–2787

Central Utah

Geographically, this part of the state is Utah's melting pot. The alpine scenery from the north flattens out, but it hasn't yet turned into the red-rock sandstone that dominates the south. This is prime farm and ranch country—and on your travels you'll drive past miles of planted crops and pastureland.

Most of Utah's tourist trade is plied to the north and the south, and this area has a slower, small-town feel. But don't let these rural surroundings fool you. There is much to do and see here, including world-famous rodeos, water slides, a national park, historic train rides, amusement parks, beaches, and theater under the stars.

The cities below are organized in a somewhat haphazard pattern because major roads do not always directly connect the destinations. As the crow flies, the route is circular, beginning and ending in the eastern end of Utah County. Be aware that in the listed order, some cities are more than 100 miles from each other, and backtracking is sometimes required. Consult a road map, and ask locally for directions.

Alpine

Peppermint Place (all ages)
From I–15 take exit 287 to Alpine; then find 119 East 200 North. Open Monday through Saturday 10:00 A.M. to 6:00 P.M. Call (800) 377–4368 for tour times or go to www.kencraft candy.com.

About 600 kinds of candy, along with porcelain dolls, cuckoo clocks, music boxes, and lots of other gifty things are sold here. You can take a tour of this cheerful outlet store (and get free candy!) any weekday between 10:00 A.M. and 2:00 P.M.

American Fork

This town, about 10 miles north of Provo, is the gateway to American Fork Canyon, one of the most rugged and beautiful canyons in Utah.

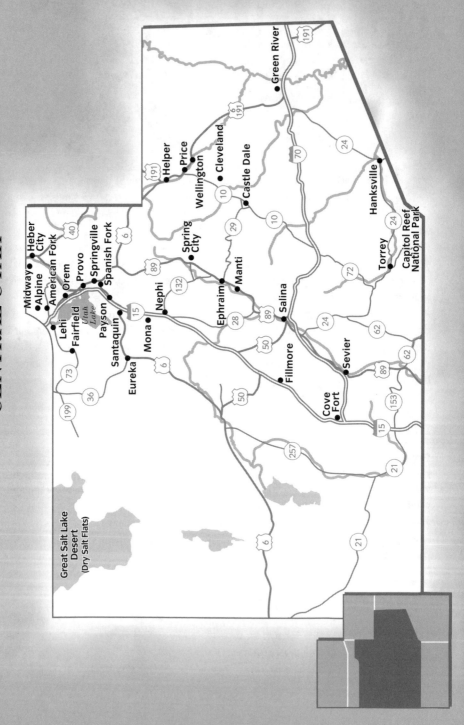

CENTRAL UTAH

Michael's
TopPicks for fun in Central Utah

1. Mount Timpanogos LDS Temple, American Fork; (801) 763–4540

2. Fish Lake, Fishlake National Forest, east of Richfield; (435) 425–3702

3. Capitol Reef National Park; (435) 425–3791

4. Goblin Valley State Park; (435) 564–3633

5. The Alpine Loop (American Fork Canyon outside of American Fork)

6. The Nebo Loop (Nebo Canyon outside of Payson)

7. Brigham Young University, Provo; (801) 422–4431

8. Provo River

9. Cascade Springs

10. Nine Mile Canyon

Paradise Pond (all ages)

1100 West Main Street; (801) 756–7821. Open weekdays noon until dark and weekends 10:00 A.M. until dark. The cost depends on how many fish you catch.

For the very small fisherpeople in your family, American Fork has a child-sized, stocked body of water where many kids have caught their first fish.

Timpanogos Cave National Monument (not recommended for very small children)

In American Fork Canyon. Follow Utah Highway 92, which is well-marked with signs. Open from mid-May through mid-September. The visitor center is open, and cave tours are available, daily from 7:00 A.M. to 5:30 P.M. Call (801) 756–5238 or, for advance tickets, write Timpanogos Cave National Monument, R.R. 3, Box 200, American Fork 84003, at least two weeks before your trip. Adults $$, children $.

Three miles up from the entrance to American Fork Canyon, you'll find the trailhead for Timpanogos Cave National Monument. A very steep, zigzaggy, 1½-mile hike is required to reach the cave, but the rewards are well worth the effort. On your way you'll have the opportunity to sit at rest areas and enjoy extraordinary views of American Fork Canyon, the Wasatch Range, and Utah Valley. If your children aren't eager hikers, plan plenty of extra time for this climb; you might consider bringing along treats with which to bribe small people "up just one more switchback." Once you reach the cave, you'll be greeted by a guide who will take your ticket and escort you through one of the most colorful and multiformationed caves anywhere. It consists of three primary chambers cluttered with stalactites, stalagmites, draperies, flowstone, and other goodies. Look for the **Great Heart** and the **Chimes Chamber.** And take a jacket—the cave has a constant temperature of about 45 degrees Fahrenheit, the temperature inside a refrigerator. Treats are sold in the lower parking lot June through August, and there are many lovely picnicking sites near the cave trailhead.

Alpine Loop (all ages)

Follow the signs from the Timpanogos parking lot to Utah Highway 92. The Alpine Loop is closed during midwinter.

This is a spectacular scenic drive that is often compared to a trip in the Canadian Rockies. The views of Timpanogos and Lone Peak Wilderness areas are stunning, and fall color enthusiasts come from all over the world to make this drive in September and October. However, be warned—the road is steep and curvy (and narrow!) and may not appeal to small, seat-belted people who can't see out of the window very well. If you do manage to navigate this road all the way to its junction with Provo Canyon, be sure to follow a connecting road to **Cascade Springs.** This small area just off the highway is a pleasant surprise, a natural wonder of crystal-clear, bubbling springs cascading merrily over limestone terraces. The Forest Service has built a series of boardwalks over the springs, providing first-rate views of the many plants and fish that thrive here. A series of signs interpret the surround. Admission is **free.** The Alpine Loop continues its winding way down Provo Canyon and into the city of Provo, which is described on page 76.

Heber City

This friendly small town is known particularly for its railroad past, but it has also become a recreation mecca. Deer Valley Reservoir offers summertime fun, while Heber City is a perfect destination for a family interested in winter recreation.

Heber Valley Historic Railroad (all ages)

450 South 600 West; (435) 654–5601; www.hebervalleyrr.org. Departure times vary. The train runs year-round, with a reduced schedule in the winter months. A special "Santa Claus Express" runs from the end of November through Christmas. Murder mysteries, which include a train ride, dinner, and lively entertainment, are hosted on the train at various times during the year. Adults $$$$, children $$$.

Railroad buffs in your family will love the history and authenticity of the Heber Valley Historic Railroad. This service still runs old-time trains up and down Provo Canyon and through the Heber Valley, just as it has for almost one hundred years. Once a vital link between Heber and Provo for the transportation of passengers and sheep, the railroad now is fully turned over to

sightseers and recreationists. In the last decades railroad enthusiasts have overseen the complete restoration of several vintage coaches and open-air cars, as well as a working steam locomotive originally built in 1904. From May through October you can choose from two round-trip excursions that leave Heber City twice daily. A two-hour trip travels through the farmlands of Heber Valley and along the shores of Deer Creek Reservoir. A longer three-and-a-half-hour trip continues from the reservoir, follows the Provo River down Provo Canyon, and terminates at Vivian Park. The park also serves as an onboard location (and is a wonderful place for a picnic!). Snacks may be purchased on board.

Soar Utah Incorporated (adventurous souls only) 🌀
2002 Airport Road; (435) 654–0654. Open May through October. "Intro" rides $$$$.

If your family is feeling particularly adventurous, you might want to check out a glider ride offered by Soar Utah. Family members sit in the back seat, and a pilot guides the engine-less plane from the cockpit.

Deer Creek Reservoir and State Park (all ages) 🔺Ⓐ
South of Heber City on Highway 189; P.O. Box 257, Midway 84049; (435) 654–0171.

Deer Creek is a 7-mile-long water recreation area popular with windsurfers, sailors, and boaters. It's also a primary source of water for both the Utah and Salt Lake valleys. Facilities at Deer Creek include a launching ramp, docks, campground, rest rooms, and showers. There are camping and day-use fees.

Midway

Midway is just west of Heber City and shares the same green valley. This town calls itself "Little Switzerland," because of both its favorable geographic comparisons with that country and its large number of residents who share a Swiss heritage. This proud fact translates each Labor Day weekend into **Swiss Days,** one of the state's most popular festivals. Thousands of people flock to Midway for food, entertainment, and homemade craft items. For more information write Swiss Days, Box 428, Midway 84049.

The Homestead Resort (all ages) ⊖
700 North Homestead Drive; (435) 654–1102 or (888) 327–7220; www.homesteadresort .com. $–$$ for crater tours and swimming, $$$$ for accommodations.

The Homestead is a wonderful destination for families that provides lodging, horseback riding, tennis, bicycle paths, hiking, golf, hayrides, and hot-air ballooning. An indoor heated swimming pool makes for a relaxing soak and swim at the end of the day. The Homestead is a good choice for a winter vacation, with miles of groomed cross-country ski trails just steep enough for children. Horse-drawn sleigh rides and dinner rides are also available.

Mountain Spaa Resort (all ages)

800 North Mountain Spaa Lane; (435) 654–0721. Open during warm-weather months only. Pool admission $.

Old-time Utahns will remember the "hot pots," a bowled depression in the Heber Valley with a miraculous bubbling of hot mineral pools. Today the Spaa Resort encompasses some of the old hot pots, with indoor and outdoor pools that are constantly fed with naturally hot (90-degree) mineral water. Cabins may be rented here, and camping is available. An old-fashioned soda fountain dispenses ice-cream treats, and a snack bar has sandwiches.

Wasatch Mountain State Park (all ages)

Follow Homestead Drive in Midway until you reach the park; (435) 654–1791. The visitor center is open from 8:00 A.M. to 5:00 P.M. daily. Day use $, camping $$$.

Utah's largest and busiest state park offers camping, picnicking, miles of hiking and biking trails, a children's fishing pond, and a twenty-seven-hole golf course. If your family enjoys wildlife watching, this park is a good destination; big-game animals are abundant here, along with waterfowl, shorebirds, and small mammals. In winter, cross-country skiing and snowmobiling are popular activities. Each February, snow permitting, brings sled dog races to the park. The races begin and end at the golf course pro shop, and your family will enjoy watching from the deck while drinking hot chocolate. Wasatch Mountain State Park has a visitor center with directions, maps, travel guides, and local information. For more information, call the number listed above.

Geology Facts: **Pass Me the Salt**

We tend to take salt for granted. Nevertheless, Utah, especially Western Utah, is a very salty place. It's little wonder only a few hearty plants survive.

As you look at the salt flats, ask your kids how much salt is there. Tell them that Utah has such a large supply of salt, we could completely support the world's salt needs for the next 1,000 years!

Lehi

John Hutchings Museum of Natural History (all ages)

55 North Center Street; (801) 768–7180. Open Tuesday through Saturday 11:00 A.M. to 5:00 P.M. Admission $.

One man's love of collecting has resulted in one of the more likable museums in the state. The museum features just about anything that is related to the American West. Your children will love the Native American and pioneer artifacts, as well as the rare rock specimens, fossils, and marine and bird exhibits. A gift shop sells items that relate to the exhibits. John Hutchings died in 1977, and today the museum is run by his son Harold, who follows his father's great sense of family history.

Thanksgiving Point Botanical Gardens (all ages)
Take exit 287 from I–15, and go west on the frontage road for about 1 mile to 2095 North West Frontage Road; (801) 768–2300; www.thanksgivingpoint.com. Open year-round, Monday through Saturday; closed Sunday. Hours vary seasonally. Farm area $, gardens $$.

A few miles from town is a back-to-nature getaway called Thanksgiving Point, which has twelve acres of "idea gardens" through which you and your family can stroll. This is especially dramatic at Christmastime, when the gardens are decorated with a million tiny lights. Your children will probably best like the Animal Park here, with its barnyard atmosphere and stables full of rabbits, goats, ducks, pigs, baby chicks, and even llamas and a buffalo. A garden center, gift shop, and restaurant are also here, as is an old-fashioned soda fountain where shakes and sundaes can be enjoyed.

If you have some time, drive down the road to the fifty-five-acre Thanksgiving Gardens. The themed gardens hold something for everyone. Individual gardens include the Monet Garden, complete with bridges and water lilies; the Secret Garden, inspired by the children's classic; the Butterfly Garden; and the Waterfall Garden. The Children's Discovery Garden is particularly fun for families, because you are encouraged to touch and explore everything. Model railroads, two mazes, and a Noah and the Ark fountain are only some of the surprises here.

Round-up Rodeo (all ages)
Rodeo grounds in Lehi. The rodeo is in June. Call (801) 763–3117 for dates.

Lehi is famous for its June Round-up Rodeo, which has been thrilling folks for almost sixty years. Cowboys and cowgirls from all over the country come to Lehi to test their skills and to take part in the carnivals, parade, and good food that are all a part of the roundup.

Fairfield

Fairfield is a small farming town today, but 150 years ago it was witness to a particularly rowdy era in Utah's history. In 1858 then-president Buchanan sent 5,600 soldiers to Utah to break up a perceived Mormon rebellion. After negotiations with Mormon leaders, the army agreed to locate close enough to Salt Lake City to keep an eye on the citizenry, but far enough away to not seem oppressive. That location proved to be Fairfield, and the army's home became Camp Floyd, now a historic state park. Back then Fairfield boasted more than three hundred buildings and was a typical hell-raising frontier settlement. Today your family can visit the only building left standing, the commissary, as well as the army cemetery, where eighty-four soldiers are buried.

The Pony Express Trail (all ages) 🏛
Utah Highway 73 (the main road through Fairfield).

Imagine a horse galloping past at high speed, carrying bags marked U.S. MAIL. The horse is the best that money can buy, and its rider, a boy, is wearing a bright red shirt and blue pants and is carrying a small brass horn that he blows to signal his arrival. The boy, of course, is a Pony Express rider, and this route served as the Pony Express Trail for nineteen months in 1860 and 1861. The invention of the telegraph ended the need for a horse-and-rider mail-delivery system.

Pony Express **Trivia**

How fast was a Pony Express rider?

About the fastest time we have on record was set by Billy Fisher, a young whippersnapper. Billy rode 300 hard miles in 36 hours. In the process, he wore out six horses and two mules.

Camp Floyd and Stagecoach Inn State Park (all ages) 🏛 🏕
18035 West 1540 North (entrance located on Utah Highway 73). Call (801) 768–8932 for more information. Open Easter weekend through October 15. Admission $.

Visit this park to see where Pony Express riders exchanged mail and stopped to rest. Stagecoach Inn was built in 1855 and also served travelers on the Overland Trail.

Day Trip: **A Drive into the Pony Express Past**

It's a blast from the past and one of our kids' favorite day trips. The route isn't dangerous any longer, but it once was. As you drive down the miles of dirt road that once hosted the brave Pony Express rider, imagine bad guys waiting to rob you, Indians who felt threatened wanting to scalp you, grizzly bears, blizzards, and heat.

Take the kids on a historical day trip into Utah's Pony Express past. Even in this age of cell phones and computers the country is wild, rugged, and lonely. I love it.

Look for coyotes, rattlesnakes, and antelope. Have your kids imagine what it was like more than 140 years ago. This is still pretty close to the Wild West. Cows are still rustled in these parts, and you could get lost real easy if you wanted to.

Okay, pard! Fill that tank very full—maybe even carry some extra gas. Take along extra water, a jacket, food, and step into the past.

Pony Express Trail National Backcountry Byway (all ages)
Call (801) 977–4300 for route information.

If your children are captivated by the lore of the Pony Express, you might want to head out on the 133-mile-long official Pony Express Trail National Backcountry Byway, which begins at Stagecoach Inn. A number of monuments and buildings along the road tell the history of the Pony Express. If you choose to travel this road, be sure to get a descriptive brochure at Stagecoach Inn and ask for advice—the sand-and-gravel road is not always passable.

Orem

Timpanogos Storytelling Festival (children 3 and up)
Evening events at the Scera Shell Theater, 400 East 600 South; (801) 229–7436; www.timp fest.org. Festival takes place Labor Day weekend. All-event tickets $$$$.

A wonderful, two-day family event takes place each Labor Day weekend in the Orem area. The festival features renowned storytellers from all over the country, who come here to dress up, sing, act out, and sometimes just tell the stories that describe their lives and heritage. Typically, the daytime activities include stories interspersed with music and art activities; there are food and craft booths nearby. In the evening stories are told at the Scera Shell Theater. Only children over three are invited to the festival, and all children are invited only with adult accompaniment.

The Trafalga Fun Center (all ages)
168 South 1200 West; (801) 224–6000. Open year-round. Admission $–$$.

Trafalga is a biosphere of recreation activities. Your family could spend a day or more running from one enterprise to the next, including talking basketball hoops, a huge arcade, three eighteen-hole mini-golf courses, a miniature race car track, and batting cages . . . whew! Trafalga provides a pavilion, picnic tables, and food service for its patrons.

Classic Skating (all ages)
250 South State Street; (801) 224–4197; www.classic skating.com. Hours and rates are different every night, but generally the rink is open from about 6:00 to 10:00 P.M. weekdays and until midnight on weekends. Family rate on Monday $$ (for up to eight family members).

If you have not yet satisfied your indoor recreation urge, move on to Classic Skating. Bring your own skates or rent them here, and be prepared to roller skate around in a big circle while listening to music.

Where to Eat

Mi Ranchito. 1109 South State; (801) 225–9195. Excellent Mexican. $

Provo

Provo has one of the prettiest locations of any Utah city. It sits directly below the most rugged mountains in the Wasatch Front, and the view from any city street is straight up and awe-inspiring. All sorts of advance information on what to do and see here can be had by calling the **Utah Valley Convention and Visitors Bureau** at (800) 222–8824 or by going to www.utahvalley.org.

Brigham Young University (all ages)

LDS Church–owned Brigham Young University is here, the largest private institute of higher education in the world. BYU has an eclectic collection of museums on campus, three of which hold particular appeal for children (and all of which have **free** admission!). The **Monte L. Bean Life Science Museum** (801–378–5051) owns huge collections of things-that-were-once-alive, including 200,000 mounted plants, more than one million preserved insects, 6,000 birds, 10,000 fish . . . and much, much more. Children love the exhibits on eggs and shells and enjoy the user-friendly visitor displays and educational programs. BYU's **Earth Science Museum** (801–378–3680) shows off one of the world's largest fossil collections, ranging from Ice Age mammals to ancient sea life and dinosaurs. The **Museum of Peoples and Cultures** (801–422–0020) attempts to trace the anthropology of world cultures. Fascinating exhibits include ancient artifacts and displays from all over the world. BYU campus is also home to two art museums, which have rotating exhibits: The **B. F. Larsen Gallery** (801–378–2881) in the Harris Fine Arts Center highlights contemporary artists, and the lovely new **Museum of Art** (801–422–8287) features major traveling collections. Most of the BYU museums are open six days a week, and hours vary. See www.byu.edu for more details.

McCurdy Doll Museum (all ages)

246 North 100 East; (801) 377–9935. Open Tuesday through Saturday 1:00 to 5:00 P.M. Admission $.

Unique in all the world is Provo's McCurdy Doll Museum, an elegant, old carriage house that has been restored into a home for more than 4,000 dolls, toys, and miniatures. In 1910 Laura McCurdy Clark began a lifetime of collecting dolls, and this museum celebrates her treasures, as well as other collections. You'll see kachinas, provincial Spanish dolls, "rare and glorious boy dolls," ballerina dolls, Japanese dolls, Shirley Temple dolls . . . and many, many more. The museum has a wonderful gift shop full of doll-related paraphernalia, including books, kits, and patterns, as well as a doll hospital for repairs. Call for special events, such as the McCurdy Storytelling Princess, lectures, and craft classes.

Ottavio's Ristorante Italiano (all ages)

71 East Center; (801) 377–9555. Open from 11:30 A.M. to 10:00 P.M. Monday through Saturday. $$

Our favorite restaurant in Provo is Ottavio's. It's a touch of Italy and certainly the best dining in the city. The prices are reasonable and the food is an adventure in eating. The service is wonderful.

Utah Lake State Park (all ages) ⚠️ 🏕️

On the far western end of Center Street, at 4400 West Center Street; (801) 375–0731. Summer entrance fee: vehicles $$, winter admission per person for skating $.

Lying serenely at Provo's western boundary, Utah Lake is Utah's largest freshwater lake. Utah Lake State Park offers boat ramps, a marina, boat slips, and picnic and food-service facilities. This park is particularly popular with anglers and water skiers; kayakers and canoers enjoy boating adjacent to the Provo River. In the winter your family will enjoy ice skating on the park's Olympic-sized rink. Utah Lake State Park is also the head of the Provo River Trail, a paved trail running along the Provo River up to Provo Canyon, enjoyed by bikers, bladers, and pedestrians alike.

Seven Peaks Water Park (all ages—adult supervision recommended) 🌊

1330 East 300 North; (801) 373–8777; www.sevenpeaks.com. Call (801) 377–8777 for ice rink hours. Water slides open Memorial Day through Labor Day, Monday through Saturday from 11:00 A.M. to 8:00 P.M. Rink is open weeknights and Saturdays from about 1:00 to 11:00 P.M. Summer all-day pass: adults $$$$, children $$$, under 3 free. Ice skating $.

Seven Peaks boasts the "tallest water slides in the world," and after one look up, your family will most likely believe that claim. Water-park enthusiasts from all over the state come here for high-flying free falls and thrills "beyond compare." There are more than forty-five water attractions from which to choose, including a slide through total blackness, offset by smoke and neon lights, and a tube-hurtling experience that ejects the rider onto a three-story-high, open-air waterfall. For the less venturesome there is a gently flowing "lazy river" and a very nice kiddie pool area. Dominating the park is a huge pool that features regularly timed ocean-like waves. Seven Peaks has an adjacent ten-acre grass and sports complex as well, with food, beverage, and catering facilities. In the winter Seven Peaks provides a water sport of the frozen variety—a skating rink.

The Rock Garden (only children with some rock-climbing experience) 🌐

22 South Freedom Boulevard; (801) 375–2388. Open year-round, 10:00 A.M. to 10:00 P.M. Admission: 12 and older $$$$, children 4 to 11 $$$, and toddlers and senior citizens free.

If your family wants to continue the pursuit of adventure at a high altitude, check out the Rock Garden. In this indoor setting you'll learn the basics of rock climbing and the intricacies of the myriad ropes and harnesses and metal clamps that comprise climbing equipment. Classes include beginning technique and introduction to lead climbing. Passes can be purchased that allow practice climbing on the simulated canyon walls lining the Rock Garden.

America's Freedom Festival (all ages)

July. Call (801) 370–8052 or go to www.freedomfestival.org for dates and times. Many events are free.

Provo hosts one of the bigger Fourth of July events in the state with its America's Freedom Festival. This is a month-long hoopla, culminating in a Balloon Festival in the early morning hours, a huge Grande Parade down Center Street and University Avenue, and the biggie— the Stadium of Fire, a fireworks-set-to-rock-music extravaganza at Lavell Edwards Stadium, the 65,000-seat amphitheater on the BYU campus.

Rutter Family Adventures: **The Provo River and Provo Canyon**

I'll admit it. I'm a fanatic fly fisherman. I'm also a serious picnicker.

The Provo River is only a few miles from my house in Orem. It's a true blue-ribbon trout stream—with really, really big brown trout. I couldn't write this book without telling you this.

Provo Canyon is one of the nicest spots on Earth—especially for a family picnic. We love Vivian Park. To kill several birds with one stone, we frequently head up the canyon with roast chicken, baked beans, and other goodies for a picnic. After a great dinner, Shari reads and I take one of the kids fly fishing.

Yes, I love to fish, but in this case I become the guide. Decked out in waders, I take Abbey or Jon-Michael to a likely stretch and try to get them into some fish. The water is cold, so I have them wear waders. I also have my kids wear life jackets until they are ten.

It's a great bonding experience. And I want my kids to love fishing. One kid at a time is all I can safely handle. We don't fish fancy. We fish with nymphs— pheasant tails, hare's ears, and brassies (#16–18). For more details look at *Fly Fishing Made Easy* (Globe Pequot Press).

Huck Finn Day (all ages—especially young children) 🐟

Footprinters Park, 1150 South 1350 West; (801) 852–6632. Admission is free.

Provo sets aside one day in the middle of June for small people who love to fish. Bring your children, their rods, reels, and fishing licenses to Footprinters Park for the Huck Finn

Day fishing derby. You will find food, games, and a contest for the most authentic Huck Finn and Becky Thatcher costumes. Call for specific dates and activities.

Provo Canyon (all ages)

Take U.S. Highway 189 to University Avenue north until it enters the canyon. For reservations and camping information, call (801) 370–8640.

The city of Provo has the lucky circumstance of sitting near the foot of Provo Canyon—a wide, beautiful alpine expanse filled with recreation opportunities. Provo Canyon summits at the top of American Fork Canyon, and the road that connects these areas is called the Alpine Loop (partially described in the section on American Fork). The city of Provo maintains a series of parks with interlinking hiking and biking trails in the canyon. All of these parks have picnic areas, and some have campgrounds and volleyball courts. Just a few miles up Provo Canyon is the trailhead for **Squaw Peak Trail,** which offers spectacular views of the Utah Valley. A terrific family outing is a short side trip off the main canyon road to **Bridal Veil Falls,** a much-photographed, double cataract waterfall, which takes a plunge from more than 600 feet above the Provo River. The falls takes its name from the intricate, lacy pattern the water makes as it flows over rock boulders.

High Country Tours (older children)

Follow U.S. Highway 189 a few miles up Provo Canyon. Call (801) 224–2500 or go to www.highcountryrafting.com for details. Adults $$$$, children $$$.

If you are game for an exciting float trip down the Provo River, strap on a life jacket at Frazier Park, located about halfway up Provo Canyon. High Country Tours offers two-hour guided raft trips through the canyon, and all ages are invited.

Sundance Resort (all ages)

Northwest at the junction of Provo Canyon and Utah Highway 92. Horseback riding (801) 225–4107, skiing (801) 225–4107, or (800) 892–1600 for reservations.

Sundance, owned by movie star Robert Redford, is famous for family skiing in the winter and outdoor theater in the summer. During the summer, you can enjoy hiking and biking the trails, and then eat a picnic dinner while watching a classic movie on a giant outdoor screen. The Utah Symphony also holds regular concerts on the outdoor stage, surrounded by the wooded mountains. Sundance offers guided horseback rides in the canyon during the warm-weather months. Skiing at Sundance is especially rewarding for young children—long, flattish bowls stretch down the mountain, with opportunities for gentle turnings and incredible mountain views. For skiing information at Sundance, including rates, rentals, and lessons, call the number listed above.

Stewart Falls (all ages)

Drive about 2 miles beyond Sundance Resort, and park at the Aspen Grove pullout on your left.

A very pleasant and educational afternoon is waiting for your family on the trail to Stewart Falls. The trailhead is plainly marked and leads you on the 1½-mile walk to the falls. Along the way markers explain the surrounding flora and fauna. You'll return along the same route; allow about two hours for this outing.

Geology Facts: Benches on the Wasatch Front

If you are near the Wasatch Front, you're going to hear the term "benches."

When we refer to the benches, we are referring to the benchlike geography above the valley floor on the sides of the steep mountains. (Many of the finer homes are located here since the view is very good.)

At the end of the Ice Age, the weather warmed up and the giant ice flows melted, flooding the land. The body of water we call Lake Bonneville formed, covering much of the Great Basin.

The windswept waves of the great water pounded against the steep sides of the Wasatch Mountains. The effect of these crashing waves caused flat terraces, or benches, to form along the sides of the mountains above the lake floor. When the lake receded and the water dried, great benches were left—favorite places for humans to build upon.

Where to Eat

Chuck-a-Rama. 1081 South University; (801) 375–0600. Buffet. $

Ottavio's Ristorante Italiano. 71 East Center Street; (801) 377–9555. $

Ruby River. 1454 South University Avenue; (801) 371–0648. Steak, American. $$

La Dolce Vita. 61 North 100 East; (801) 373–8482. $

Where to Stay

Best Western Columbian. 70 East 300 South; (801) 373–8973. $$

Days Inn. 1675 North 200 West; (801) 375–8600. $–$$

Howard Johnson. 1292 South University Avenue; (801) 374–2500. $

Springville

This quiet town, just south of Provo, with its wide streets and tall trees, is home to an art museum that documents Utah's art from pioneer days, beautiful outdoor recreation, and a rich cultural atmosphere. In short, there is very little that Springville does not have to offer.

The Springville Art Museum (all ages)

126 East 400 South; (801) 489–2727. Open Tuesday through Saturday 10:00 A.M. to 5:00 P.M. (Wednesday also 5:00 to 9:00 P.M.) and Sunday 3:00 to 6:00 P.M. Admission is free.

The museum was built in 1937. Its nine permanent galleries display about 275 pieces, arranged in chronological order. Most major styles and artists of Utah are represented. Each spring the art museum hosts the **Spring Salon,** a showcase for living Utah artists; it is modeled after the salons in Paris that feature local artists. Older children will love the scale of this museum as well as the historical art that is exhibited here.

Art City Days (all ages)

The first full week of June. Call (801) 489–2700 for dates and events information.

This festival hosted by the town of Springville includes a carnival, concerts, baby contest, food and craft booths, a car show, and other fun activities.

The Daughters of the Utah Pioneers Museum (all ages)

175 South Main Street. The museum is open irregular hours. Call the Springville city offices (801–489–4681) for specific information. Admission is free.

The museum is a historic building that houses mementos from the pioneers, including clothing, furniture, handwork, musical instruments, and photographs.

Springville's State Fish Hatchery and Game Farm (all ages)

1000 North Main; (801) 489–4421. Open daily from 8:30 A.M. to 4:30 P.M. Admission is free.

In a museum you might find fish interpreted as art, but at the hatchery you will find the real thing. Stroll around the hatchery raceways and view the million-or-so rainbow trout and kokanee salmon that begin life here and are eventually sent to stock Utah's fishable waters.

Annual Springville World Folkfest (all ages)

Spring Acres Arts Park at 620 South 1350 East; (801) 489–2700; www.worldfolkfest.com. Adults $$, children $.

Each July Springville offers the opportunity to "travel the world in just one night" with the Annual Springville World Folkfest, one of the largest international festivals of folk dance in the world. The weeklong event includes nightly performances at the Spring Acres Arts

Park. More than 500 dancers and musicians from around the world dress in native costumes and perform authentic folk melodies and exotic dances reflecting the heritage and culture of their homelands.

Spanish Fork

Utah Valley Llamas (all ages)

8628 South Main Street; (801) 798–3559; www.utahvalleyllamas.com. Open year-round. Hours vary. Admission is free. Visitors are urged to call ahead for specific farm information.

For a truly unique family outing, head for Utah Valley Llamas, an actual llama "farm" that welcomes visitors who are curious about these South American pack animals. Thirty to forty llamas are generally on the premises, ready to be petted. The animals are also available for pack trips on Utah County trails and for rental as party entertainment. The llamas are deemed "safe and rideable" for youngsters and may be visited during the spring, summer, and fall. Each July the **Utah Valley Llama Fest** is held here, a one-day event that celebrates llamas and the South American culture from which they originate. Your family will see llamas sheared and their wool spun and woven into cloth (nominal entry fee). South American dances and music are performed, and food from that continent is sold. Your children can pet and ride the llamas and get their picture taken while doing so. The llamas also participate in contests of skill, featuring obstacle courses and pack demonstrations.

Watch Out **for Spitting Llamas!**

I guess I have another confession to make: I love llamas. It all started a few years ago. A friend and I continually passed by a llama farm and, well, I got curious. Now I'm hooked, and with good reason. These are some amazing animals.

Llamas are extraordinary pack animals for a couple of reasons. They have padded feet, not hooves like a horse. This makes the llama very sure-footed on treacherous mountain paths. Llamas are also especially loyal. They often become attached to their owners and make great travel companions. They will even lie down in the back seat of a car—perfect for a Sunday drive.

My favorite animal has only one problem: spit. Llamas are known for their ability to spit long distances. They often do so when upset or agitated. These unique South American mammals use their saliva as a defense.

While visiting the llamas at the fabulous farm in Spanish Fork, appreciate the amazing animals and watch out for the spit!

Spanish Fork Community Water Park (all ages)
North of the high school parking lot, at 200 North 500 West; (801) 798–5091; www.spanish fork.org/dept/recreation/waterpark/. Admission $.

When you need to cool off, head for Spanish Fork Community Water Park. It has an 18-foot-high, 150-foot-long water slide and a nice picnic area nearby. Call for information.

Canyon View Park (all ages)
On Power House Road, just past the golf course; (801) 798–5000; www.spanishfork.org/newsevents/festivaloflights/. Vehicles $.

Canyon View Park is another nice place to spend an afternoon, with a fishing pond for children, nature trails, a picnic area, and playground activities. During the month of December your family can drive through the park and see the **Festival of Lights,** when thousands of colored lights are made into pictures of candy canes, Santas, dinosaurs, skiers, and more. For more information call the Spanish Fork city offices at the number listed above.

Helper

Fifty years ago trains of heavily laden coal cars would load in Price and make their way north. Getting up the steep hills of Price Canyon was so difficult that "helper" trains would be attached for a temporary locomotive boost. This tiny town thrived in that era, and its saloons and hotels were famous with the railroading crowd.

Western Mining and Railroad Museum (all ages)
296 South Main; (435) 472–3009; wmrrm.org. Open Monday through Saturday from 10:00 A.M. to 6:00 P.M. May through September and Tuesday through Saturday from 11:00 A.M. to 4:00 P.M. the rest of the year. Donation requested ($).

Helper's old-fashioned Main Street is part of a national historic district and is home to the Western Mining and Railroad Museum. Your children will love the eccentric collections of early coal and uranium mining paraphernalia, WPA paintings by young, Depression-era artists, personal and household artifacts, an old-fashioned dental office (which will make you grateful for modern medicine), a replica of a 1930s store, and two coin-operated model railroads. Outside exhibits include a 1917 railroad caboose and mining equipment that spans a century.

Centennial Parkway (all ages)
Behind Main Street in Helper.

After touring the museum, the perfect place for a picnic is the Helper Centennial Parkway. Find your way behind Main Street to the winding Price River, which is the backdrop for this black-topped pathway with picnic tables, a sandbox area for children, bocce ball courts, and horseshoe pits.

Helper Intermountain Theatre (all ages)
On Main Street; (800) 842–0789. Call between 9:00 A.M. and 5:00 P.M. for current information on productions and prices.

The theater stages live, family-oriented productions during the months of July and August as well as a holiday production in December.

Electric Light Parade (all ages)
Parade starts at 7:00 P.M. Friday and Saturday night, the second weekend in December; (800) 842–0789. Admission is free.

It's worth a trip to Helper during the holiday season to witness the Electric Light Parade, an extravaganza held in December. About twenty-five floats, lit with thousands of tiny lights, make their way down Main Street while an awestruck crowd watches from the sidewalks. After the parade on Saturday, enjoy a fireworks display. Before the event your family is invited to enjoy a chili dinner at Helper's Civic Auditorium at 19 South Main. There is a nominal cost for this meal.

Price

Price's thriving industry is coal mining, and you'll see much evidence of the mining trade all over town. In the **Municipal Building** on Main Street is a famous mural, commissioned by the WPA in 1938, which details the history of the surrounding county. A brochure describing each historically correct scene is available here.

Price hosts a number of events that families enjoy. If you are in Price during the first week in May, ask about the activities scheduled for **Pre-History Week.** One day of this week is dedicated especially for children, with games, food, and fun, which might include dinosaur-related crafts and bone-filled "fossil sites" ready to be unearthed. Another annual event your children will enjoy is **Greek Festival Days,** usually the second week in July, when Price celebrates the ethnic heritage of many of its citizens with dancing, authentic food, crafts, and church tours. During the last week of July is the **International Folk Festival,** when Price hosts performers from all over the world, who come to town to perform their native dances. A major rodeo on the pro rider circuit takes place the third week in June at the Carbon County Fairgrounds. The **Black Diamond Stampede** has several events especially for children, including "mutton busting," where local, future rodeo champs test their bareback skills on sheep, trying to stay astride for the longest time. For information, including dates, call (435) 637–5010 or (800) 842–0789.

The College of Eastern Utah Prehistoric Museum (all ages)

155 East Main Street; (435) 637–5060; museum.ceu.edu. Open 9:00 A.M. to 6:00 P.M. daily from Memorial Day through Labor Day and 9:00 A.M. to 5:00 P.M. Monday through Saturday the rest of the year. Donation requested ($).

The geology that forced the formation of plentiful coal beds also created the perfect conditions for the preservation of ancient fossils. More complete dinosaur skeletons have been excavated in the area surrounding the town of Price than anywhere else in the United States. The College of Eastern Utah Prehistoric Museum displays some of these finds, including full-sized skeletons of dinosaurs and a huge Columbian mammoth in real-life poses. Learn about the discovery of the Utahraptor, the scary, clawed dinosaur featured in the movie *Jurassic Park.* Dinosaur footprints that were fossilized in coal beds are laid out on the floor—your children will most likely want to compare their own size with these prehistoric bigfoots. The museum also exhibits artifacts of the area's ancient human inhabitants; pictographs and figurines of the Fremont people can be seen here as well.

Shaman Lodge (all ages)

3645 West Gordon Creek Road; (800) 710–7842; www.shamanlodge.com. Horseback rides $$$$, lodging $$–$$$$.

Horseback rides, by the hour or by the day, can be booked at Shaman Lodge, a bed-and-breakfast facility. Guides will teach your children to saddle, mount, and ride a horse, and, if needed, lead them along the trail. Dutch-oven dinners and nighttime cowboy poetry readings are also available by reservation.

Price City Desert Wave Pool (all ages)

240 East 500 North; (435) 637–7946. Open year-round. Call for hours and admission fees.

When it's time to cool off, your children will enjoy the ebb and flow at the Price City Desert Wave Pool. The giant pool here simulates the ocean's waves at regularly timed intervals. In winter a bubble covers the pool.

Price Canyon Recreation Area (all ages)

Follow U.S. Highway 6 north from Price for 12 miles, and turn onto a dirt road at the sign. Call (435) 636–3600 for camping fees and reservations.

A favorite summer escape for Price natives is the Price Canyon Recreation Area. Located on a ridge above Price Canyon, it offers cooler temperatures under the shade of ponderosa pines. A self-guided nature trail interprets the surrounding flora, and a campground has picnic tables, barbecues, and rest rooms.

Scofield State Park (all ages)

From U.S. Highway 6, turn off onto State Route 96 and proceed for 10 more miles; P.O. Box 166, Price 84501; (435) 448–9449.

Scofield State Park offers excellent boating and year-round fishing. In winter the area is a base for snowmobiling and cross-country skiing. There are three separate facilities that comprise this state park: two full-service campgrounds and a day-use area.

Wellington

This small town east of Price is named after the nearby carbon dioxide gas wells, which for decades have produced gas for the coal, refrigeration, and beverage industries.

Rutter Family Adventures: **Amazing Fish Springs**

In the middle of a major desert, in some of the most desolate, wildest country in the "Lower 48," there's a place called Fish Springs. If you're into wildlife, it's a must see. We go there every year.

Fish Springs National Wildlife Refuge is 45 miles west of Simpson Springs down the Pony Express Trail. It's a pretty good dirt road, but no place for a new Cadillac or a Lexus.

This 10,000-acre marshland seems out of place in an arid desert, but you soon get used to it. There are 11 miles of road—perfect for animal watching and enjoying. Look for deer, antelope, and dozens of species of waterfowl. Your kids will loves the ducks, geese, and swans.

Our favorite time is early spring; spring and fall are the best times to visit. Summer can be very hot. Winter is not bad, but you'll want to dodge snowstorms—the wind and snow can really blow.

Take binoculars and a bird book. Keep an eye out for rattlesnakes. If you don't have a four-wheel drive, call (435) 831–5353 to check on conditions.

Nine Mile Canyon (all ages)

From Wellington follow the signs for the canyon, heading north on a paved road that soon turns to gravel. Travel about 20 miles until reaching the bridge over Minnie Maude Creek.

One of the more interesting backroads in Utah is reached from Wellington. Nine Mile Canyon passes through historic ranch country, beautiful cliff walls, and waterfalls; but its most outstanding features are the ancient Indian structures and rock art that line the canyon in profusion. Nine Mile Canyon is actually about 40 miles long—so plan about six hours for this trip, which could include frequent stops, some hiking, and a picnic. The bridge over Minnie Maude Creek marks the unofficial beginning of Nine Mile Canyon. For many years the canyon was the main route between the Uintah Basin (described in "Northeastern Utah") and the railroad in Price. Some of the old ranch houses you see alongside the road were waystations for travelers, where they could stop to rest and water their animals.

Farther on, evidence of the ancient Fremont Indian culture is apparent. The rock structures you see high on the cliff walls are most likely granaries where the Fremont stored their dried crops. The petroglyphs (carvings in the rock) and pictographs (pictures drawn on the rock) you see are their pictorial legacy. More than 1,000 of these sites have been found in the canyon; however, if your family is not experienced in finding rock art, it can sometimes be hard to spot. There is a helpful brochure available, which can be obtained by calling (800) 842–0789 or asking at the College of Eastern Utah Prehistoric Museum in Price. A local guide business, **Reflections on the Ancients** (800–427–0738), conducts excellent custom tours of Nine Mile Canyon. They can be reached at the number listed above. Be aware that this area is extremely remote, and there are no services available once you enter the canyon. Be sure to carry water and start out with a full tank of gas. The gravel road may be impassable in bad weather. For road conditions and more information about Nine Mile Canyon, call the BLM office in Price at (435) 636–3600.

Cleveland

Cleveland Lloyd Dinosaur Quarry (all ages)
From Wellington, head south on U.S. Highway 6, take the turnoff onto Utah Highway 10, and follow the signs to the tiny town of Cleveland and the quarry; (435) 636–3600. Open 10:00 A.M. to 5:00 P.M. daily from Memorial Day through Labor Day, and weekends only 10:00 A.M. to 5:00 P.M. from Easter through Memorial Day and Labor Day through October. Admission $.

If you count a junior paleontologist among your family members, don't miss the quarry and its incredible close-up view of fossil excavation. More than 12,000 bones representing seventy different animals have been dug from this site, which has been designated a national natural landmark. The visitor center displays two of these creatures, an allosaurus and a stegosaurus. Other bones from this area are displayed in more than sixty museums worldwide. A short walk from the visitor center leads to a covered area where your children can learn about the excavation process firsthand. Paleontologists continue to remove bones from this site, and their half-unearthed work is on display. Picnic facilities and a self-guided nature trail are nearby. The quarry site is located 30 miles south of Price, and some of the drive is on a gravel road. Before you make the trip, it is recommended that you inquire at the College of Eastern Utah Prehistoric Museum in Price or the local BLM office at 125 South 600 West, or call for road conditions, maps, and quarry hours. There is no telephone service at the quarry.

Castle Dale

Emery County Pioneer Museum (all ages)

161 East 100 North; (435) 381–5154. Open weekdays 10:00 A.M. to 4:00 P.M. and Saturday noon to 4:00 P.M. Admission is **free.**

The Emery County Pioneer Museum authentically re-creates life as it was in pioneer times. The museum has assembled a schoolroom, a typical pioneer home, and a dry goods store exactly as they would have looked in the mid-1800s. Early farming tools are displayed, and a pioneer handcart is outfitted with items the pioneers used for early survival.

Museum of the San Rafael (all ages)

96 North 100 East; (435) 381–5252. Open Monday through Friday 10:00 A.M. to 4:00 P.M. and Saturday noon to 4:00 P.M. Admission is **free.**

The Museum of the San Rafael celebrates the local ecology. It features life-sized dinosaurs that are mounted on a rotating platform. A group of world-famous Fremont Indian artifacts, the "Sitterud Bundle," is here, along with other cultural and geologic displays.

Fast
Utah Facts

- The rugged San Rafael Swell region was nearly untouched by white men until Cold War uranium prospectors wandered its canyons with a Geiger counter.
- Utah's Colorado Plateau covers nearly half of the state (in the south and east).
- All of Utah's national parks are found on the Colorado Plateau.
- As you study Native American petroglyphs, remember this is not graffiti—there is no such thing as swearing in the Indian culture.
- Utah is the third most popular state for filming American movies.

San Rafael Swell (all ages)

East of Castle Dale. For more information call the BLM office in Price at (435) 636–3600. Several local outfitters offer guided trips in the swell, including Reflections on the Ancients (800–427–0738) and Hondoo Rivers and Trails (800–332–2696).

Just east of town lies an incredible place called the San Rafael Swell; it is one of the more remote regions on the planet. It was formed hundreds of thousands of years ago, when earth shifts created a huge dome of rock. The elements beat on the rock for several eons, until it collapsed into a gigantic pile of rocks, from which canyons and gullies and buttes emerged, creating a "swell" on the landscape. The swell has no services in its huge interior (approximately 60 by 80 miles), but camping, hiking, and sightseeing are extraordinary here. Inside the swell you'll find a maze of dirt roads that lead to a number of destinations.

The **Wedge Overlook** offers an incredible view from atop the San Rafael Gorge. You will look down 600 feet over layers of red canyons into the San Rafael River. The area around the overlook is home to a cactus that doesn't grow anyplace else on earth. The cactus was discovered just a few years ago: It is called pediocactiwinklerii (say that twice, fast), after the graduate student who discovered it. (It's also known as the San Rafael cactus.) You'll have to look carefully to find it—it sits flush with the dirt and is about the size of a nickel. This cactus actually recedes into the ground in the winter and has a brief bloom in the spring.

Buckhorn Draw's primary feature is an extraordinary rock-art panel. You'll also find towering cliffs, dinosaur footprints, and an unforgettable swinging bridge, which is now used only for foot traffic. One of the few campgrounds in the swell is here, with picnic tables and campsites.

Eagle Canyon Overlook offers a bird's-eye view of Sid's Mountain Wilderness Study Area, a formation similar to Zion National Park, and, some say, just as beautiful. Swasey's Cabin offers a glimpse of the hardships that frontier people endured. Here you'll get a taste of what life was like for the Swasey brothers, who ran cattle in this area more than a hundred years ago.

Now, a word of caution: The San Rafael Swell is huge and dry and often empty. Road signs sort of exist, but not enough to depend on. And if it rains, you could be in trouble on some of the less-graded dirt roads. Get directions and weather information before you go. There is a good informational brochure available at any visitor center in the area. The remoteness of the swell can make it seem unfriendly, but it's also what makes this region worth visiting.

Green River

Driving down this city's main street, you'll probably notice that many of the businesses here are engaged in the sport of river running. The **Green River** is a world-class rafting river, and it runs right through the middle of this town, which has taken its name. Commercial river trips vary from a few hours to several days, and you can choose an exciting whitewater adventure or a lazy meander under the desert sun. To check out individual outfitters, rates, and reservations, call the **Green River Visitors Center** at (435) 564–3526.

Green River State Park (all ages)

Just off I–70 in Green River; P.O. Box 637, Green River 84525. Call (435) 564–3633 for more information. Day-use and camping fees are charged. Vehicles $.

A park on the banks of the river is a favorite starting point for many river trips. Green River State Park has beautiful shaded lawns perfect for a picnic, as well as a full-service campground and boat launching ramp.

John Wesley Powell Museum (all ages)

900 East Main; (435) 564–3427. Open 8:00 A.M. to 8:00 P.M. daily, April through October, and 8:00 A.M. to 5:00 P.M. the rest of the year. Admission $.

Whether or not your family chooses to take a river trip, be sure to stop at the John Wesley Powell Museum, which interprets the history of river running. It is named after the man who first charted the local waters and has a replica of the boat and equipment he used. Also displayed are boats used by early Native Americans, primitive rafts used by early sportspeople, and the modern equipment used today. The geology and geography of the Colorado Plateau (the huge formation that includes much of southeastern Utah) is explained. There is an excellent video presentation here, and a fun gift shop.

Crystal Geyser (all ages)

Travel east from the John Wesley Powell Museum for 1.3 miles, and turn left onto a frontage road. Follow this well-marked road for 10 miles.

On the east bank of the Green River is a weird-but-wonderful phenomenon, the Crystal Geyser. It is a rare, cold-water geyser that erupts at irregular intervals, about three or four times a day. The mineral deposits left by the geyser are interesting to look at anytime.

Melons **in the Desert**

While traveling through the arid region that surrounds the small town of Green River, you might find yourself in need of a refreshing treat. Don't worry—you've come to the right place.

You see, Green River is famous for its sweet, juicy melons. A number of elements combine in this area to create an environment perfect for growing wonderful watermelons, heavenly honeydews, and all kinds of other melons.

First, water from the Green River is plentiful. Second, the sun is hot and steady. Third, and most important, the alkaline soil makes the melons grow fast and oh-so-sweet.

It was just over one hundred years ago that farmers accidentally discovered that melons were the ideal crop in this desert landscape. Now you can enjoy the best melon in a highly unlikely place—the desert community of Green River.

Melon Days (all ages)

In September. For more information call the Green River Visitors Center at (435) 564–3448.

Besides river running, Green River is known for growing melons, and the third weekend of each September the entire town makes merry at Melon Days. One and all are invited to this celebration, which includes a fair, parade, dances, food, and, of course, plenty of sliced watermelon.

Hanksville

This small desert town is a popular gearing-up spot for the major attractions that surround it. To the south is Lake Powell, to the east is Canyonlands National Park (both described in "Southeastern Utah"), and to the west is Capitol Reef National Park (described in the next few pages).

Goblin Valley State Park (all ages)

Travel about 30 miles on Utah Highway 24 and take a left at Temple Mountain Junction; P.O. Box 637, Green River 84525. Call (435) 564–3633 for admission fees and seasonal information or (800) 322–3770 for reservations.

North of town is one of the most unique and fun places for kids anywhere. You only have to travel about 30 miles to find Goblin Valley State Park, a place beloved by children—and with good reason. Their imaginations run wild in this enchanted valley filled with soft limestone hoodoos and elves and goblins. These magical rock sculptures have been carved by the wind and rain over centuries. Look for Skull in the Sky, Parade of Elephants, and Dance of the Dolls formations. Bike riding is great fun on the long, flat roads in the park, traffic conditions and weather permitting. Campsites are available, as well as a covered picnic area that overlooks the valley. Plan at least a half day for exploration of the park, with plenty of time for climbing and hiding among the formations.

Torrey

For many years this sleepy little town near the junction of Utah Highways 12 and 24 and its adjacent national park remained a Utah secret. In the 1990s all that changed, however. Torrey thrives with new hotels and restaurants, and visitation at Capitol Reef National Park grows by leaps and bounds. This park is a wonderful choice for a family vacation, with a dozen small hikes that offer views up, down, and all around this colorful red-rock sanctuary.

Capitol Reef National Park (all ages)

Located in Boulder, south of Torrey. Take the Burr Trail south. The trail is paved for the first 7 miles; where the pavement ends, Capitol Reef begins. For information on staying in or near the park, write Capitol Reef National Park, HC 70, P.O. Box 15, Torrey 84775, or call the visitor center at (435) 425–3791. Vehicles $.

Capitol Reef's defining rock formation is called the **Waterpocket Fold.** In very basic terms, the Waterpocket Fold is a big ridge (100 miles long) that was thrust higher than its surroundings about seventy million years ago. The ridge has one many-colored, steep-cliffed side that faces the main road through the park, and another side with a more gradual decline. The "waterpocket" comes from the many erosion-formed depressions in the fold, which are now the natural holding tanks for water after a storm. Capitol Reef is the most grandiose section of the Waterpocket Fold. The "capitol" comes from huge rocks shaped like government buildings, one rock in particular resembling the Capitol in Washington, D.C. The "reef" designation reportedly comes from the early Anglo explorers of this area. They had seafaring backgrounds, and the reef provided an impenetrable barrier to travel, just as a coral reef in the ocean would bar ships from a direct route. The most-visited sections of the park extend from the **visitor center.** Directions to all Capitol Reef hikes and drives can be found here, as well as books, maps, exhibits, and a short film. Bathrooms, drinking water, and a soft-drink machine are located just outside. The nearby park campground is beautiful, located along the Fremont River with a surround of spectacular red-rock views. In warm-weather months the first-come, first-served sites are usually gone by midmorning, so it is wise to plan ahead for alternative lodging. In the fall, visitors are invited to pick fruit for their own use, for a small fee. A brochure in the visitor center will give you more information about this attraction.

The area called **Fruita** is a favorite haunt in Capitol Reef. The Fremont River runs through here, creating an oasis in the red-rock desert. A hundred years ago settlers established a township, planting hundreds of fruit trees, and the original orchards are still maintained today. One roadside exhibit features an old blacksmith shop, where you can press a button and the blacksmith will tell you his story. The same device is used at the tiny, one-room, log schoolhouse, where Mrs. Torgerson tells us her true-life teaching experiences. The school was built in the 1890s and used until the 1940s. While you're here, think how the world has changed—just fifty years ago children sat in this school and learned to read! You might recognize the beautifully restored hay barn in Fruita, as its photograph graces some of the park publications. Fruita has a large grass area that is perfect for a picnic, a game of Frisbee, or an afternoon nap. You will probably notice the abundance of deer in the area, many of which are extremely tame. One deer in particular is fond of getting his picture taken while eating an apple from your hand.

When your family is ready for a hike, grab a **Hickman Trail** pamphlet at the visitor center, so you will be able to interpret each of the eighteen markers along the way. This relatively easy 2-mile-round-trip hike is probably the most popular in the park, and deservedly so. It features 125-foot Hickman Bridge, a spectacular stone arch. Try to be the first one to spot Hickman, as it is camouflaged quite cleverly on its approach. On the way you will pass the foundation of an ancient pit house and granary, probably built by the Fremont Indians. There are all sorts of rock hiding places along the trail, including small rock fins and cliffside depressions the perfect size for a human. Once you reach the bridge, continue on the path. You will loop back around to the original path after a while, but first you'll be treated to good views of Fruita.

Grand Wash is another great hike. This ancient riverbed makes for a nice, no-uphill stroll through a magnificent rock canyon. Caution: If it looks like rain, you will want to make other plans. This is not a good place to be during a flash flood. A one-way trip through Grand Wash is 2.4 miles. You can start in two places—a marked pull-off a few miles south of the visitor center, or a marked side road on the scenic drive. Whichever way you begin, you might want to arrange for a car to pick you up at the other end. You'll squeeze through narrow cliff passages, see arches (look up!), find smooth river stones of every possible color, and feel the power of the canyon walls surrounding you.

Take the turnoff to Panorama Point. Just before dusk, try heading to **Sunset Point Trail,** which is, yes, an excellent place to be during a sunset. You might want to take refreshments and make a dinner party out of your visit. From Panorama Point, take the short walk to Gooseneck Point. Stop and gaze down in wonder at the path Sulphur Creek has wrought, and then continue for ½ mile to Sunset Point. Looking to the east, with the sun at your back, you'll get a good view of the Waterpocket Fold and the pink and orange world beyond.

A scenic drive begins at the visitor center, passes through the picnic area and national park campground, and then heads out into desert country (nominal admission). There is a free pamphlet available at the visitor center that is very helpful in interpreting your surroundings. This is a narrow, twisty road at times, with plenty of pullouts and short hikes. Eight-or-so miles into the scenic drive, you'll see the sign for **Capitol Gorge,** an especially fun destination for children. Weather permitting, this turnoff onto a graded dirt road is easily managed in a passenger car. There are picnic tables and displays at the trailhead inside Capitol Gorge—this was the main road from Hanksville to Torrey for many years, and some of the trials and tribulations of maintaining the road are documented. There is an easy, 1-mile hike deeper into the narrowness of Capitol Gorge—look for the Pioneer Register, where pioneers signed their names on the rocks, and the natural Water Tanks, which hold good supplies of rainwater.

Cathedral Valley

If your family is happy taking a half-day drive on a bumpy dirt road, consider touring **Cathedral Valley.** Ask for directions and road conditions at the visitor center. This road requires a high-clearance vehicle, some driving skill, and is not for everybody. The valley is extremely beautiful, with several unmatched viewpoints—especially memorable are the Temple of the Sun and Moon monoliths. Cathedral Valley is named for its many-spired formations that resemble church architecture and also inspire spiritual thoughts.

Where to Eat

Boulder Mesa Cafe. 155 East Burr Trail; (435) 335–7447. American. $$

Burr Trail Cafe. 225 North Highway 12; (435) 335–7500. American. $$

Where to Stay

Wonderland Inn. Junction of Highways 12 and 24; (435) 425–3775. $$–$$$

Best Western Capitol Reef Resort. 2600 East Highway 24; (435) 425–3761. $$–$$$$

Salina

Mom's Cafe (all ages)
On the corner of State and Main; (435) 529–3921. Open Monday through Saturday 7:00 A.M. to 10:00 P.M. $

You'll find several good reasons to visit this small ranching town. The first is Mom's Cafe, an institution of sorts, where friendly service and old-fashioned, home cooking reign. Even if you're not hungry, stop in for a scone, one of Mom's specialties.

Burn's Saddlery (all ages)
79 West Main; (435) 529–7484. Open Monday through Saturday 9:00 A.M. to 6:00 P.M.

When you are feeling well-fed, walk half a block to Burn's Saddlery, a "real" cowboy store stocked with all sorts of interesting stuff. The selection of children's cowboy boots is first-rate, and the clerks here know how boots should fit. Some of the ranching equipment for sale is downright confusing to a city slicker—have your children guess the uses of some of the more exotic looking paraphernalia.

Fish Lake (all ages)
East of Richfield; take Utah Highway 24 (following the signs), and turn north on the well-marked turnoff, which is Utah Highway 25.

Fish Lake is a natural body of water (2,700 acres) in the middle of God's country. At 8,800 feet, the cool, blue water is one of Utah's best fisheries. You can catch rainbow, splake, perch, and lake trout. Indeed, the lake is known for its lunker lakers!

The surrounding mountains are covered with spruce, fir, and aspen. Look for moose, elk, and deer, and an occasional bear. Bring the field glasses along to see the abundant waterfowl.

Fish Lake is a perfect spot for fishing, hiking, backpacking, biking, hunting, photographing—or just plain relaxing. For us, a visit to Fish Lake is a yearly occurrence. We wouldn't miss it. Of course, we fish. But we also love to wander on the paths and absorb nature at her best. The valley is peaceful.

Fish Lake and the fall go hand in hand. A visit in September is something you'll always remember. The leaves turn early in the high mountain country, and it's a visual feast. Bring along a warm coat, however.

Fish Lake Resort (all ages)

10 East Center Highway 25. Call (800) 638–1000 or go to www.fishlake.com for reservations and information. Lodging $$–$$$$.

We stay at Fish Lake Resort on the north shore. It's a lovely place, the prices are very reasonable, and the folks are nice. The resort has complete accommodations, including cabins and motel rooms, as well as boat rentals and a marina. However, we park our trailer in the trailer park. We have visited Fish Lake for more than twenty years and have always been well cared for by the staff. Now open in winter, the resort's cabins are warm and cozy.

Sevier

Fremont Indian State Park (all ages)

Located just off I–70 southwest of Sevier, at 3820 West Clear Creek Canyon Road. Open daily, except major holidays, from 9:00 A.M. to 6:00 P.M. in the summer and 9:00 A.M. to 5:00 P.M. in winter. A campground and picnic area are nearby. Vehicles $. Call (435) 527–4631 for more information.

Just up the road from Sevier is Fremont Indian State Park. The park's creation was rather serendipitous—state road crews were clearing a path for I–70 through this area, called Clear Creek Canyon, when they uncovered remnants of an ancient Indian tribe. This park now protects that archaeological find and honors the Fremont tribe, which lived and worked here as early as 3500 B.C. You'll see the Fremonts' pit houses and stone granaries as well as their cliff dwellings built high up on the canyon walls for protection. The Fremont Museum, located in the park, has an exhibit room and twelve interpretive trails that show off Fremont rock-art panels.

Where to Stay

Days Inn. 333 North Main (travel east on I–70 from the Fremont Museum), Richfield; (435) 896–6476. $–$$

Easy Travel Tips: **Each Kid Should Have a Bag of Stuff**

If your kids have their way, each child will pack about a ton-and-a-half of personal junk for your trip.

To simplify the issue of what can go and what stays home, we've held to a simple rule. Each child can take a blanket (for napping), a pillow, and a bag for personal "stuff."

We tell them, "If you can't get it in your bag, you can't bring it." Those bags get stuffed, but it works well for us. It goes without mentioning that each should be the same size to avoid conflict. We've used duffle bags with success. We've since switched to knapsacks (day packs), since they're easier to carry about.

Within reason, kids can take what they want. The car rules are: Play with your stuff, but put it back when you're done. Don't leave it on the seat or floor.

A few hints: If your kid has a Game Boy or similar computer game, make sure he or she has ear phones. We also provide a Walkman-style tape player with ear phones for music and stories. Even in a car full of kids, this gives your child a few private moments.

Cove Fort

Cove Fort (all ages)

Near the junction of Interstates 15 and 70 and easily found by following the directional signage; (435) 438–5547. Open daily from 8:00 A.M. to dusk. Admission is free.

This place is actually a historic site to which a small town has attached itself. Cove Fort is one of the better re-creations of pioneer life anywhere. Cove Fort's original purpose was as a way station for travelers between the cities of Fillmore and Beaver. The "cove" part of the fort is easy to understand, because there are a steady water supply and a natural rock surround here that lend themselves to a cove designation. The "fort" part of the equation has to do with "Indian troubles" that cropped up nearby around 1867. Mormon Leader Brigham Young asked that a sturdy rock fort be built, capable of sustaining life within and fending off attacks from without.

The fort was built according to his specifications from rock quarried nearby. It never had to prove its mettle, however, as peace was made with the local Indians, and there was no need for armed shelter. When you pass through the gates of the fort, you'll most likely be greeted by a Mormon guide, who will stay with you during your visit. You'll see a real frontier kitchen, replete with all sorts of utensils. You'll see bedrooms and parlors and eating rooms, all re-created to look just as they did a century ago. Once you leave the fort itself, there are surrounding grounds to explore. Don't miss the blacksmith shop, where a modern-day guide will work the bellows if you ask. The enormous barn has been built to absolute specifications, matching the original that once stood on this spot. This is a nice place for a picnic, with plank tables set out under big, shady trees.

Fillmore

If you look at a map of Utah, you'll notice that Fillmore is almost smack in the center of the state, which might account for Mormon leader Brigham Young's declaring this town the state capital in 1851. He commissioned an elaborate capitol, and work commenced. After two years, only the south wing of the building was completed, however, and shortly afterward the seat of government was transferred to Salt Lake City.

Territorial Statehouse State Park (all ages)
50 West Capitol Avenue. Open Monday through Saturday 8:00 A.M. to 8:00 P.M. and Sunday 9:00 A.M. to 6:00 P.M. in the summer, and Monday through Saturday 9:00 A.M. to 6:00 P.M. in winter. Admission $. For more information call (435) 743–5316.

The existing structure, now called Territorial Statehouse State Park, served as the site for only one full session of the territorial legislature. It fell into disuse and in 1930 was restored and reopened as a museum. In 1957 it became Utah's first state park. It now houses a collection of pioneer artifacts. Be sure to go to the lower level and find a favorite exhibit of children, an example of an early jailhouse. Outside the building is a picnic area and award-winning rose garden.

Where to Stay

Best Western Paradise Inn of Fillmore.
905 North Main; (435) 743–6895. $–$$

Manti

Mormon Miracle Pageant (all ages)
This outdoor pageant is held in midsummer near Manti's LDS Temple; (888) 255–8860. Admission is free. Dinner is available: adults $$, children $. Call for specific dates and more information.

This tiny town greets 30,000 visitors during the run of its annual, midsummer Mormon Miracle Pageant, played out against the dramatic backdrop of Manti's LDS Temple. This extravaganza, held the last two weeks of June, requires the volunteer services of just about everybody in town. Hundreds of people are cast in the pageant, which depicts the story of the Book of Mormon, and the history of the American continent. Scores more of the townfolk are involved in feeding the influx of visitors; arrive early for the barbecued turkey dinner served at the Manti Tabernacle at 100 South and Main Street, and also at the Manti Stake Center at 300 South and Main Street. The pageant begins at nightfall, about 9:30 P.M. Bring a blanket, as the chairs fill up quickly, and most pageant watchers sit on the grass.

Fishing the Skyline Drive **with the Kids**

Yes, Utah is the second most arid state. Nevertheless, we also have some of the best fishing in the world! That's a major reason my family lives here.

One of the nicest drives on earth is the Skyline Drive, outside of Fairfield and Manti. The scenery is breathtaking—watch for elk and mule deer. The fishing is really good, too. There are a number of lakes, and catching fish isn't that tough for kids. If one lake isn't too hot, try another.

If you want to catch native cutthroat, Electric Lake is your best bet. It's catch and release, but bank fishing can be fast and fun; lures and flies only. For kids, tie a fly #20 below a plastic float or bubble and cast. Keep tension on the line and reel in very slowly, with occasional pauses.

Huntington Creek is a great place to dry fly cast. Gooseberry is a wonderful place to catch browns from the bank (use worms, hoppers, or flies). Use worms or PowerBait on the dozen other waters.

There is something for everyone. If the fish aren't biting, you'll at least have a visual feast.

Where to Eat

Bright Spot. 156 South Main; (435) 835–4871. Fast food. $

Pepperbelly's Restaurant. 61 South Main Street, Ephraim; (435) 283–8000. $

Don's Gallery Cafe. 115 North Main Street; (435) 835–3663. $

Ephraim and Spring City

These towns have separate annual festivals, but since the festivals are always held on the same day and the towns are only 10 miles apart, a visit to both makes a nice day trip. Ephraim's **Scandinavian Festival** honors the area's heritage with a Little Denmark supper, booths, crafts, an ugly troll contest, a rodeo, and more. Spring City is a historic Mormon town, with a century of architecture still intact. For its **Heritage Days,** many of the townsfolk open their doors to visitors, allowing a glimpse inside these beautiful old homes. Both of these festivals fall on the Saturday before Memorial Day. Call (435) 283–4321 for more information on both. Ephraim is on U.S. Highway 89, 7 miles north of Manti. Spring City is just off the same highway, a few miles farther north.

Where to Stay

Iron Horse Motel. 670 North Main; (435) 283–4223. $$

Fiddler's Green Inn. 3564 West Highway 116, 10 miles north of Ephraim in Mt. Pleasant; (435) 462–3276. $–$$

Larsen House Bed and Breakfast. 805 East 100 South, Mt. Pleasant; (435) 462–9337. $$

Fast Utah Facts

- Utah County has the most apple and peach trees in Utah.
- Fish Lake National Forest provides 4 million board feet of timber, and 9,000 Christmas trees.
- The blue spruce *(Picea pungens)* was chosen by the Utah state legislature in 1933 to be the state tree.
- Kings Peak, at 13,528 feet, is the highest point in Utah.
- Notable in Utah's ancient history is the abundance of dinosaurs that once roamed the region.
- The Uinta Mountains run east and west (one of the few ranges in the world to do so), and are part of the Rocky Mountains.

Nephi

Ute Stampede (all ages)

Usually takes place during the second weekend of July. Call (435) 623–5608 or go to www.utestampederodeo.com for details. Tickets $$–$$$ depending on the night.

Hold onto your hats! One of Utah's largest rodeos is held here. The Ute Stampede's festivities include a parade with horses, band, and floats, as well as a carnival, foot races, a street dance, and golf tournament. The rodeo features top cowboys and cowgirls from all over the West showing their bareback, roping, bull riding, and barrel racing skills. The three-night run includes a Thursday Family Night.

Eureka

Tintic National Historic Mining Area (all ages)

One hundred and thirty years ago Eureka was a boom town, and a mother lode of gold, silver, lead, and other metals was mined from the nearby mountains. Today Eureka is a living history museum of sorts, a town still standing, but barely inhabited. This area is now called the Tintic National Historic Mining Area. Wandering the streets of Eureka and imagining what once was is an interesting way to spend an afternoon. The cemetery near town will appeal to children who are old enough to interpret the stories on the gravestones. In the nearby town of Tintic is the **Tintic Mining Museum,** a nice **free** (donations accepted) little museum in the old city hall on Main Street that chronicles the area's history. Children especially enjoy a model of the inside of a silver mine. To visit you need to make advance arrangements by calling (435) 433–6842, as the museum does not have regular hours of operation.

Little Sahara Sand Dunes (all ages)

Travel south from Eureka on U.S. Highway 6 for 20 miles. Look for the turnoff sign. Call the BLM for more information at (435) 743–3100. Vehicles $.

You and your family don't want to miss out on the geologic oddity known as Little Sahara. These 60,000 acres of dunes are popular with families who enjoy driving ATVs and dune buggies over the rolling sand. Some areas are fenced off for "sand play," and no vehicles or horses are allowed in these. The dunes are a moving force, traveling an incredible 18 inches a year; it is estimated that Little Sahara started out 150 miles from its present location. Sand drags and racing events are held regularly. Four campgrounds and several picnic areas surround the dunes.

Young Living Family Farm (all ages)

Call (435) 465–5550, or write to 3700 North Highway 91, Mona 84645, to get their calendar of events.

The farm is 40 miles south of Provo, just off I–15 in the small community of Mona. Here you will find an exotic zoo with a rare white buffalo, Goliath horses, miniature ponies, yaks, camels, llamas, zedonks (a mix between zebras and donkeys), and wild Watusi goats. There is also a duck pond with paddleboats, a Western village with a child-size Wells Fargo stagecoach drawn by miniature ponies, and an Indian village. Its newest feature is the Medieval Heritage Center, complete with jousting tournaments, medieval fare, and performances of Shakespeare. In addition, you can explore what the farm is here for; they grow herbs for essential oils that are used in holistic medicines.

Santaquin

Chieftain Museum (all ages)
100 South 100 West. Open on Friday and Saturday 1:00 to 4:00 P.M. April through August. For more information call the Santaquin city offices at (801) 754–3603. Admission is free, but donations are encouraged.

The charming Chieftain Museum is divided into themes, displaying memorabilia from each and every war veteran in town, a handcart used by the pioneers, old farm machinery, and more. This historic building was originally built as a schoolhouse.

Payson

Nebo Loop Scenic Byway (all ages)
Follow the signs in town to reach the Nebo Loop.

Payson Canyon is a gateway to the Nebo Loop Scenic Byway, which travels through the Uinta National Forest between the cities of Nephi and Payson, up and around the highest mountain in the Wasatch Range—Mount Nebo's 11,877 feet. This 38-mile road is famous for its spectacular views of Utah Valley and the Wasatch Mountains and is particularly popular in September and October with lovers of fall colors. If you travel this road, be sure to pull off when you see the sign for Devil's Kitchen. This red-rock formation is most unusual in its alpine surround. The Nebo Loop is very popular with families who enjoy fishing, canoeing, and hiking. There are several campgrounds along the road, and many picnic areas.

Golden Onion Days and The Scottish Festival (all ages)
Payson celebrates the local bounty with **Golden Onion Days** each Labor Day weekend. Carnival rides and booths are open all weekend, and horse races are scheduled for specific days. Call (800) 222–UTAH for more information. The city honors its many Scottish residents with a **Scottish Festival** each July. A parade features Scottish bands and Highland games and dancing competitions in the city park, at 255 South Main Street. Call (800) 222–UTAH for specific dates.

Top Annual Events in Central Utah

MEMORIAL DAY WEEKEND
Scandinavian Festival and Heritage Days, Ephraim and Spring City; (435) 283–4321

JUNE
Art City Days, Springfield; (801) 489–2700

Black Diamond Stampede Rodeo, Price; (800) 842–0789

Round-up Rodeo, Lehi; (801) 763–3117

JULY
America's Freedom Festival, Provo; (801) 370–8052

Annual Springville World Folkfest, Springville; (801) 489–2700

Scottish Festival, Payson; (801) 465–2634

Ute Stampede, Nephi; (435) 623–4407

LABOR DAY WEEKEND
Timpanogos Storytelling Festival, Orem; (801) 229–7161

Swiss Days, Midway; (435) 654–1271

SEPTEMBER
Melon Days, Green River; (435) 564–3526

DECEMBER
Electric Light Parade, Helper; (800) 842–0789

Northeastern Utah

N ortheastern Utah is known as dinosaur land. While significant fossil quarries have been found in other parts of Utah (most notably in Emery County), the geographical area known as the Uintah Basin is famous worldwide for the plentitude and pristine condition of its dinosaur fossils. For the dinosaur aficionado, there are quarries and parks and museums devoted to dinosaurs—and even biking and hiking trails, rodeos, and dinner menus that pick up on the "terrible lizard" theme. If you want to, you can spend two or three days totally immersing yourself in dinosaur artifacts. If your interests spread to ancient stuff in general, some of the oldest geologic eras on earth are exposed here—you can get your picture taken next to a billion-year-old rock.

The area also boasts Flaming Gorge, a flamboyantly colored rock formation that skirts the trout-laden Green River, described in "Central Utah." When you're near the Green River, remember that the sport of river running was first practiced in this part of Utah and is still going strong today. The Ashley National Forest sprawls across the Uinta Mountains here—home of wild, scenic beauty and excellent stream fishing. If you saw the movie *Butch Cassidy and the Sundance Kid,* you'll want to check out the real-life haunts of Butch and his gang near Vernal, where they headquartered for a time.

Duchesne

Much of eastern Utah enjoys the bounty of a petroleum-rich landscape, and as you travel U.S. Highway 40 through Duchesne and the other small towns in this part of the state, you will see evidence of the oil industry.

Strawberry Reservoir (all ages)
Located on U.S. Highway 40. Call (435) 654–0470 for more information.

On your way to Duchesne, you will also cross two of Utah's major reservoirs and water recreation havens: Strawberry and Starvation dams. Strawberry Reservoir is the largest in Utah, with a water surface of 27,000 acres. It is a popular trophy fishing spot, with a lodge, marina (with boat and equipment rentals), and numerous campgrounds on its shores. The **Strawberry Visitor Center** is a wonderful rest stop, with two short nature

NORTHEASTERN UTAH

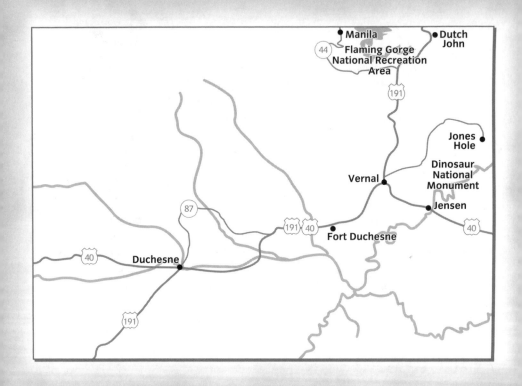

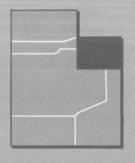

trails that are perfect for stretching your legs. One is land based—look for hawks overhead. The other has a water view leading to a protected part of the reservoir. During spawning seasons (spring and fall), fish are trapped here for a short time while their eggs are harvested, and the fish activity is fast and furious.

Michael's
TopPicks for fun in Northeastern Utah

1. Dinosaur National Monument, Jensen; (435) 789–2115

2. The Green River, Dutch John/Manila

3. Field House of Natural History, Vernal; (435) 789–3799

4. Red Canyon Overlook, Manila

5. Flaming Gorge Reservoir, Manila

6. Utah Waterfowl Management Area, Manila

7. Brown's Park, Flaming Gorge/Manila

8. Strawberry Reservoir, Duchesne; (435) 654–0470

9. Sheep Creek Geological Loop, Manila

10. Red Canyon Lodge, Vernal; (435) 889–3759

Starvation Reservoir (all ages)
Located on U.S. Highway 40. Call (435) 738–2326 for information.

Just outside of town, you will find the second body of water, Starvation Reservoir. This manmade lake hosts a state park on its beaches that provides a campground, rest rooms, showers, fish-cleaning facilities, and sewage dumps.

Where to Stay

Falcon's Ledge. P.O. Box 67, Altamont 84001; (435) 454–3737. $$$$

L.C. Ranch. P.O. Box 63, Altamont 84001; (435) 454–3750. $$$$

The Mirror Lake Highway: **Drive into God's Backyard**

Many of the Native Americans believe that God lived in the high Uinta Mountains. They weren't wrong. The Mirror Lake Highway is the way in. This is a must-see if you are in the region from May to October (the road is closed during the winter).

Take Utah Highway 150 out of Kamas. You'll start at an elevation of about 6,000 feet and climb to nearly 11,000 feet as you go over Baldy. Stop at the top and take a good look—see if you don't also think that God lives here. Let your kids run about in the thin air chasing squirrels and collecting wildflowers. Tell them that this is the only range on this continent that runs east and west—not north and south.

There are dozens of pull-offs. This isn't a race—stop and smell the mountain flowers and deep-scented pines. Sit on a boulder and explore the many trails. There are dozens of great fishing spots and numerous campgrounds. Watch for bear, moose, and elk. Play close attention to deer on the road during mornings and evenings.

Tip: Administer motion sickness pills to kids before you leave home (check with your doctor first). There are some curves.

Fort Duchesne

Fort Duchesne still looks like the army post it was in the 1880s, but its modern-day function is to serve as headquarters for the 2,500-acre **Uintah-Ouray Indian Reservation.** The Uintah-Ourays host a **Bear Dance** (nominal fee) every spring, and if you're lucky enough to be in the area during this three-day festival, do go out of your way to participate. The tribe also hosts a **Powwow and All-Indian Rodeo** (nominal fee) over the Fourth of July weekend. Call (435) 722–5141 for information on all events at Fort Duchesne. The complex is open from Monday through Thursday from 8:00 A.M. to 4:30 P.M.

Vernal

Vernal, about 40 miles northeast of Duchesne on U.S. Highway 40, is heaven for the dinosaur enthusiast. Just by driving down Main Street, you'll see scores of dinosaurs adorning the town's establishments. Dino motels, restaurants, and gift shops abound (even the taxi service in town is called T-Rex Taxi). There is one water slide in town, with the tantalizing name of **Hydrosaurus Slide** (435–789–1010). If you call the **Dinosaurland Travel Board** at (800) 477–5558 before your visit, you will receive an official "dinosaur hunting license" and a brochure describing the area. This office can also give you information on the region's festivals and rodeos. If you pass this way in midsummer, chances are your visit will coincide with a festival or rodeo celebration. Early June brings **Rough Rider Days** and its rodeo to Roosevelt. The second weekend in July is the **Dinosaur Round-Up Rodeo** and **Dinosaur Days** in Vernal; the rodeo runs for four nights and is billed as one of the biggest and best in the West. Dinosaur Days takes place at the Field House and offers food and craft booths and special activities. Vernal also hosts the **Outlaw Trail Festival** in June and July, with an outdoor play that enlivens local history.

Ouray National Wildlife Refuge: Raptor Heaven

Whenever we're in Vernal, which is often these days, we always stop at the Ouray Refuge, even if it's just for a few minutes. It's 12,000 acres of marshland fun.

Fifteen short miles from Vernal, this refuge is one of the best places I know to get a bird's-eye view of raptors. Of course, the place is also loaded with waterfowl, pheasants, and shorebirds.

On any given day, you'll see the large golden eagle, bald eagles, osprey, hawks, and owls. You might also spot a whooping crane. On the 9-mile drive, you might even see a raptor catch a duck or a pheasant for supper. While somewhat brutal, this is an exciting part of nature not to be avoided.

Field House of Natural History (all ages)

235 Main Street; (435) 789–3799. Open 8:00 A.M. to 9:00 P.M. in summer and 9:00 A.M. to 5:00 P.M. the rest of the year. The building is closed for renovation until spring 2004; however, the gardens will remain open. Admission $.

A good first stop for orientation is the Field House of Natural History, a Utah state park that also houses a visitor information center. Natural history displays describe the people who first settled this area; Fremont Indian artifacts and Ute Indian ceremonial clothes can be seen. A mural describes the geologic formations in the area, which reveal three-billion-year-old rocks. Rocks and fossils are on display; don't miss the fluorescent mineral room. In the visitor center you'll find brochures, videos, maps, and helpful people to explain the area and its attractions.

Pictographs and Petroglyphs: **Indian Rock Art**

Both pictographs and petroglyphs are types of rock art—images produced on rock.

Pictographs are images *painted* on rock, probably with a crude stick brush or fingers. The medium might be blood, minerals, crushed plants, ash, charcoal, or a mixture of these.

Petroglyphs are images *etched* into the rock. Using some sort of sharp object, the artist etched the image into the "desert varnish" on the rock. This "varnish" is a natural stain and is rather dark. When it's removed, the brighter colored rock is revealed.

We know what the artists were drawing: bighorn sheep, deer, bears, lizards, and snakes. What they meant is another story. There are a number of theories, but no one really knows for sure. Whether these works of art were a religious expression or a form of communication is still debated.

The admission fee includes a visit to the adjacent **Dinosaur Gardens,** a (you guessed it) dinosaur-filled garden. Fifteen life-size sculpted dinosaurs, tinted in authentic hues, roam a two-acre park. Your children will see the terrible *Tyrannosaurus rex,* a pterodactyl, and a Utah raptor, an ancient bird first discovered in this state. The plantings are carefully chosen to imitate food that would have tempted real dinosaurs; a small lake and waterfall echo the more temperate climate that reigned here 200,000 years ago. At night the dinosaurs are lighted, and informational talks are given each evening during the summer. During the month of December thousands of tiny Christmas lights surround the dinosaurs to celebrate the holiday season.

Ladies of the White House Doll Collection (all ages)

At the Uintah County Library at 155 East Main, next door to the Field House of Natural History. Open Monday through Thursday 10:00 A.M. to 9:00 P.M. and Friday and Saturday until 6:00 P.M. Call (435) 789–0091. A small donation is requested.

The Uintah County Library is the home of the Ladies of the White House Doll Collection. A doll represents each of the first ladies of the White House and is draped in an authentic reproduction of the gown she wore at her husband's inaugural ball.

Daughters of the Utah Pioneers Museum (all ages)
200 South and 500 West; (435) 789–0352. Open during the summer Tuesday through Saturday 10:00 A.M. to 4:00 P.M.; Friday and Saturday in September, during the same hours. Admission is **free.**

Just down the street is the Daughters of Utah Pioneers Museum. It contains artifacts and pictures describing the history of the area from the time Vernal was settled in the 1800s. This museum is open only on summer afternoons.

Rutter Family Adventures: **Camping at Christmas Meadows**

We've camped all over the Uintas. However, one of our favorite spots is Christmas Meadows, off Utah Highway 150, nearly to Wyoming. Maybe it's the great fishing, the tall trees, and rugged mountains. Maybe it's because we camp there every year and it's familiar.

The campground is on a rise overlooking a stream packed with cutthroat trout near a backpacking trailhead. It's not a large campground, but it's comfortable.

We have a ritual. Abbey and I set up the tent; Shari and Jon-Michael break out the Coleman stove and make a very large afternoon lunch. Then Shari kicks back with a mystery novel, and I go fishing with one or both kids.

That night we eat leftovers, take a stroll down the trail to find moose, and wander back to camp about dark. We build a glorious fire, roast too many marshmallows, tell stories (not too scary), fire up the Coleman lantern, unroll the bags, and read ourselves to sleep in the green tent.

Next morning, we sleep in since the fish don't mind. I make a big breakfast on the stove, and we eat in the clean, mountain air. Then we take a hike, focusing on interesting things like cool rocks, pieces of wood, grass blades—whatever a six-year-old wants to do.

Western Heritage Museum and Convention Center (all ages)
302 East 200 South; (435) 789–7399. Open Monday through Saturday 9:00 A.M. to 6:00 P.M., Memorial Day through Labor Day; Monday through Friday 9:00 A.M. to 5:00 P.M. and Saturday 10:00 A.M. to 2:00 P.M. the rest of the year. Admission is **free.**

Vernal's biggest and newest museum is the Western Heritage Museum and Convention Center. The theme here is the Old West, and there are memorabilia explaining Uintah County's outlaw past, as well as an art gallery and gift shop.

Fun and Games (all ages)
1781 West 1000 South; (435) 781–0088. Call for rates and hours.

Older children in your family will especially enjoy the amenities at Fun and Games, where teens gather to enjoy each other's company while playing mini-golf and video games. Batting cages and a snack bar complete the scene.

Red Canyon Lodge (all ages)
Utah Highway 44 northwest of Vernal, at 790 Red Canyon Road, Dutch John; www.red canyonlodge.com. Call (435) 889–3759 for reservations.

If you're looking for a destination resort, try Red Canyon Lodge, about an hour's drive northwest of Vernal, on Utah Highway 44. The resort is perched on the south rim of Red Canyon in the Ashley National Forest. There is a spectacular 1,500-foot overlook here of Flaming Gorge and the Green River that runs through it. The lodge is open most of the year—all of the warm months and on winter weekends for snowmobilers. Dinner here is a treat, to be enjoyed out on the deck or in the wall-to-wall-windowed dining room. Look for blue herons and other fabulous birds, chipmunks, and deer. Horseback rides can be arranged, and the lodge keeps a stocked fishing pond for children.

U-Bar Ranch (all ages)
In Uintah Canyon above Roosevelt. For information and reservations call (800) 303–7256 or (435) 645–7256.

U-Bar Ranch sits on the edge of the officially designated High Uinta Wilderness Area. Here you'll stay in a rustic cabin, share a bathroom with another family, eat family style, and truly "get away from it all." Expect to see elk and moose, and maybe even a black bear. Horseback riding, fishing, and hunting are all available.

Easy Travel Tips: **The Activity Bag**

No matter how carefully you plan, there will be times when you wish you'd left your children at home with Grandma. To survive Utah with your children, plan an activity bag.

Before you leave home, pack a bag with games, books, tapes or CDs, colored pencils—maybe even treats. As you begin each day on the road, with great ceremony, reach into the activity bag and pass out the entertainment. Plan to have a new activity for each kid each day. It doesn't have to be very large or elaborate.

Some of our favorite activity bag items are stories on tape or CD. Shari goes to our local library and selects family-oriented stories we can listen to on the vehicle's stereo. She gears each story to a certain kid, but we all listen and enjoy the show.

Where to Eat

Betty's Cafe. 416 West Main; (435) 781–2728. $

Country Grub. 2419 South 1500 East; (435) 789–7000. $

Stella's Kitchen. 3340 North Vernal Avenue; (435) 789–5657. $$

Breathtaking Ranch **Rock Art**

This is a MUST, MUST see! This is one of the finest, most accessible collections of rock art I've ever seen. When you're in Vernal, stop at the Dinosaurland Travel Board (800–477–5558) for a map. See the work left by those who walked the land before the white man.

This majestic collection of pictographs and petroglyphs is among the finest in Utah (which means it's among the finest in the world). It will be a hit with your children since you can get very close to the walls. The rock art is located on private property, but the owners welcome visitors. Please leave a donation of a few dollars for trail upkeep.

From the parking lot, you'll walk a few hundred yards to the side of the canyon and wander the trail that takes you past dozens and dozens of displays. Look for the flute player, the lizard, and the grizzly bear.

Ask your kids to imagine what the pictures mean. Enjoy and take pictures, but don't touch. The oils from your hands are detrimental to the art. We have our kids take their sketch books and draw reproductions.

Where to Stay

Best Western Antlers. 423 West Main Street; (435) 789–1202. $$

Best Western Dinosaur Inn. 251 East Main Street; (435) 789–2660. $$

Jensen

Jensen is just a short drive from Vernal, about 20 miles east on two-lane U.S. Highway 40. The visitor center here provides maps, brochures, and hiking and biking routes, as well as rest rooms.

Tour of the **Tilted Rocks**

When you're in Dinosaur National Monument, the visitor center is a must see. However, don't rush out of the park.

Take the Tour of the Tilted Rocks. It's a car tour that starts at the Dinosaur Quarry and takes you on a 22-mile tour of the park. It is supposed to take about two hours, but it takes us four, and is very informative. Don't miss it.

Pick up a 50-cent tour guide, stop at each of the suggested points, and read about how the park was formed. The Josie Morris Cabin is very interesting.

If you have a four-wheel drive, consider taking the Blue Mountain Road.

Dinosaur National Monument (all ages)
Call (435) 789–2115 for more information. The visitor center is open daily 8:00 A.M. to 7:00 P.M. from Memorial Day to Labor Day, and 8:00 A.M. to 4:30 P.M. the rest of the year. Vehicles $$.

You'll want to save at least a half day for a visit to Dinosaur National Monument and a hike on the Cub Creek Trail (see below). If it is near lunchtime, consider stopping for food in Vernal (the grocery stores have deli sections, and most of the restaurants will gladly pack lunches), because there is great picnicking to be had in this area.

At Jensen's visitor center, look for the Dinosaur Monument sign, and turn left. A winding road takes you to the Dinosaur Visitor Center and Quarry. Dinosaur National Monument stretches 100 miles into Colorado, but the area here is the only place to actually view dinosaur bones. During the summer a shuttle bus operates from the main parking lot; the rest of the year you may drive directly to the quarry building. What you'll find here are four walls and a roof, which literally sit atop one of the most dense fossil discoveries in the world. About 145 million years ago, this site was a bend in a river, which neatly snagged an accumulation of dead animals. It efficiently buried more than 2,000 bones, and the rest, as they say, is history. This find was discovered in the early 1900s by a paleontologist named Earl Douglass. He was exploring the Uintah Basin when he came upon the exposed spine of an apatosaurus. (Can you imagine?) The fossils can still be viewed in their natural state, mostly exposed and lying in their original, 200-foot-long graveyard. During the summer, on the hour, rangers give talks explaining the ongoing excavations in the quarry and out in the field. The quarry also has real dinosaur bones that kids can touch, re-created dinosaurs, and a gift shop that has an excellent selection of dinosaur books as well as coloring books, replicas of petroglyphs, and other cool prehistoric items.

Once you've had your fill of dinosaur bones, make a left turn out of the parking lot of Dinosaur National Monument, and follow the road signs to the **Cub Creek Trail.** To find the trail, just watch for the numbered signs on the road that indicate SOMETHING SIGNIFICANT along the roadside. A helpful printed guide with a map and descriptions may be purchased at the Dinosaur Quarry visitor center for 50 cents. On the trail, you'll see **Split**

Mountain, a mountain effectively divided in two by the Green River. There is a hike here called **Desert Voices Trail,** a 2-mile loop with a long, uphill grade. **Split Mountain Campground** has picnic tables, but it's exposed to the sun in summer, and is probably too hot for comfort. A short drive down the road to **Green River Campground** provides shadier tables for lunch. You'll pass a boat ramp that is a popular take-out point for river trips, and you may see rafters unpacking their boats here. Continuing on, look for **Turtle Rock** on your left. You'll know it when you see it.

When you reach the dirt road, don't be daunted. In wet weather it can be impassable, but if the road is dry, continuing on from here is worth the effort. Take the left fork and cross Cub Creek. A bit farther and you'll see superb rock art on your left. This creek and canyon provided safety and a water supply for ancient Indians. At the road's end is the **cabin of Josie Bassett Morris,** a farmer and rancher who took advantage of the same reliable water supply several millennia after the first inhabitants. Josie Bassett was raised in Brown's Park, lived a long and very full life, and ended her days here, at this wilderness cabin. Her exploits as a cowgirl and adventuress are legendary—she married and divorced five times and reportedly shot one husband, poisoned another, and ran one off while wielding a frying pan. There are rumors, but no proof, that Butch Cassidy was one of her suitors. She settled in Cub Creek in 1914 and built this cabin in 1935 or so. Josie lived here for fifty years, all by herself, and raised pigs, chickens, field crops, and a variety of fruits and vegetables. She had no indoor plumbing or modern conveniences. Next time you're feeling a little blue, remember Josie's remarkable determination.

The nearby trailhead leads 1 mile up **Hog Canyon** and is a nice, easy, one-hour hike. *Note:* While you're here, stop and listen to the quiet. This corner of the world has no major airplane traffic above, and you're far enough from the highway to escape ground noise.

Geology and Natural History Facts: **Utah Land Regions**

Utah can be divided into three basic regions: The Colorado Plateau Region, the Mountain Region, and the Great Basin Region.

The Colorado Plateau covers the southeastern part of the state, which is rather dry. All the water drains into the Colorado River system, eventually ending up in the Pacific Ocean. This area produces some fantastic rock forms. All five of our natural parks are in this area.

The Mountain Region is in the northeastern part of the state. This area is covered with forests and is home to the Uinta and Wasatch Mountain ranges. This is the home of the best snow on earth.

The Great Basin Region is the western part of the state. All the water here flows into the basin and has no outlet to the ocean. The largest cities are in this region.

Hatch River Expeditions (older children only)
200 North 400 East in Vernal; (435) 789–4316 or (800) 342–8243; www.hatchriver.com.
Lunch is included. $$$$.

If your inspection of this area has sparked your family's interest in a river trip, call Hatch River Expeditions in Vernal and book a trip on the Green River in the Split Mountain area. For this daylong trip, you will meet your guide in Vernal and then take an hour's ride to the put-in spot in Rainbow Park. This is a challenging whitewater trip, with gorgeous canyon scenery along the way. In the spring the water is high and fierce, and children under eight may not participate on this ride. Later in the summer, when the water has gentled, children six and older are welcome.

Buy Books, Not Junk

Vacations are fun and educational.

Visitor/interpretive centers are very instructive and worth stopping at. However, most come equipped with a trusty gift shop loaded with stuff your kids are going to want.

Avoid the temptation, and pressure from your kids, to buy a lot of junk. It's stuff that will be forgotten and broken before long, anyway. Get in the habit of buying educational items.

Our kids are finally trained. No, we'll not buy that ridiculous wood popgun (which will drive us nuts in the car and break after the second day). We might, however, buy you a book about the place in question.

This type of parental pedagogy will pay lots of dividends, reinforcing what you show your children. Books, and other educational materials, have a much greater value than trinkets.

Dutch John and Manila

Dutch John, more than thirty years old, is a town that literally arose during the course of one year, built by the U.S. Bureau of Reclamation to house the constructors of Flaming Gorge Dam. Manila is home to the Forest Service headquarters for **Flaming Gorge National Recreation Area.** These towns flank Lake Flaming Gorge, with Dutch John on the east shore and Manila near the west. Both are reached by traveling north from Vernal on U.S. Highway 191, and there are several worthwhile stops along the way. In mid-July the **Cow Country Rodeo** draws visitors from all over the West to Manila. Then on the Saturday night of Labor Day weekend, Manila is famous for its **Festival of Lights.** The celebration begins at dusk, when hundreds of local boaters entertain an onshore crowd by lighting up their boats and traversing in formation on Lake Flaming Gorge. Afterward, a dazzling fireworks display can be seen from the lakeshore. For more information on these events, call (800) 477–5558 or (435) 784–3445.

Steinaker Reservoir State Park (all ages)

4335 North Highway 191; (435) 789–4432. Call for more information. Vehicles $, camping $$$.

Beginning a few miles out of Vernal, you will see a series of signs that interpret the surrounding geology. Called **Drive Through the Ages,** this road passes over rocks laid down one billion—that's correct, one billion—years ago. You will pass Steinaker Reservoir State Park, popular with anglers and water-skiers. There is a sandy beach here, along with a self-guided nature trail, rest rooms, a thirty-one-unit campsite, and a waterski slalom course. This water is an important source of irrigation for the valley below. Continuing on, you will look down at the open pit phosphate mine that has been in operation since 1959.

Red Fleet Reservoir State Park (all ages)

8750 North Highway 191; (435) 789–4432. Call for more information. Vehicles $, camping $$$.

About 10 miles out of Vernal is Red Fleet Reservoir State Park, named for the sailing "fleet" of red rock surrounding the water. Again, fishing and boating are the main activities. There are covered picnic tables, a nice sandy beach, and twenty-nine campsites. A dinosaur trackway dating back 200 million years was recently discovered nearby. As the road continues its rise, you will head into Ashley National Forest. The surroundings turn green, and the wildlife is plentiful.

Red Canyon Overlook (all ages)

Just west of the junction of U.S. Highway 191 and Utah Highway 44.

Forty miles outside of Vernal you will meet the junction of U.S. Highway 191 and Utah Highway 44. Heading west toward Manila, pull over for a spectacular view at the Red Canyon Overlook. This is an excellent choice for a picnic and/or pause-and-reflection. The canyon is 1,500 feet deep. Lake Flaming Gorge spreads out in two directions, with the red slash of rock, for which the gorge is named, providing an electrifying background. There is a Forest Service visitor center here, and a campground nearby.

Sheep Creek Geological Loop (all ages)

Drive west from the Red Canyon Overlook. Follow the road signs.

If your family wants to continue the quest for really old rocks, you will want to proceed west from Red Canyon Overlook and take the side road to Sheep Creek Geological Loop. This area sustained some very weird earth rotations about two-and-a-half billion years ago, and a drive through here is sort of eerie and fantastical. Today it is called the Uinta Crest Fault, and if you look closely you can tell how it was formed: The south side of the fault was thrust up from the earth more than 15,000 feet, while the north side didn't move much at all. The in-between, bent-up parts expose billions of years of geologic history. If you look carefully, you might see the encrusted fossils of sea creatures who lived here when this area was under water.

Oscar Swett Historic Ranch (all ages)

From Manila, retrace your route east, back to the junction of Utah Highway 44 and U.S. Highway 191. Continue northeast on U.S. 191. You will see the signs for the Oscar Swett Historic Ranch; veer left. (435) 789–1181. Call for hours and admission fees.

About a hundred years ago one of the last homesteading projects in the country began here. Oscar Swett and his family used nothing but sweat (no pun intended) and horse-power to create this beautiful ranch, and it is preserved on the National Historic Register as "a vivid example of man learning to live in harmony with nature in order to survive." The ranch is open seasonally, in warm-weather months only.

Fast Utah Facts

- Today Utah is home to two of the largest dinosaur graveyards in North America: Dinosaur National Monument, in the northernmost part of the state, and the Cleveland Lloyd Quarry in east-central Utah.
- The bridge across Starvation Reservoir is the longest one in Utah— ¼ mile long.
- Duchesne is located near the largest cedar forest in the world.
- There are 1,253,142 acres of aspen trees in Utah.

Flaming Gorge Dam (all ages)

In Dutch John, on U.S. Highway 191. Call (435) 885–3135 for visitor information.

This is one of the more massive western dam sites, and its sheer bravado as an engineering feat demands notice. The impressive dam rises 502 feet above the mighty Green River, creating Lake Flaming Gorge, which extends 91 miles. The **Flaming Gorge Dam Visitor Center** (435–885–3135) is open year-round. Stop here and grab a brochure and fact sheet, and take the self-guided tour of the dam. The tour takes you, via an elevator, into the bowels of the earth. Inside the dam you are surrounded by more tons of concrete than you most likely ever will be again (one million cubic yards), and you are offered a fascinating look at the changes humans can effect on their environment. Guided tours of the dam and special programs for kids are available in the summer.

Hiking with the Kids **on the Crystal Lake Trailhead**

Taken an alpine hike with the kids recently? Smelled the wildflowers? Looked at the pristine real estate? Walked within 30 yards of a lazy moose? Let the kids run across a grassy meadow at 10,000 feet?

A lot of high-mountain trails are pretty rough. You have to be half mountain goat—the going isn't kid (or adult) friendly. Well, have I got a trail for you! We love to hike Crystal Lake Trailhead (Tail Lakes off Highway 150) and head for Long Lake. The going is gentle, and the scenery is breathtaking.

The flowers are likely to be in bloom, since spring in this country is June and July. It takes about an hour to get to the lake with kids. Pack a good lunch and take water—the lakes and streams look pure, but they're not for drinking. Once you are at Long Lake, you can relax, fish, or hike other trails. There are at least half a dozen lakes within a mile.

Fishing is very good right from the bank. For a special treat, wander over to Majorie Lake and fish for grayling. They are easy to catch and fun to look at. (They have a long dorsal fin.)

In the Uintas, always take a jacket, even on nice days. Rain gear is also standard equipment.

Green River (older children only)

The controlled flow of the Green River below Flaming Gorge Dam is excellent for family **river rafting.** Half-day trips from just below the dam to Little Hole can be booked at Flaming Gorge Lodge (435–889–3773). The trip costs $175 for up to six people, and you can usually arrange your own departure time. This trip takes about four hours. There are a half-dozen river companies in Vernal that will book one- to five-day trips on this river, as well as other rivers in the area. Do-it-yourselfers can rent rafts for self-guided excursions from the lodge, or from Flaming Gorge Recreation Services (435–885–3191).

Trout fishing is extremely popular here—this stretch of the Green River, below the Flaming Gorge Dam, is oft cited as one of the premier spots in the world (a trophy mackinaw was taken from the river weighing 51½ pounds). Boaters and anglers flock here year-round, and you will find complete marina facilities, including boat rentals, launching ramps, lodges, and campsites of all comfort levels.

Fishing the Green **Below the Dam**

The Green River below the Flaming Gorge Dam is one of the most famous fishing waters in the United States. If you spin cast, it's a paradise. If you fly fish it's high heaven. If you bait fish, you're out of luck (bait is against the law).

The fishing in the clear green waters is wonderful. The fish are big and feisty. It's enough to make an angler fall to his or her knees and give thanks. This water, however, at least if you wade, is not for young kids. The wading can be a little bit technical. I'd have my kids wear a life jacket and I'd want them to be pushing close to five feet. Your kid needs to be at least ten—or stay in the gentlest sections.

The river is wide, but the fish are found on the edges. You won't have to wade very far out. Check at the local fly shops for the best offerings.

Even if you don't fish, swing by the Green and take a look. It's a very pretty river. It's also a great place to raft.

Brown's Park (all ages)

On U.S. Highway 191, 20 miles north of Flaming Gorge Dam. Tours of John Jarvie Historic Ranch conducted May through October, 10:00 A.M. to 5:00 P.M. Call (435) 885–3307 for more information. Admission is **free.**

A full gas tank and provisions are advised when you head for Brown's Park because there are no services. This area is famous as the home to many turn-of-the-century eccentrics, who reportedly loved the remoteness here because it kept everybody else away. One of those people was John Jarvie, and his legacy is seen at the **John Jarvie Historic Ranch,** about 20 miles in from U.S. Highway 191 (travel is via a dirt road). Jarvie chose this spot because it was an important river crossing, and a hundred years ago he created a resting place for travelers from Utah, Wyoming, and Colorado. His ranch included a store, post office, river ferry, and a reportedly busy cemetery. There was a lot of outlaw activity here in Jarvie's time, and many violent deaths. The area's most famous gunman, Butch Cassidy, was said to do business here, along with his cohort, the Sundance Kid. Jarvie himself was murdered during a robbery at his store. Today the ranch exhibits include an old stone house, a blacksmith shop, and a collection of Western artifacts. A **Utah Waterfowl Management Area** is located just east of the Jarvie Ranch, and this area is a very popular birdwatching site in the spring and fall.

Where to Stay

Flaming Gorge Lodge. 155 Greendale, U.S. Highway 191, Dutch John; (435) 889–3773. $$$

Red Canyon Lodge. Highway 44, Vernal; (435) 889–3759. $$$

Jones Hole

Call (435) 789–4481 for information on Jones Hole.

Jones Hole National Fish Hatchery (all ages)

Get on 500 North Street in Vernal, and head east for 40 miles, until just before you reach the Colorado border. Then follow the signs to Jones Hole and Diamond Mountain. Open 7:00 A.M. to 3:30 P.M. daily. Admission is free.

Another fun trip in this region requires a trip back through Vernal, as the road to the Jones Hole National Fish Hatchery isn't really on the way to or from anything else. You will go up and over Diamond Mountain and end up at this little oasis of a place, where people live and work to raise fish for the stocked waters in Utah. There is a visitor center here, bathrooms, picnic tables, and grassy running-around areas. You can go inside the fishery, with its tanks and fish smell, or view the fish outside, from fifty different raceways. Two million fish begin life here each year. Each is one of four different kinds of trout, and most of them are one of five different strains of rainbow. There are no formal tours here, but you can find out everything you need to know, because the nice people who work at the hatchery are very forthcoming with information. If you are in the mood for a walk, consider the **trail down to the Green River,** which begins near the hatchery raceways. It is 4 miles long, but it's flat, and considered an easy walk. You will see petroglyphs and waterfalls, and if you're extremely lucky, a bighorn sheep or two.

Top Annual Events in Northeastern Utah

JUNE
Rough Rider Days, Roosevelt; (800) 477–5558

JUNE AND JULY
Outlaw Trail Festival, Vernal; (800) 477–5558

JULY
Dinosaur Round-Up Rodeo, Vernal; (800) 477–5558

Uintah-Ouray Powwow, Fort Duchesne; (435) 722–5141

LABOR DAY WEEKEND
Festival of Lights, Manila; (800) 477–5558

Southeastern Utah

his corner of the state is part of a larger area called the Colorado Plateau. Colorado is a Spanish word for "red"—and red is definitely the characteristic color of the landscape. Brightly colored sandstone tumbles and falls for hundreds of miles through this country, pausing sometimes to allow a valley oasis to thrive and a town to grow.

The climate differs greatly from northern Utah's alpine terrain. Winters here are mild, making outdoor sports popular all year long. Mountain bikers have made this area their mecca, hiking and backpacking are spectacular, and river running is a major industry—on both the thrilling rapids of the Green and Colorado Rivers and the tamer waters of the languid San Juan River.

There are many sacred Native American sites here, both ancient and modern, and incredible rock-art panels. Enjoy the beauty of two national parks as well as Lake Powell and Rainbow Bridge National Monument. Monument Valley, made famous in dozens of Western movies, guards the southern border.

Moab

For its first half century of settlement, Moab was a quiet, dusty town, pretty much in the middle of nowhere. That changed dramatically in the 1950s, when huge uranium deposits were discovered in the area. Moab became the center of a booming mining industry that drew thousands of hopeful prospectors. Much money was made and lost, but the most lasting effect was that Moab was "discovered" and has never been the same since. The town is now a bustling activity center for the tourist trade. Thousands of vacationers flock here to enjoy the scenic and recreational beauty nearby.

Shopping is a pleasant diversion in Moab's bustling downtown area. The jewelry shops on Main Street make for great browsing and buying. Look for silver jewelry hand-crafted by Utah Indians and decorated with native rock such as turquoise and topaz. The bookstores in town have good selections of natural history and western geology books; local art galleries feature unique Native American sculpture and paintings; and rock collectors will find a great selection here. A couple of fun shops are **Marc II** and the **Trading Post,** where your children will find clever toys, gadgets, and collectibles. Both of these stores

SOUTHEASTERN UTAH

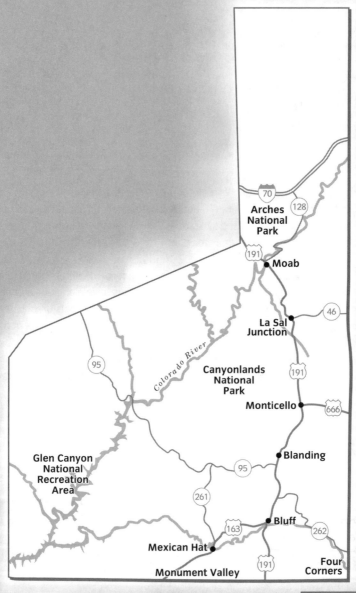

Arches National Park

70
128
191
Moab
La Sal Junction
46
95
Colorado River
Canyonlands National Park
191
Monticello
666
Glen Canyon National Recreation Area
Blanding
95
261
Bluff
262
163
Mexican Hat
Monument Valley
191
Four Corners

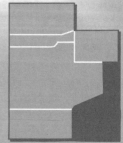

are located in a small mall on Main Street and 50 South next to a popular brew pub called Eddie McStiffs.

Moab Information Center (all ages)
On the corner of Center and Main; (435) 259–8825.

A good first stop is the Moab Information Center. The nice people here can help you with directions as well as restaurant and lodging selections. They also know about evening activities and seasonal goings-on. Great maps and a selection of books describing the area are for sale. The spectacular scenery in and around Moab has provided the backdrop for many movies, from *Rio Grande,* made in 1950 and starring John Wayne, to *Thelma and Louise,* made in 1992. Many of these movie locations can be visited, and some have sets that remained after the Hollywood crews returned home. Pick up a **"Movie Locations Auto Tour"** brochure at the visitor center, and show the cinema buffs in your family where more than a dozen movies were filmed.

Michael's
Top Picks for fun in Southeastern Utah

1. Arches National Park; (435) 719–2100

2. Canyonlands National Park; (435) 259–7164

3. Dead Horse Point; (435) 259–2614

4. Moab, Utah; (435) 259–8825

5. Delicate Arch, Arches National Park

6. Newspaper Rock, Moab

7. Horseshoe Canyon Rock Art, Canyonlands National Park

8. Hovenweep National Monument, Bluff

9. Colorado River Scenic Byway

10. Glen Canyon National Recreation Area

Dan O'Laurie Canyon Country Museum (all ages)
118 East Center; (435) 259–7985. Open Monday through Saturday 1:00 to 8:00 P.M. April to November; Monday through Thursday 3:00 to 7:00 P.M. and Friday and Saturday 1:00 to 7:00 P.M. the rest of the year. Adults $, children free.

The museum interprets the history and prehistory of both man and beast who lived in this area. The Pierson History Hall traces the development of ranching, early transportation, and the Old Spanish Trail. The museum is named after its modern-day benefactor. For more information call the museum.

Escape to the **Sunshine**

Sometimes the snow and cold weather of northern Utah can be depressing, and we often make a trip to southern Utah during the winter months. It's almost always sunny and warm in the south, and the change can be refreshing after a big snowstorm.

Whether you decide to head for the southwest or southeast, be sure to check the weather forecast. There's nothing worse than leaving bad weather behind and ending up in another storm.

If you head for the Moab area, plan on spending a day hiking or riding the fabulous mountain bike trails. The fresh air, sunshine, and exercise will have you feeling like a new family.

Perhaps the best part about heading south in the winter is that the motels drastically slash their rates. It is not uncommon to find rooms in Moab for under $30 a night. So load up the gear and get away!

Butch Cassidy's King World Waterpark

(all ages) 😊

Located in the north end of town on U.S. Highway 191, at 1500 North Highway 191. Call (435) 259–2837 or go to www.butchcassidyskingworldwaterpark.com for more information. Admission $$$.

Butch Cassidy's King World Waterpark is a good way to cool off in Moab. Open during the summer season, the winding tubes and open slides here are very popular with preteens. No other water park in the world can boast King World, a weird, very old carving done in stone that sits a few hundred feet above the water activity. King World was named by its now-forgotten sculptor, and features a king's head and a horse's head. If you want a close-up look at this oddity, ask and a guide will accompany you to the site. The water park takes its name from the original natural pond located here, which was reportedly a watering hole for the outlaw Butch Cassidy. In season, the park is open seven days a week.

Ya Gotta Wanna Fun Park (all ages)

60 West Cedar Avenue. Call (435) 259–8007 or go to www.yagottawanna.com for admission prices and park hours.

Another fun place for kids is Ya Gotta Wanna Fun Park, located behind McDonald's on Kane Creek Boulevard. Mini-golf, paddle boats, pool tables, and a go-cart track will entertain the older children in your family.

Geyser Pass (all ages)
Follow U.S. Highway 191 south of town until the Pack Creek cut-off, and then follow the Scenic Loop road to the signed turnoff.

In winter, Geyser Pass is a favorite place with families for sledding, snowmobiling, and cross-country skiing. Geyser Pass has miles of groomed trails that branch from its trailhead; ask locally for a route that will fit your skiing ability.

Colorado River Trips (all ages)
The La Sals are one reigning natural force in southeastern Utah; another is the Colorado River. The Colorado may look fairly tame as it runs through town, but a few miles north and south are wild, whitewater canyons famous for rafting. Moab is the put-in point for a dozen rafting companies that take adventurers on both calm water and whitewater trips on the Colorado and Green Rivers, which join together just south of town. If you're a novice, it's highly recommended that you book with a guide for this experience. Among the many rafting outfits in town are some that cater to families. They offer shorter trips for small children; older children can ride along on anything from half-day to multiple-day trips. Be aware that in spring the water is high and fast, and often children under eight are not allowed on the river. Later in the year, when the water is tamer, children over six may join the fun. A typical guided trip involves a boat guide who is thoroughly acquainted with the rapids and the history and the geology of the area, an inflated rubber raft that holds between eight and ten rafters, and oars and life jackets for everybody. The companies to try are **Adrift Adventures** (800–874–4483), **NAVTEC Expeditions** (800–833–1278), and **Tag-A-Long** (800–453–3292; www.tagalong.com). Expect to pay about $30 per person for a half-day trip.

Rafting **with the Family**

A raft trip is a great family value, and often the only way to see rock formations that otherwise go unnoticed.

Depending on the time of the year (and runoff), the ride has varying degrees of "wild." I wouldn't take really young kids. But unless the rafting company has other regulations (or the water is really wild), I'd have no fear about taking a six- or seven-year-old.

A rafting trip is a lot of fun. Certainly, you can book a camping raft trip. However, many trips are only a few hours. Most companies have very good safety records, and the guides are very professional. It's an adventure your kids will never forget.

A river and camping trip designed just for families is offered by **Sheri Griffith Expeditions** (800–332–2439; www.griffithexp.com). Called Coyote Run, the two-day, one-night trip takes children as young as four years old down a mild stretch of the Colorado River in paddleboats and inflatable kayaks. At night you'll camp at an old ranch homestead on the riverbank, and, if you're willing, you can sleep in an authentic reproduction of a Sioux Indian tepee. Dinner is cooked by your river guide in Dutch ovens over an open campfire. This outing is meant to re-create life along the river as it was at the turn of the century—except with less work and a lot more fun. A similar but longer trip is offered on the Green River. For prices, dates, and more information, call the number above.

Slickrock Trail (all ages)

Bicycling has been made famous in Moab by the Slickrock Trail, perhaps the best-known fat-tire route in the country. This is a difficult trail, with the only guide an occasional slash of paint on the rock, requiring about five hours for completion of its loop. The Slickrock Trail is noteworthy for its thrilling ups and downs over colorful sandstone, especially lovely at sunset or sunrise. If you and your family are not seasoned bikers, you might want to try the 2.3-mile "practice loop" located nearby. Moab's annual **Fat Tire Festival** (435–260–1182; www.moabfattirefestival.com), always the week of Halloween, features fun family rides and activities.

Day Trip: **The Colorado Drive**

Outside of Moab, take a drive up the Colorado River. Before you do, though, stop and drink from the water that flows out of the rocks—fill your canteens.

As you drive along the river, you'll wonder at the deep-red canyons carved out by the muddy Colorado River. Ignore the catfish angler and the half-crazy rock climbers as they hang in midair. Take a close look at the Colorado red rock and the surreal shapes.

Watch for desert mule deer, rabbits, and birds. Feel free to take a side dirt road up a good-looking canyon. How many shades of red do you see?

Colorado River Scenic Byway (all ages)

About 2 miles north of Moab on U.S. Highway 191, you will see the turnoff to Utah Highway 128; this is the byway.

This is a gorgeous road, and your family will enjoy the great hiking and sightseeing along the way. The road travels 44 miles and requires about two hours to travel to its terminus, Cisco, and back. Notable features on the byway are Big Bend Picnic Area, with its wide, sandy beach on the Colorado River; Castle Valley Junction, with a view of Castle Rock, an improbable, slender monolith of stone made famous in rock music videos and car commercials; the crumbling flanks of Fisher Towers, with a picnic area and hiking trails; and the historic Dewey Suspension Bridge, built in 1916 and used until 1986, and listed on the National Register of Historic Places.

Arches National Park (all ages)

To get to Arches, travel 4½ miles north from Moab on U.S. Highway 191 until you see the turnoff sign. For advance information on Arches and its amenities, call (435) 719–2100, or write Arches National Park, P.O. Box 907, Moab 84532. For information on private campgrounds and other lodging possibilities, call (800) 635–MOAB. Vehicles $$, good for seven days.

You may have viewed some spectacular red-rock formations in Utah, but until you have been to Arches National Park, you have not seen 2,000 stone openings spanning their way across a 73,000-acre protected reserve. Your family is in for a treat! The arches are everywhere, great big ones and little tiny ones, interspersed with wonderful rock spires and turrets and monoliths. It's recommended that you leave at least half a day for this adventure, and bring along a picnic lunch. Every family member should have plenty of portable water to take along on the many hikes in the park. There are friendly rangers at the visitor center and all sorts of good orientation information.

If you want to hike the **Fiery Furnace** (this is a terrific family hike and highly recommended, even if you have to come back on another day—more info below), now is the time to sign up for this unforgettable only-with-a-ranger guided expedition. Look at the pictures that describe the plant and animal life you'll see here. It's amazing to discover the

Making Shapes from Rocks and Clouds

The Canyonlands-Arches-Moab area has haunting skies and rock formations. Indeed, I've often wondered if it's not my spiritual home.

Most adults forget what they've learned as a child—it's only when you become a parent that, at least for a moment, you can rediscover a child's perspective again. It's easy to be a child in this part of the world. The cares of the adult world seem to lose importance.

Take your cell phone and drop it in the nearest pit toilet. Take your pager and drive over it. Pawn your personal computer for pocket change. Take your kid's hand and go for a walk among the giant cookie-dough rock formations.

Lay on a slick rock with your children and watch the clouds drift by. Make pictures from the drifting vapor and let your mind wander to worry-free days when you were young. Look at the great forms of rock and make shapes from them.

If you've forgotten how to relax like this, let your child show you how it's done.

variety of life that manages to thrive in this high desert country. Take time to study the geology tables. The sandstone all over this region was laid down in different geologic eras, and each one has a name and a history. There are many unique formations here—on your drive through the park see if you can spot the **Penguins, Sausage Rock, Three Gossips,** and **Adam and Eve.**

Now you are ready to hit the park's 41-mile loop road. Wind around for a mile to **Park Avenue,** the first stopping spot. The main feature here is the vertical slab on your right, which forms a huge "storefront" to the "avenue." Strolling down the avenue is an easy mile if you arrange to get picked up at North Park Avenue. The next stop is another 1½ miles up the road, at **Courthouse Towers.** These monoliths were probably arches at one time. The largest is called **Sheep Rock,** and you can see the "sheep" looking longingly across a breach to their sandstone grazing grounds. Look just to the left for **Baby Arch,** and you will have a lesson in how arches are formed. On to **Petrified Dunes,** which, in fact, were real sand dunes a couple of million years ago. You will notice the rock's whiter color here—this is Navajo sandstone, which contains a smaller amount of the iron that colors the rocks nearby. About 9 miles from the visitor center is **Balanced Rock**—a perfect example of two varieties of sandstone, with different hardening agents at work against the elements. A huge boulder (about 3,500 tons) sits on top of a smaller boulder, performing one of nature's more precarious balancing acts. This is a good spot to take pictures of the red rock with the green La Sal Mountains courteously making a perfect backdrop.

A short drive down the road brings you to the **Windows** section of the park; if your family enjoys hiking, you'll want to get out of the car and walk around for an hour or so. Remind your family that nature really did make these arches—they are so whimsical and perfect that it seems Disney might have had something to do with it instead. North and South Windows are so named because both arches provide a perfect frame for the gorgeous scenery beyond. These are two arches formed inside the same huge fin, and if you face them directly but back up a couple hundred feet, you will see why they are also known as The Spectacles (as in eyeglasses, not public embarrassments). **Turret Arch** is just across the way, with its castlelike capstone.

Back in the car, drive just a few minutes on, to **Double Arch.** This requires an easy five-minute walk to see its twin image. These arches were formed differently—see if you can tell which was originally a pothole, and which was formed by water and wind beating against its rock fin. Stand at the end of the trail, and you can see the **Parade of Elephants** leading a billion-year-old circus march. Less than 2 miles beyond is **Pothole Arch,** so named because water that once rushed down from above formed a depression in the rock, which after an inconceivable amount of time formed a hole in the cliff side, which after another very long time wore away to leave only this span of stone.

Hang on. The next stop is the Big One. **Delicate Arch** is an extraordinary formation. It has become Utah's signature arch, celebrated on license plates and official road signs. You can see Delicate from a roadside turnout, but this is a must-see-close-up kind of thing, and its 3-mile round-trip hike is worth the effort. If your children hike this trail in the full heat of summer, you will need a lot of water and rest stops. If you visit the area during

A Rutter Family Adventure: **Camping on the Desert Outside of Moab**

Yes, summers in this part of the world are a bit warm. And winters can be rather cool. Spring and fall are lovely—and great for camping.

You can select one of the many campgrounds, or do what we sometimes do. We find a dirt road, drive down it, find another dirt road, drive down it, find a nice-looking arroyo, and set up the Coleman tent.

While we set up camp, the kids collect dead sagebrush and mesquite for the evening fire. After a foil dinner over the coals, we band the fire and watch the sunset change the sky. Drinking cups of hot chocolate, we listen to the coyotes yip and feel the cool night replace the desert warmth. (It gets cool fast on the desert.)

For breakfast, we eat sourdough pancakes, followed by a hike on which our geologist, Shari, points out how it all happened to form.

the cooler months, the hike seems easier and you will need less hydration. Be warned that you are exposed to the full sun for much of this hike; it's a 500-foot elevation rise, and it's officially labeled "moderately strenuous," so plan accordingly. Just past the trailhead to Delicate are the remains of Wolfe Ranch, where a hardy family lived for twenty years at the turn of the century. Take a moment to marvel at the hardships they must have faced.

Shortly, you'll reach a sandy path, then cross a bouncy bridge. Just past the bridge, look for a side trail on your left. Follow this around the corner for about a hundred yards and you'll see a large **Ute Indian petroglyph panel.** Continuing on, after the switchbacks, the boulder portion of the hike is the most strenuous, as it climbs over rolling slickrock marked by rock cairns. Nature provides suspense as you near the arch, hiding it from view until the very end. When you turn the final bend—voila!—a 45-foot arch inside a sandstone bowl the size of a small town, gleefully teetering on sandstone high heels. A natural stone bench provides an excellent view, and if you're feeling brave, you can hike into the slippery bowl and actually stand under the arch. Like every good thing, Delicate has been discovered by the hordes, but if you are lucky and see it on an uncrowded day (which probably will not happen in the summer), it is unbeatable as a picnic/contemplation spot.

Back in the car, the next pullout point is **Fiery Furnace,** but you will notice this intense cluster of rock flame-fins before you get there. The Furnace is so winding and convoluted that a ranger's accompaniment is needed, which requires a sign-up at the visitor center, and often at least a day's notice. This is an especially great expedition for kids—all sorts of squeezing through narrow places and jumping off things and poisonous plant sightings. The naming of the Fiery Furnace is an obvious choice, but if you see this formation at sunset, you will view it in its fullest, flaming beauty. Next up is **Sand Dune Arch.** Small kids love the 30-yard walk to this arch, because it requires squeezing between two rock fins to see it. Nature has made a terrific sandpile here, and this place is shady for most of the day. If you feel like walking farther, you will come to **Broken Arch,** named because it looks broken from a distance (it really isn't).

Another mile up the road you will pass **Skyline Arch,** on your way to the third, and final, big hike of the day, in **Devil's Garden.** The hike in Devil's Garden can be split up a number of ways. The main trail will take you to **Pine Tree Arch** (a short side trip and well signed—when you get to the "T" in this trail, go right for a view of **Tunnel Arch,** left to Pine Tree), **Landscape, Navajo, Partition, Double O,** and **Dark Angel** arches. If you make it all the way to Dark Angel you deserve a merit badge. The length is not prohibitive—7.2 miles round-trip—but you are walking in sand for much of the way, and after Landscape Arch the trail gets iffy as you are following cairns, and it is just plain tiring. The most popular destination is Landscape Arch—about a mile in from the trailhead on a well-marked path. Landscape is the longest known natural span in the world, with an inside width of 306 feet. You can hike up the short side trail to Landscape, sit under it, and contemplate man's small place in the universe. The very apparent land restoration going on here is an educational lesson in what it takes to save an area from being "loved to death."

Near the Devil's Garden parking lot, you will see the **Devil's Garden Campground.** It has fifty-two beautiful sites, many of them clustered with juniper and bordered by big mounds of sandstone. From March through October, weather permitting, the campground has running water, and the nightly fee is $8.00. During the colder weather months water is not available in the campground (bring your own or else fill up at the visitor center), and the nightly fee is $5.00. Advance reservations are not taken; these campsites must be registered for at the visitor center the day of your arrival. Be aware that this is the only camping possibility in the park, and it is nearly always full. There are many privately owned campgrounds within 10 miles of Arches. After an hour or two at Devil's Garden, it's an 18-mile drive back to the visitor center. Activities at Arches include campfire chats every night of the week during the summer. Topics include "Why scorpions live in the parks," "Shaman's paint box," and "Why Arches?"

Canyonlands National Park (all ages)

For information write Canyonlands National Park, 2282 Southwest Resource Boulevard, Moab 84532, or call (435) 259–7164. Vehicles $$, backpacking permit $$, four-wheel permit $$$$; all good for seven days.

Another Very Big Deal near Moab is Canyonlands National Park, a park so big it's been split into three very distinct sections: the Maze, the Needles, and Island in the Sky. These areas adjoin each other but are neatly trisected by the Colorado and Green Rivers and must be reached from different entry points. A fourth section of the park, Horseshoe Canyon, is reached by yet another road. Canyonlands' vast expanse dwarfs Arches National Park and makes Arches, with its paved roads and signed trails, seem almost tame. This is not the place to fool around with Mother Nature. Get directions, have provisions on hand, and be careful. Throughout Canyonlands National Park backcountry camping, accessed by backpackers and four-wheelers, is allowed. Reservations and permits for this type of camping must be arranged at park visitor centers or by calling (435) 259–4351.

The Maze (all ages)
Accessible by Utah Highways 24 or 95 and passable only in a four-wheel-drive vehicle or on a mountain bike.

The Maze is known as one of the most remote places on earth—not in terms of distance but in terms of how-many-tons-of-sandstone-between-you-and-others. Once you enter this 30-square-mile tangle of rock wilderness you'll truly be away from it all. If you're extremely hardy, you might make it all the way to the Doll's House, 40 miles in on a dirt road. You'll be rewarded with an incredible surround of colorful rock formations, and a stunning view downward of the Colorado River.

The Needles (all ages)
Travel 50 miles south of Moab on U.S. Highway 191, and turn right onto Highway 211 at the Canyonlands National Park road sign. The visitor center is open from 8:00 A.M. to 5:00 P.M. in summer, 8:00 A.M. to 4:30 P.M. in winter. Vehicles $$, good for seven days.

The Needles section is more family-friendly than the Maze. Named for its predominant red-rock spires, the Needles is about an hour-and-a-half drive from Moab. *Note:* You will pass a turnoff for the Bureau of Land Management's (BLM) Needles Overlook Road. About 20 miles in on this road you'll pass **Newspaper Rock**—a great introduction to rock art for kids, and a very worthwhile stop. From prehistory through frontier days, people felt the need to make their mark here, and the result is a crowded mix of messages on a huge rock wall. Perhaps it was the black oxide surface of this rock, which makes carving through it easy and distinct, or perhaps it was its location as an ancient trail—but for whatever reason, Newspaper Rock is an amazing amalgam of history. Moving on, it is about 25 more miles to the Needles themselves. The park service has thoughtfully put a visitor center here, because you will probably need directions and a bathroom. Here your family is treated to a view of artifacts, displays, a short film, and a book shop.

Squaw Flats Campground (435–259–7164) and its wonderful sites are nearby; however, they are first-come, first-served, and the campground fills up most summer nights. Running water is available here during the warm-weather months; in winter you are asked to bring your own. Picnic tables in the campground and at the visitor center are pleasant for lunch, although with all the wildness surrounding you, your family might prefer a more remote spot down the road.

Back on the road, look for the **Wooden Shoe** formation—when you spot it, you will definitely know what you're looking at. Two excellent family hikes in this area are recommended. **Roadside Ruin** is a short, easy, loop trail. Pick up the interpretive pamphlet for this hike at the visitor center, so you can identify the flora and fauna along the way. This area was occupied a century ago by Indians who used this same flora and fauna for sustenance. One of their better-preserved storage houses constitutes the "ruin" of this hike. Just down the road is the pullout parking area for the **Cave Spring Trail,** a 0.6-mile loop. This hike involves lots of fun things including climbing two ladders, viewing an old cowboy camp, and finding Indian markings on boulders. If you are prepared with a four-wheel-drive vehicle, continue on the Cave Spring dirt road to **Paul Bunyan's Potty,** the fodder for many grade-school jokes. This giant rock formation could be described, but you probably get the idea.

The BIG things in the Needles are **Chesler Park,** the confluence of the Green and Colorado Rivers, and Angel Arch. However, all three of these natural phenomena are hard to reach. The access roads are classified for difficulty, and they are all pretty high up on the scale. They require not just a four-wheel-drive vehicle, but an experienced driver. The trade-off is that this area provides high adventure and solitude. Ask a ranger before you head out on any of these potentially dangerous roads. Chesler Park is a huge, scrub-grass meadow rimmed by the needle-shaped rock for which this park is named. In Chesler you get your best sense of how the needles were formed, and of their size and shape. To view the **confluence of the Green and Colorado Rivers,** follow the road to the Big Spring Canyon Overlook, and then set out on dirt for a hefty four-wheel drive. Park at the sign and hike the last mile or so of this trail. When you reach the terminus, you're rewarded with a heart-stopping view, straight down, of the joining of these two mighty rivers. As mentioned at the beginning of this chapter, Colorado is a Spanish word for "red," you know what green is, and the rivers are actually green and red. When they join, they turn a third, marvelous color. This is not for the vertigo-impaired. You'll probably see pictures of **Angel Arch** in the visitor center. Again, this trail follows a long four-wheel-drive route into Salt Creek Canyon (it's a lot of fun if you're equipped), and requires a strenuous hike. But this 150-foot-high winged arch is simply breathtaking.

Island in the Sky (all ages)

The entrance to the Island is on Utah Highway 313, reached by heading north on U.S. Highway 191 from Moab. The visitor center is open from 8:00 A.M. to 5:00 P.M. in summer and 8:00 A.M. to 4:30 P.M. in winter. Vehicles $$, good for seven days.

A vivid contrast to the Needles and the Maze, Island in the Sky is not about rock scrambling, hidden picnic spots, or dirt roads. This lofty perch offers sweeping mesas and an eagle's-eye view of the world. Bonus—the road is paved almost the entire way! There are rest rooms and a drinking fountain in the visitor center, as well as a bookstore and a theater showing films that describe the area. *Note:* It is recommended that you bring plenty of water along on your visit; there are no water stations on Island in the Sky. After a short drive out onto this section of the park, it becomes apparent how the Island got its name. This high peninsula towers above the winding rivers below, offering fabulous viewpoints from the pullouts that dot its scenic route. You'll see canyon after canyon rolling into the far distance. Three mountain ranges rim the horizon—they catch all of the water that would fall here, which is one reason why the mountains are blue-green in the distance but the closer view is of barren red rock. The Henry Mountains are to the southwest, the Abajos (a Navajo word for "blue") are to the south, and the La Sals are to the east. The closest mesa you'll see is the massive White Rim, which runs almost continuously below the Island. You'll also view both the Needles and the Maze from this elevated point.

There are a couple of easy hikes on the Island. The **Mesa Arch Trail** is a short route looping across a piñon and juniper plain to the edge of the mesa. The arch here is a perfect frame for the La Sal Mountains in the distance. Pick up a guide to the geology and plant life of this trail at the visitor center. The Upheaval Dome Crater View Trail leads just 500 yards to the remains of an incredibly turbulent geologic event. Tons of layers of rock were pushed up, and others fell down—and the result is a big bowl of . . . rock. Your family will enjoy this dome because its scope is small enough that kids can grasp its geologic significance. Again, a pamphlet can be found at the visitor center explaining just exactly what happened here. **Buck Canyon Overlook** and **Grand View Point Overlook** complete the scenic drive.

Horseshoe Canyon: **Hiking into the Past**

If you're into Native American rock art, or just want a good view of the canyon country from the bottom up, take a hike into the past.

At the bottom of the canyon, a mile or so down the mostly dried streambed, there are some of the most stunning, large panels of Native American rock art in this country.

You'll park at the top of the rim and hike down. It's a good family hike, if your children are at least eight (or they're sturdy hikers). You'll travel down a trail, steep at times, for about a mile. Then it's another mile more. Coming up can be taxing on younger children, so take plenty of rests.

When you hike the canyon trail, have your kids take your hand if they are young (it's quite a drop in places). Keep a watchful eye for rattlesnakes—especially in the shade on hot days and in sunny places when it's cool. I've seen at least one each time I've been down.

Take along a walking stick, moleskin for blisters, plenty of water, sunscreen, snacks, and film. Plan on at least half a day—why rush something this rare? Do not drink the water.

Horseshoe Canyon (all ages)
Reached via Utah Highway 24; more easily accessed from the town of Green River than from Moab. Hans Flat Ranger Station is open daily from 8:00 A.M. to 4:30 P.M. Vehicles $$.

Horseshoe Canyon, a non-adjoining section of the park, is federally designated to protect its rare rock art. Horseshoe is a magical place, but entrance to the canyon requires a bumpy ride on a dirt road and then a strenuous hike—straight down a cliff side, with much of the trail in deep sand. The return, of course, is straight up a cliff side in deep sand. The destination in Horseshoe is the Grand Gallery—a bigger-than-life-sized ancient drawing of fifty figures, stretching for more than 80 feet along the canyon wall. Perhaps because of its isolated location, the rock art has not been disturbed by humans for the last 2,000 years or so. A walk through this canyon evokes the magic and mystery that were integral to the Indians who lived here so long ago.

Utah's Three Major **Climate Zones**

Utah has a wonderfully varied climate. For example, St. George, in southern Utah, has about 204 growing days without frost. The Heber Valley, not far from my house, has about 75 days without frost.

The state is divided into three climate zones: The Mountain Zone takes up about 26 percent of the state; the Desert Zone makes up 37 percent of the state; and the Steppe Zone (the land between the desert and mountains) makes up about 37 percent of the state.

Dead Horse Point State Park (all ages)

Take the turnoff on Utah Highway 313. Follow the signs. Reservations may be made by calling (800) 322–3770 at least three days in advance. Campers are asked to bring their own water. For more information write Dead Horse Point State Park, P.O. Box 609, Moab 84532-0609, or call (435) 259–2614. Vehicles $$, camping $$.

The perfect time to reach Dead Horse is just as the sun is starting to think about setting. You can take the short walk to the overlook and sit and relax and let the 1,000-mile view out there sear itself into your consciousness. But beware, there are all sorts of ways to fall off a cliff here—don't discover any of them. Dead Horse is a narrow, high mesa jutting out into heaven atop cliffs called the Orange Escarpment. It is not named after a bunch of horses that jumped off these cliffs. It seems a few genera-tions ago, this spot was used as a corral because it required a minimum of fencing, the cliffs providing an effec-tive barrier for horses. One story tells of an errant cowboy who penned up a herd of horses and then apparently for-got about them. When the poor beasts were discovered, they had died of thirst, probably looking longingly down the 2,000-foot cliffs at the rushing waters of the Colorado River. Speaking of the Colorado, it takes a very show-offy turn just below Dead Horse Point. One of its better goose-necks performs in perpetuity right in front of your eyes. Try to figure out which way the flow goes.

Where to Eat

Moab Diner. 189 South Main Street; (435) 259–4006. American. $

Arches Pancake Haus. 196 South Main Street; (435) 259–7141. American. $

Fat City Smoke House. 36 South 100 West; (435) 259–4302. BBQ. $

Where to Stay

Apache Motel. 166 South 400 East; (435) 259–5727. $–$$

Best Western Canyonlands. 16 South Main; (435) 259–2300. $$$

Moab Valley Inn. 711 South Main; (435) 259–4419. $$–$$$

Red Stone Inn. 535 South Main; (435) 259–3500. $–$$

Aarchway Inn. 1551 North Highway 191; (435) 259–2599. $$

La Sal Junction

Just a few miles south of La Sal Junction, on U.S. Highway 191, are **Looking Glass Rock** and **Wilson Arch.** Looking Glass requires a 1-mile drive on a dirt road to see its large, round opening-in-a-rock. Wilson, another big hole, is just off the road. A bit farther on, to the west, you'll see the turnoff to **Canyon Rims Recreation Area.** This is a 22-mile paved road that skims along a narrow, mile-high peninsula with powerful vistas all around. The terminus is **Needles Overlook,** a picnic-tabled area, where you'll look down into Canyonlands National Park. Do take time to stop at **Anticline Overlook,** one of the more fabulous lookout points in the state. Picnic tables, interpretive displays, and hiking trails are located here.

Hole 'N the Rock (all ages)

On U.S. Highway 191, 5 miles north of La Sal Junction. Call (435) 686–2250. Open 8:00 A.M. to 8:00 P.M. from Memorial Day to Labor Day; 9:00 A.M. to 5:00 P.M. the rest of the year. Tours begin every ten to fifteen minutes. Admission $.

Fifty years ago, this was just a rock (without 'n hole). Then along came a sculptor named Christensen, who saw some potential, and began blasting away to create the present site. This was the Christensen family's home for many years, and now the original owners are buried nearby. Today Hole 'N the Rock is a gift shop, snack bar, and American original.

Monticello

This bustling town 60 miles south of Moab sits on the edge of the Manti–La Sal National Forest and takes its green scenery and cooler climate from the nearby mountains. Yes, it's named after Thomas Jefferson's home, but in Utah it is pronounced "Mon-ti-sello." A casual restaurant in town with a great children's menu is **MD Ranch Cookhouse** (435–587–3299), found on South Main Street. The **Monticello Museum** is located inside the city library, with Indian and pioneer artifacts and rocks. The **San Juan County Travel Council** is located at 117 South Main, ready and waiting with books, brochures, and maps that interpret the area. For information call (435) 587–3235 or (800) 574–4386.

Monticello's **Horse Head**

While traveling in southeastern Utah, you will see dozens and dozens of amazing rock formations. Monticello, just an hour south of Moab, has another sort of natural wonder that is sure to catch your attention.

If you look to the east, you will see a beautiful mountain range. On the face of the range, you will also see an intriguing group of trees that look just like a horse's head.

Residents of Monticello take great pride in this natural spectacle and have even adopted it as a sort of mascot. If you ever have trouble picking it out, just ask the local gas station attendant, grocery store worker, or anyone you run into.

It is interesting to note that the trees actually grew naturally in this shape. However, just a few years ago crews trimmed the trees to prepare for the town's centennial celebration.

Where to Eat

Bev's Barn. 216 East Central; (435) 587–2550. Sandwiches. $

Lamplight. 655 East Central; (435) 587–2170. American. $$

MD Ranch Cookhouse. 380 South Main; (435) 587–3299. American. $$

Grandma's Kitchen. 133 East Central; (435) 587–3017. American. $$

Where to Stay

Days Inn. 549 North Main; (435) 587–2458. $$$

Best Western Wayside Inn. 197 East Central; (435) 587–2261. $$–$$$

Blanding

Shopping for handmade Indian crafts is rewarding here. **Huck's Museum and Trading Post,** ½ mile south of town on U.S. Highway 191 (435–678–2329), has a large display of Indian artifacts and a shop that sells Navajo-crafted gifts. **Cedar Mesa Pottery,** 333 South Main (435–678–2241), sells handmade pottery, and during the week you can watch the potters ply their craft in the factory next door. The **Blue Mountain Trading Post,** just south of town on U.S. Highway 191 (435–678–2218), has a big selection of jewelry, art, and kachina dolls. For information about Blanding, write to P.O. Box 490, 117 South Main Street, Blanding 84535, or call (435) 587–3235.

Dinosaur Museum (all ages)
754 South 200 West; (435) 678-3454; www.dinosaur-museum.org. Open June through August, Monday through Saturday 8:00 A.M. to 8:00 P.M.; mid-April through May and September through mid-October, Monday through Saturday 9:00 A.M. to 5:00 P.M. Admission $.

A serendipitous circumstance has left Blanding with a wonderful museum. It seems a family of paleontologists with a private collection of fossils fell in love with the area and decided to live here. A suitable building to house the collection became available and—voila!—a world-class museum. Several of the displays here don't exist anywhere else, including rare petrified wood and ancient fossils. There are lots of little cases with neat displays, and dioramas that explain ancient life. Real-life dinosaur bones have been pieced together to their original state. One of the dinosaur builders is a skin specialist and believes that dinosaurs were very brightly colored. You'll see his work on display.

Easy Travel Tips: Map Out the Next Day's Trip

Keep your kids excited about the trip.

In the evening, open up a map and show your kids where you plan to travel the next day. Show them the towns and roads you plan to travel. Also, tell them what you plan to see the next day.

Doing this will help kids get involved in the vacation adventure. You can even have your children mark the map as you pass certain points.

Edge of the Cedars State Park (all ages)
Follow the signs from Main Street around lots of corners, and just when you're sure you're lost, there it is, at 660 West 400 North. Call (435) 678–2238 for more information. Vehicles $.

In a residential neighborhood in Blanding is **Edge of the Cedars State Park.** This park is dedicated to the ancient inhabitants of this neighborhood and features the remains of an Anasazi Indian pueblo and its ceremonial kivas. The Anasazis, also called "the ancient ones," flourished in southeastern Utah between A.D. 700 and 1220. They irrigated and grew crops and raised livestock. Then, suddenly, their population vanished, and nobody knows why. The Edge of the Cedars Museum has collections of artifacts and pottery, and the only known metal Anasazi artifacts in Utah. Navajo, Ute, and early Anglo cultures are interpreted as well.

For lunch in the great outdoors, you can get take-out at several of Blanding's restaurants, including pizza and pasta at the **Cedar Pony** at 191 North Highway 191 and burgers at the **Patio Drive-In** at 95 North Highway 191. Armed with food, find the park and tables in the center of town, or else enjoy the nice picnic area at Edge of the Cedars State Park.

Where to Stay

Best Western Gateway Motel. 88 East Center; (435) 678–2278. $–$$

Bluff

This beautiful oasis was settled in the late 1800s by Mormon pioneers and was the first Anglo town in this quarter of the state. The pioneers had been directed by LDS Church leaders to explore and settle this area and to establish friendly relations with the local Indians. The story of their journey south from Salt Lake City is one of horrific hardships and sacrifice. Today the entire town of Bluff is designated as a historic district. The main road through town doesn't really show off Bluff's history. Turn west onto any side road and you'll be treated to wide, shady streets lined with original pioneer homes. Look for the **Jens Nielson House** as one fine example of pioneer enterprise. You'll notice right away that farming is an important industry here. You'll notice soon after that river running is also of economic importance to the town. A major put-in point for rafters on the San Juan River, **Sand Island,** is just a few minutes west of town. In May, Bluff hosts **Head Start Days,** a child-centered celebration with a parade, concessions, and Indian dances. If you're in town in early June, ask about the annual **Indian Day Celebration,** a festival of games, good food, and horse races. The first weekend in September brings the **White Mesa Ute Council Bear Dance,** a three-day affair featuring contests, a cook-out, games, and, of course, native dances. In mid-September Bluff hosts the **Utah Navajo Fair,** with a rodeo and powwow. For information on events in Bluff, call (435) 587–3235 or go to www.bluffutah.org.

Hole-in-the-Rock (all ages)
Travel to the town of Escalante, head 5 miles east of town, and then head south on a rugged dirt road for 60 miles.

The Anasazi's legacy is literally etched in stone at Hole-in-the-Rock. This "hole" is a small break in the sheer cliffs of Glen Canyon, with a drop into Lake Powell. The rugged pioneers pushed their wagons and cattle through the hole and lowered them by rope to the water, where they then ferried their possessions across to dry land. This labor took months longer than the pioneers had planned for the trip. Their destination was about 15 miles east of Bluff, at Montezuma Creek. But by the time the settlers arrived at Bluff, they were too exhausted to continue. This proved to be fortuitous, as Bluff, with its artesian wells, proved to be a more hospitable environment.

The Anasazi Indians

The prehistoric Anasazi lived in the southernmost part of Utah, from St. George to the Four Corners area.

Like the Fremont Indians, their culture also disappeared around A.D. 1000. They planted corn, squash, and other vegetables and did some hunting. Unlike the Fremont culture, the Anasazi lived in large cliff dwellings (Mesa Verde–style). Some had hundreds of rooms in them.

They also left records of their presence on the rock walls. They made fine baskets and pottery for storing food.

Twin Rocks Trading Post and Cow Canyon Trading Post and Restaurant (all ages) 🔲 🍴
On the north end of town on U.S. Highway 191, at 913 East Navajo Twins Drive; (435) 672–2341; twinrocks.com. $

This is major silver-jewelry-buying country. You're on the northern tip of a huge Navajo Indian reservation, and there is evidence everywhere of that rich cultural influence. Look for beautiful workmanship and great buys. Twin Rocks Trading Post, named for the Navajo Twins rock formation nearby, has a big selection of Navajo and Zuni jewelry, belt buckles, hair fasteners, and other good stuff. Across the street, Cow Canyon Trading Post and Restaurant sells wonderfully small, handmade, clay farm animals and figurines, and there are beautiful rugs and fabric bolts here as well as good food.

Sunbonnet Cafe (all ages)
Along the Historic Loop through Bluff; (435) 672–2201. $

If you've never had a Navajo taco, run, don't walk, to the Sunbonnet Cafe, found on the Historic Loop. Also, take time to visit **St. Christopher's Episcopal Mission,** established by a hardworking priest more than fifty years ago. Find the mission by heading east from town on U.S. Highway 163 for about a mile. About 2 miles farther on from the mission is a **swinging bridge,** which is fun to walk across. It was used by children from the reservation for access to school in town. The cemetery on the hill provides a great view and some local history.

Recapture Lodge (all ages)
On U.S. Highway 191 in Bluff, at 220 East Main Street. For reservations call (435) 672–2281. $

Lodging here is not plentiful, so book ahead. Recapture Lodge is a good bet, with a helpful staff, historic surroundings, and evening lectures. Try to stay upstairs, where the surrounding deck offers a shady spot at day's end.

Paddling Down the San Juan River (recommended for older children)

A river trip in this part of the world is highly recommended. The San Juan River is user-friendly (although rapids do exist—don't be fooled by first impressions!) and perfect for those who aren't ready for the thrills of whitewater. Two popular trips depart from near Bluff—put-in at Sand Island and take out at Mexican Hat, and/or put-in at Mexican Hat and take out at Clay Hills. If you go to Sand Island, find the rock panel that displays the five ancient images of **Kokopelli**—easily distinguished by his humpback and flute. Kokopelli is a popular Hopi Indian legendary figure, who among other things, could supposedly stop winter weather with his flute. An outfitter in Bluff called **Wild Rivers Expeditions** (435–672–2244 or 800–422–7654; www.riversandruins.com) takes families on one- to seven-day trips on the San Juan.

Valley of the Gods (all ages)
West of Bluff, off U.S. Highway 163.

There are many easy, scenic bike trails near Bluff. One of the best is in Valley of the Gods, a 27-mile loop trail. Pedal just a few miles in and out, and you'll find a level road and lots of good scenery. The valley is named for its stately stone formations—you'll see empirical monoliths and mighty beasts. The predominant butte at the start of the trail is 400-foot-high Seven Sailors.

Hatch Trading Post (all ages)
From Bluff, take U.S. Highway 191 north to the intersection with Utah Highway 262, turn right, and follow the signs.

If you want to see a traditional Indian trading post, stop here. This is the equivalent of a corner grocery for the Navajo tribe.

Hovenweep National Monument (all ages)
On Highway 216. For more information call (970) 562–4282. Vehicles $$.

Farther on down the road is Hovenweep National Monument, an exceptionally well-preserved ancient Indian city, with 20-foot-high tower walls still standing, generally agreed to be at least 700 years old. From the parking lot you'll approach the most accessible ruins, a grouping called Square Tower. Square Tower is one of six groups of ruins at Hovenweep. Trails emanating from here include three short loop trails that total about 1½ miles. This is an easy, cairn-led hike, perfect for small children if the weather cooperates—it gets VERY hot here in summer. Borrow a trail-guide pamphlet at the ranger station, or buy one for 50 cents. As you're walking through this place, remember that these towers and rooms were built about the same time as the medieval castles in Europe. A network of dirt roads connects the five outlying ruin groups. There is a ranger station and visitor center here, along with a campground that is sometimes closed, rest rooms, and bottled drinking water.

Lake Powell

Look at any list of Utah's most popular tourist attractions, and you'll see Temple Square in Salt Lake City at the top of the list, and **Glen Canyon National Recreation Area** a close second. Tourists love this boating mecca for its warm, blue water and steep, red-rock cliff surroundings.

John Wesley Powell **and the Colorado River**

Major John Wesley Powell is one of the West's great explorers.

In 1869, this one-armed Civil War vet set out to explore the Colorado River—a region completely unknown, even though the territory had been populated twenty years earlier by the Mormon pioneers.

In a wooden boat, he cast off on the Green River (now in Wyoming) in a canyon area named Flaming Gorge. Little did he know the adventures he was in for as he sailed into the history books. This brave man strapped himself to a chair as he rode the waves, shouting commands to his men as they entered the boat-engulfing Colorado rapids.

It was nearly fall, after many hardships, when he drifted, half waterlogged, out of the Grand Canyon into a small Mormon settlement. Lake Powell is named for this indomitable man.

Lake Powell has backed up behind Glen Canyon Dam and is the central recreation area of Glen Canyon. Powell takes its name from John Wesley Powell, the intrepid explorer who first charted these waters in 1869. You'll see monuments and plaques documenting his journey all over the place. Lake Powell also has one of the more convoluted shorelines on the planet. The lake is 186 miles long, with almost 2,000 miles of shoreline. You read correctly—that's a shoreline more than ten times as long as its length. For every mile of lake, there are 10 miles of corrugated, wild ins-and-outs of red-rock canyon walls surrounding you. Perhaps the lake's appeal for boaters is that even though the lake is crowded, a quick cruise up any of a hundred side canyons can provide solitude and quiet. If you're on the lake at dusk, you'll notice boaters heading up these canyons, ready to stake out a private campsite for the night.

Glen Canyon is a million-acre, federally owned expanse of land stretching from Canyonlands National Park, across the southern border of Utah, and down into Grand Canyon National Park in Arizona. The government's purpose here, besides providing recreation for three million people every year, is to control the flow of the Colorado River in order to supply water and electricity to the surrounding states of Arizona, New Mexico, Nevada, and California. This was accomplished first in 1963, with the completion of Glen Canyon Dam. Before the dam, Glen Canyon was a steep, many tributaried, tangle of red rock. Today visitors "float" above the canyon floor, about halfway up the side of the old rocks. When you're on the lake, think about the grottoes, natural arches, and Indian artifacts below you. Before, during, and after the dam was built, many people objected to its invasion of environmentally sensitive landscapes. Several attempts to halt construction have since become legendary. For a fictionalized account of this time and place, read *The Monkey Wrench Gang* by Western author Edward Abbey. For more information write P.O. Box 1507, Page, AZ 86040.

There are three marinas open on Lake Powell year-round, one on each side of the lake and one at the north end. All offer boat rentals, lodging, groceries, fuel, and myriad marina and fishing facilities. **Bullfrog Marina** (435–684–3000) is a full-scale resort, with a lodge and restaurant. **Halls Crossing** (435–684–7000) has "housekeeping units"—three-bedroom suites, complete with a kitchen. **Hite** (435–684–2278) is the smallest marina, accessible off State Route 95. Both Bullfrog and Halls Crossing have National Park Service campgrounds. A fourth large marina, **Wahweap** (928–645–2433), is on the south end of Lake Powell, across the border in Arizona.

At the end of November, Wahweap hosts the **Festival of Lights.** Thousands of lights sparkle over the houseboats, many of which also sport Christmas ornaments and scenes. Santa and Mrs. Claus are aboard the paddlewheel, available for pictures, and there is lots of free chili and hot chocolate to cap off the evening.

Rainbow Bridge National Monument (all ages)

Tours leave from both Bullfrog and Halls Crossing in the morning and return mid-afternoon. The cost is $72.00 for adults and $39.80 for children 11 and under and includes a box lunch and drinks. Call (800) 528–6154 for more information.

If you don't have access to a private watercraft, an outing on a guided boat is an enjoyable way to tour the lake. Several outfitters take tourists on a daylong trip to Rainbow Bridge National Monument. This is the largest stone bridge yet discovered, and is often cited as one of the seven natural wonders of the world. Ancient Navajos believed that Rainbow was a sacred place. The bridge spans 275 feet and rises 290 feet from its rocky base. Until the dam created Lake Powell, Rainbow Bridge was accessible only by a two-day hike over red rock. Now it is accessible only by water. Several hundred thousand people now dock at the small marina each year and take the short walk to the bridge. While you're standing under it, remember that the Capitol in Washington, D.C., could fit under the bridge with plenty of room to spare.

John Atlantic Burr Ferry (all ages)
For information call (435) 684–7000. Vehicles $$.

Another fun way to see Lake Powell, and one that doesn't require an entire day, is to cross with the *John Atlantic Burr Ferry.* This hulking steel machine seems to defy the laws of flotation, as its 245 tons displace 100 tons of water. Eight cars and two buses fit on board this huge boat. The ferry crosses from Bullfrog to Halls Crossing and back, on the hour, seven days a week, for most of the year. It always begins at 8:00 A.M.; however, quitting time depends on the season. The crossing takes about twenty minutes. There's an observation deck high above the water that offers great views. John Atlantic Burr was a pioneer rancher born to an immigrant mother while crossing the Atlantic Ocean.

Fast
Utah Facts

- The Henry Mountains were named by a member of the Powell Expedition, in honor of the secretary of the Smithsonian Institution, Joseph Henry.
- The Rocky Mountain elk (*Cervus canadensis*) became the official state animal in 1971.
- Mexican Hat is named for the sombrero-like rock formation several miles to the northeast of town.
- The same year the Declaration of Independence was signed, Fathers Dominguez and Escalante, two Franciscan priest-explorers, journeyed across much of the state.

Mexican Hat

This is splendid, wide-open country, the Wild West made famous in cowboy movies and car commercials. It's also an area of the world where travelers are advised to keep plenty of water and snacks in their car, and a full tank of gas; services are few and far between. Just north of this town, look for two natural formations: The first is the unmistakable, sombreroed Spaniard for whom the town is named; the second is less distinct—a 15-mile-long strata of rock known as the Navajo Rug. **Valle's Trading Post** on the town's Main Street, U.S. Highway 163, sells cold drinks, good jewelry, and guidebooks.

Easy Travel Tips: **Young Kids and Coloring Books**

Most visitor/interpretive center gift shops will have coloring books dealing specifically with the material you have just seen.

Kids love to color—especially drawings of stuff they've just looked at. Also, coloring is a good way to occupy those energetic kids while you drive to the next location.

Each kid should have his or her own crayons (or colored pencils). But be aware that they will get lost. Shari always brings along a spare box, just in case.

I enjoy coloring, too. When Shari drives, I often color with the kids.

Goosenecks of the San Juan State Park (all ages)
Drive north from Mexican Hat on U.S. Highway 163, and watch for the intersection of Utah Highway 261. Turn right and be ready to veer left; (435) 678–2238. Admission is free.

For a great daylong adventure, take a trip to Goosenecks of the San Juan State Park, one of the better panoramas in the world. You'll look down a thousand feet, onto the tortured path of the San Juan River as it does an exaggerated series of s-curves, or goosenecks, through the Pennsylvania Hermosa Rock Formation. The river travels 6 miles, yet manages only 1½ miles by the crow. Bathrooms are available, but don't look for a flush toilet. Call for more information.

Cedar Mesa (all ages)
On Utah Highway 261, north of Goosenecks of the San Juan State Park.

Heading north from the Goosenecks, you'll ascend the thousand-foot cliff wall of Cedar Mesa, heading nowhere but straight up. The steep switchbacks you encounter are called the **Moki Dugway,** named after an old mispronunciation of the word "Hopi." This road is an aerial thrill—be sure and stop near the top at the **Muley Point Overlook.** You're standing a thousand feet above Valley of the Gods, which in turn, rises a thousand feet above the San Juan River. This road was blasted out of the side of this mountain during the uranium boom forty years ago. Since then it has been improved numerous times and today is fully paved and does not require a four-wheel-drive vehicle. Traveling on it does, however, require some old-fashioned intestinal fortitude.

Grand Gulch (all ages)

On Utah Highway 261. For more information call the Bureau of Land Management at (435) 587–1532.

Grand Gulch is a treasured area for backpackers. The Anasazi Indians flourished here 2,000 years ago, and many of their ruins and rock-art panels can be seen for those willing to make a long trek. There are no roads suitable for automobiles in the Gulch, but if your family can withstand the rigors of backpacking, this is a wonderful place to discover beauty and solitude.

Natural Bridges National Monument (all ages)

On Utah Highway 261. There is a 13-site campground, but there are no services here, and water is available only at the visitor center. For information on camping, hiking, and sight-seeing here, write Natural Bridges National Monument, P.O. Box 1, Lake Powell 84533–0101, or call (435) 692–1234. Admission $$, good for seven days. Camping $.

From Grand Gulch, it is just a few more miles to Natural Bridges National Monument. This place celebrates three natural stone bridges that have formed in the cedar mesa sandstone. The bridges are seen from viewpoints along a 9-mile, paved loop road, or by walking a trail that takes you close up to the bridges. Now, just because these bridges look similar to the stone arches you have seen elsewhere, don't think they are the same thing. These massive stone spans began to be formed when dinosaurs roamed the earth. When harder stone was sedimented over softer stone, and the softer stone eroded out, these bridges are what remained. Natural Bridges is open year-round. You might notice the solar panels that supply all the electricity here. This monument was chosen as a test base for the use of solar energy in the mid-1980s. When it was built, this system was the largest sun-powered plant in the world.

The Sipapu, Kachina, and Owachomo Bridges (recommended for older children)

If you're up for a challenge, the access trail to Sipapu Bridge is a lot of fun. It involves a 600-foot descent on wooden ladders and steel stairs and is a great leg-stretch for kids who've been trapped in the car for several hours. The second bridge on the route, Kachina Bridge, is the most massive of the three. It is named for the prehistoric drawings on its abutment, which resemble kachina dolls. Owachomo Bridge is the last stop on the loop road; it's the smallest and most "fragile of the bridges," at 106 feet high and 9 feet thick.

Monument Valley

Monument Valley (all ages)

To reach this far corner of Utah, you must travel almost all the way to the Arizona border on U.S. Highway 163. All of the land you see, once you leave Mexican Hat, is Navajo tribal land. From far away you'll notice the achingly beautiful, monolithic rock formations of Monument Valley, and once you've arrived, you'll find a bustling, touristy visitor center with several gift shops. There are fabulous views in every direction. Find the mittens (hint: this is two monuments), elephant, camel, three sisters, eagle, and dozens more. If you want to get closer to "what's out there" you must hire a guide. You'll most likely be approached in the parking lot by someone who is willing to take you through the valley; if you prefer a more formal arrangement, ask inside. For more information on Monument Valley, write Monument Valley Navajo Tribal Park, Box 360289, Monument Valley 84536; or call (435) 727–5870.

The Fremont Indians

The prehistoric Fremont Indians lived in the northern part of the state.

Their culture disappeared around A.D. 1000. We have archaeological evidence of their being here; perhaps most noticeable is the rock art they left.

They lived in pit houses that were partly below the ground. The Fremont people harvested grains, grew vegetables—even irrigated their crops. They hunted the abundant game in the region and stored food for the winter in baskets and pottery, which was gray. (The Anasazi had orange-colored pottery.)

Goulding's Trading Post (all ages)

On U.S. Highway 163; (435) 727–3231. The museum is open daily from 7:30 A.M. to 9:00 P.M. March through October; by appointment the rest of the year. Admission is free.

Just down the road is Goulding's Trading Post, established in 1923 by the Goulding Brothers and now listed on the National Register of Historic Places. For many years this was the primary trading post for Navajo Indians. A museum at Goulding's re-creates the old trading post, provides a history of movies made in the area, and includes a room dedicated to the Navajo Nation. There is a sixty-two-room motel here, a nice gift shop, and a restaurant. A film describing the history of the valley can be seen for a small fee.

Four Corners

From Bluff, take U.S. Highway 163 east through Navajo Country to Aneth, and keep on heading south. After a while you'll cross the Colorado border and see the signs for the Four Corners monument (nominal admission).

For those in your family who just have to experience everything, there is the Four Corners. However, I should warn you—it is just a big slab of concrete, with two dissected lines painted in its center. During the tourist season, there are usually Navajo craft booths set up around the perimeter of the square. Put a hand and foot in each square, and then . . . you will be touching four states at once! The Four Corners is the only place anywhere where four states meet. You cannot get any farther southeast in Utah, no matter how hard you try.

If you decide to continue on from here, there are many good choices nearby in the three surrounding states. **Canyon de Chelly National Monument** in Arizona, **Chaco Culture National Historic Park** in New Mexico, and **Mesa Verde National Park** in Colorado are just a few of the outstanding adventures in this part of the world.

Top Annual Events in Southeastern Utah

SEPTEMBER
Music Festival, Moab; (435) 259–7003

White Mesa Ute Council Bear Dance,
Bluff; (435) 678–3397

OCTOBER
Fat Tire Festival, Moab; (800) 635–6622

NOVEMBER
Parade of Lights, Bullfrog; (435) 684–3046

DECEMBER
Winter Festival, Moab; (435) 259–2742

Southwestern Utah

This area of the state likes to promote itself as "Color Country," and it's easy to see why. On this tour of the southwest corner of Utah you will pass up, over, around, and through fir- and aspen-covered mountains, crystal-blue lakes, flowered meadows, and some very respectable red rock.

Zion, Utah's oldest and most popular national park, is here, along with ethereal Bryce Canyon and a host of other nationally designated scenic spots. Enjoy world-class theater, catch a few rodeos, marvel at lots of wildlife, and manage to pack in a few unique shopping experiences.

This chapter moves geographically in a roundabout way, beginning and ending near Cedar City, with a notable, large leap in space from Boulder down to the city of Kanab. This progression does not always make sense for the traveler, and care should be taken to consult a map before planning a road trip.

Cedar City

During the months of June through October, Cedar City transforms itself into an Elizabethan English village, and the entire town celebrates a world-class Shakespeare Festival. For more than thirty-five years the "Festival City" has treated audiences to an array of activities that encompass the "Shakesperience."

Shakespeare Festival (all ages)
At the outdoor Adams Shakespearean Theatre and the Randall L. Jones Theatre. Tickets can be ordered by calling 800–PLAYTIX or going to www.bard.org. Call (435) 586–7880 for information on prices, dates, and specifics of all Shakespeare Festival events and workshops. Tickets $$–$$$$.

The festival includes three Shakespeare plays each summer as well as three other popular plays and musicals, all of which are performed on a rotating basis. In addition, each fall three popular plays are performed. Each evening at 7:00, before the performances, a **Greenshow** is played out on the grounds surrounding the theaters. Your children will love this **free** outdoor entertainment, which is billed as an "immersion into the song and dance of merrie olde England." On a typical night stages are set up on a huge, rolling

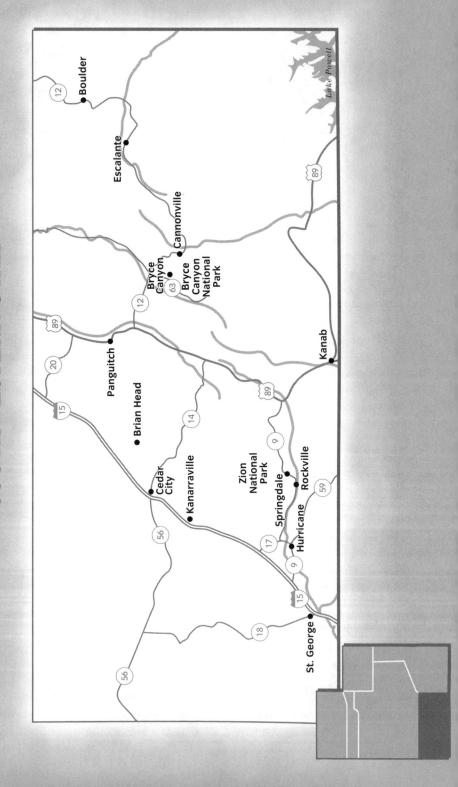

SOUTHWESTERN UTAH

Shakespeare in Cedar City:
Take Your Kids?

Cedar City is the home of the Utah Shakespeare Festival—and it's very good. Make plans to see a play if you're in the area.

"To take or not to take . . . that is the question?"

When my children were in the cradle, I played Bach, Beethoven, Jethro Tull, and Willie Nelson—the great classical masters. I also read passages from Chaucer, Edward Abbey, and Shakespeare. I called my program kids 'n culture.

It sort of worked since my kids like Shakespeare (even if they hate Brother Willie). I also started taking my kids to plays at a very early age—but not without some preparation.

If you take your kids to the play—especially the younger ones—more power to you. Kids love the pageantry of the stage and often get caught up in the magic of theater. However, if you want the evening to be a success, you have to prepare them beforehand. We took Jon-Michael at age four, but he sits well and was born loving the stage. Six or seven is normally a good age, if you think your child can handle it.

Be selective about what you see. Comedies are the best choice. Before I take a kid to a production, I spend time talking about the play and reading a story version (Charles Lamb's Shakespeare stories) over and over again so they'll know the characters. We also talk about how to act at a play—no whispering or talking. By the night of the production, they are very excited and we have a great time.

One last thing: Get aisle seats for those emergency potty calls.

lawn. Costumed performers may entertain by singing and dancing on one stage and performing farcical combat on another. Puppeteers roam the grounds, as well as sellers of food, drink, and souvenirs.

Another popular pre-play activity is the **Royal Feaste.** While dinner is served, an amusing play takes place that involves much audience interaction. Your family will be served about seven courses, and eating with your fingers is encouraged. You will leave well versed in the Elizabethan mode of speech, and ready to tackle the Bard's flowery verse. The Royal Feaste is held Tuesday through Saturday and begins at 5:30 P.M. Tickets ($$$$) must be reserved by noon the day of the Feaste. Call (435) 586–7880 for more information. Other fun things to do with a Shakespeare theme include a backstage tour, field falconry, and weeklong Shakespeare summer camps.

Bulloch Drug (all ages)

91 North Main; (435) 586–9651. Open Monday through Friday 9:00 A.M. to 9:00 P.M. and Saturday until 7:00 P.M.

This quaint drugstore has an old-fashioned soda fountain and candy counter right in the front window. Try a frosty root beer float or an ironport, a southern Utah soda. While you enjoy your ice cream, mill around the other rooms full of nostalgic gifts and toys.

Iron Mission State Park (all ages)

635 North Main; (435) 586–9290. Vehicles $.

A fun museum in town has unusual displays of old wagons, a cabin, and an Indian artifact collection donated by a man who lived with and was adopted by the Paiute Tribe. Iron Mission State Park also interprets the story of the development of the iron industry in the area.

Michael's
TopPicks for fun in Southwestern Utah

1. Zion National Park; (435) 772–3256

2. St. George LDS Temple; (435) 673–5181

3. Bryce Canyon National Park; (435) 834–5361

4. Kodachrome Basin, Cannonville; (435) 679–8562

5. The Burr Trail, Boulder

6. Anasazi Indian Village State Park; (435) 335–7308

7. Utah Shakespeare Festival at Cedar City; (435) 586–7880

8. The Boulder Mountains

9. Cedar Breaks National Monument; (435) 586–9451

10. Panguitch Lake, Panguitch

Cedar Breaks National Monument (all ages)

Follow Utah Highway 14 to its junction with Highway 148, and then turn north to the monument; (435) 586–9451. Cedar Breaks is generally closed in the winter due to snow. Call for more information. Vehicles $, camping $$.

When you are in town, take an afternoon to visit Cedar Breaks National Monument, located about 20 miles from Cedar City. In a country filled with surprises, Cedar Breaks is one of the best surprises of all. This is a huge earthen coliseum, more than 2,000 feet deep and 3 miles across. It is surrounded by juniper and filled with spectacular colored rock and rock formations that have been shaped by millions of years of wind, rain, and snow. A 5-mile scenic drive around the perimeter features four lookouts that offer different perspectives on the view below. A great hiking trail for children is the 2-mile **Alpine Pond Trail,** which leads past intricate rock shapes, forest glades, and ponds. A thirty-site campground is open June through September, and has running water, rest rooms, and an amphitheater with nightly ranger talks.

Plant Life Changes at Different Altitudes

There is a variety of plant life in our state. As you gain or lose altitude, you'll notice different species.

- At 10,000 feet, you'll notice tundralike growth.

- At 9,000 feet, look for Englemann spruce and alpine fir.

- At 5,500 to 9,000 feet, look for quaking aspen, blue spruce, and Douglas fir.

- At 4,000 to 5,500 feet, look for piñon pine, juniper, lots of sagebrush—and more sagebrush.

- At 2,700 to 4,000 feet, look for creosote brush, Joshua trees, grasses, and still more sagebrush.

Where to Eat

Adriana's. 164 South 100 West; (435) 865–1234. American fine cuisine. $$–$$$

The Pastry Pub. 86 West Center Street; (435) 867–1400. $

Brad's Food Hut. 546 North Main; (435) 586–6358. American, fast food. $

Cowboys' Smoke House Café. 95 North Main Street, Panguitch; (435) 676–8030. $$

The Pizza Factory. 131 South Main Street; (435) 586–3900. $

A Taste of Hawaii. 64 North Main Street; (435) 586–1693. Hawaiian. $

Where to Stay

Abbey Inn. 940 West 200 North; (435) 586–9966. $$

Bard's Inn Bed and Breakfast. 150 South 100 West; (435) 586–6612 or (800) 586–6612. $$$

Garden Cottage Bed and Breakfast. 16 North 200 West; (435) 586–4919. $$$

Brian Head

Just a five-minute drive from Cedar Breaks, this place has the distinction of being the highest town in Utah. It exists mostly as a resort, and its beautiful surroundings are an anomaly of aspen and fir in a red-rock world. Brian Head perches on top of a 10,000-foot-high plateau—the altitude makes for a super ski resort in winter and a cool oasis in summer. Biking is very popular here, and in warm weather the winter chairlift is outfitted with bike racks to transport cyclists and their gear up to **Mountain Bike Park,** which accesses 40 miles of single-track trails. The trails are marked like ski runs, so cyclists can choose their skill level before starting out. Guided horseback rides are also popular in these mountains. Brian Head boasts restaurants, shops, more than 1,500 lodging rooms, and special events all through the summer. In September the town hosts an **Oktoberfest** celebration, complete with German food, oom-pah bands, and a guided bike tour known as the **Fall Colors Fat Tire Ride.** For all event and lodging information in Brian Head, call (435) 677–3101 or go to www.brianhead.com.

Easy Travel Tips: **Hiking with Your Kids**

A lot of the best places to see mean a little bit of hiking.

If you have younger children, you need to remember that walking to the destination is only half the battle—you still have to walk back. I can't count the number of times Abbey has walked in like a trooper, but decided she'd had enough on the way back, so I had to carry her. This gets really old fast—and it's hard on your back.

More hints: Let your child set the pace—not vice versa. Carry energy treats and plenty of water. Kids get dehydrated very quickly in this dry climate. Keep them drinking all the time—especially when you hike. Make sure you have good shoes on those growing feet. Stop often, take plenty of rests, and keep your patience. If you have to, do the carry-the-kid thing without getting mad. You want them to have fun with you outdoors.

Panguitch

This lovely town along U.S. Highway 89 is architecturally significant for its old, red-brick homes. A hundred years ago the town operated a brick kiln; each man who worked there was given enough bricks to build his own house. Many of these structures remain and are still inhabited. By the way, *panguitch* is a Paiute Indian word for "big fish," which people are still catching today at nearby Panguitch Lake. For information on events and lodging in the area, call (800) 444–6689.

Paunsagaunt Western Wildlife Museum (all ages)
250 East Center Street; (435) 676–2500. Open daily from May to October from 9:00 A.M. to 8:00 P.M. From November to April, call (702) 877–2664 to make an appointment. Admission $.

This museum features a large collection of stuffed animals that are displayed in re-created outdoor scenes, acting as they might have when they were alive. You'll see a skunk climbing a tree, a cougar tracking game, a deer enjoying a sunny afternoon, and more. There is also a display of exotic game animals from Africa, India, and Europe. Collections of fossils, weapons, tools, and artifacts can also be seen.

Bryce Canyon and Vicinity

Bryce is not really a canyon at all, but a high plateau with hundreds of amphitheaters carved from its southern effacement. Water is the principal architect here, with sudden summer storms sending rushing water from the top of the plateau down into the soft sandstone and winter ice and snow helping the erosive process with their freeze-thaw cycle. The spires that remain are topped by harder, protective rock called capstone, which helps stave off the water's effects.

Bryce is easily navigated. The 20-mile-long, two-lane road that follows the rim of the canyon neatly widens at each of twelve major viewpoints. At Bryce you don't have to work to see the big views—they're staring at you right there through your windshield, or even better, just a few steps out of your car to the plateau's very edge.

Bryce is open year-round, and a trip here in winter features stunning views. Picture pink-rock spires, covered with a white dusting, against a surround of electric blue sky. It's not wise to try and explain the power of beauty to anyone, but if you're going to have an epiphany, Bryce Canyon in winter is a pretty good locale. Snowshoes are loaned from the national park's visitor center on a first-come, first-served basis. It is great fun for older children to strap these old, luggy things on their feet and attempt a few miles down and up the winter trails. Cross-country skiing along the plateau's edge is also an excellent way to spend a day.

Red Canyon (all ages)
On Utah Highway 12; (435) 865–3700. For camping information call the Forest Service office in Panguitch at (435) 676–8815 or write to 1780 North Wedgewood Lane, Cedar City 84720.

Utah Highway 12, which turns east from U.S. Highway 89 just a few miles south of Panguitch, is a stunning drive and a destination unto itself. Your children will ooh and ahh as you pass through Dixie National Forest's Red Canyon, and experience the thrill of driving beneath two rock "tunnels." The visitor center at Red Canyon has good information about how and why this small patch of land, in the middle of a forest, is blessed with some of the brightest red rock anywhere. Guided horseback rides are available, and if you ask you will most likely be taken back into the untouched areas of the canyons to see a favorite hideout of outlaw Butch Cassidy. The campground here is very pleasant, and sites are available on a first-come, first-served basis.

Ruby's Inn (all ages)

East of Red Canyon, just before the Bryce Canyon National Park entrance. For reservations and seasonal information, call (435) 834–5341. Motel $–$$, hotel $$–$$$$.

The history of this destination resort actually pre-dates the park, and its owners had much to do with the park's inception. The third generation of Ruby Syrett's family now runs the resort, which is a year-round amalgam of things to do. Besides the usual lodging, swimming, grocery, camping, and restaurant services, Ruby's contracts for open-cockpit biplane rides over the park, helicopter and other charter flights, as well as van tours and park shuttles. Guided horseback and buggy rides to the canyon rim are available in the warm-weather months, and chuckwagon dinners complete with Western hoedowns can be booked Memorial Day through September. Your children will especially enjoy the Petting Farm at Ruby's, where various barnyard pets can be fed, as well as the nightly rodeo that shows off the considerable horse sophistry of the families and children who live in the area. In winter cross-country skiing is popular on miles of groomed trails.

Bryce Canyon National Park (all ages)

For all information, including campground, area lodging, and overnight facilities, call the park at (435) 834–5322 or write to Bryce Canyon National Park, P.O. Box 170001, Bryce Canyon 84717. There are a lodge and two campgrounds inside the park, along with a restaurant, grocery store, and gas station. North and Sunset campgrounds are open in late spring and close when water starts to freeze in the fall. They have a total of 218 sites, available on a first-come, first-served basis. No reservations are accepted. There is one group campsite available. The lodge is open April through October, and Western cabins and motel rooms are also available. Call (435) 834–5361 for reservations. Attractions within the park are highlighted below. Vehicles $$$$, good for seven days; camping per night $$.

Bryce is the "fairy princess" of Utah's national parks, and its hundreds of acres of densely placed, delicate pink spires and turrets are the most feminine of rock formations anywhere. The early Anglo settlers' names for the rocks remain today—Queen's Garden, the Grand Staircase, and Fairy Castle, to name a few. Earlier Paiute Indian residents saw the rocks in a more surreal light. They named the area Land of the Legend People, and believed the chimney-shaped rocks were evil folks who had been turned to stone, right in the midst of saying bad things. If you're ever down inside the canyon at dusk, look up at the monolith "faces," and remember this legend—you'll know just what those Indians had in mind. The park takes its name from one of the first Mormon pioneers who tried to run cattle in the area. Ebenezer Bryce will forever be remembered by his statement of exasperation over the myriad hiding places in the canyon: "It's a hell of a place to lose a cow!"

The top of the plateau remains intact, and is a surprise to people who come looking for the rock expanses and sunset colors for which Bryce is famous. The flat top of Bryce supports a vast evergreen forest and many kinds of wildlife. Wildflowers bloom throughout summer, spring, and fall. Autumn is a wonderful time to visit, when the aspens turn bright yellow against the green of the pines. One note of warning: The ground squirrels in the area have become so tame that they harbor no fear of humans. Don't feed these animals—park signs everywhere warn that they may carry disease.

Fairyland Point is located just inside the park boundary, and you'll see its turnoff sign before you reach the pay station. You're overlooking Fairyland Canyon here, a petite, self-contained bowl well worth the mile drive off the main road. Immediately after passing the pay station, you'll find the **visitor center** on your left. This is a good place for all sorts of information including weather, hikes, wildflowers, ranger talks, and an orientation slide show. If you would like to take a guided walk with a ranger, ask for the schedule. You will also find rest rooms here.

Easy Travel Tips: **Diaper Wipes Are the Greatest Invention**

It doesn't matter if you have a baby or not. Diaper wipes (sometimes called moist towelettes) are a must for any traveler. This is the greatest invention since sliced bread.

Sure they're great for baby bottoms, but did you know they are one of the best stain removers ever invented? Spill something on your shirt or pants and notice how a baby wipe lifts the stain.

Here are a few other uses: napkin after a messy meal, hand washer, face washer. They work great for spit baths, for cleaning shoes, for when that outhouse is out of paper. You can also use wipes for cleaning picnic tables and cooling off hot feet.

Throw a box in your car!

Next up are **Sunrise** and **Sunset Points,** with their exponentially expanded views. You're overlooking the **Bryce Amphitheater** from both of these pullouts, and it seems as if you can see most of the world in the distance. Closer up, just below the concrete, find the famous exposed-root pine trees, which continue in a most steadfast way to survive, even though their underpinnings are continually being washed downward. Notice the birds that enjoy showing off their skills here, swooping through the canyon and making sudden, picture-perfect stops on top of the pinnacles.

Inspiration Point is a favorite viewpoint because of its vista of **Silent City.** If you've seen any of a dozen science fiction movies that portray an abandoned metropolis, you'll have something of an idea of Silent City's power. Narrow ridges topped by thousands of delicate spindles lie packed together, resembling the most ethereal, golden-pink interpretation of urbanity. It's made absolutely eerie by its lack of emanating sound—in other words, this is well worth the short climb down a trail to get a better look.

Following a spur road from Inspiration, you'll reach **Paria Viewpoint,** where you'll look down 500 feet and beyond, witnessing the work of the Paria River. The cliffs that span out from this point are "failing," in geographical terms. Their broken spines have quit trying to shake off the prevailing erosional forces, and are quietly, magnificently, being returned to the canyon floor. Luckily for your family, this process will take another thousand-or-so years, and your children's children will look out on approximately this same view. Nearby is **Bryce Point,** also named after Ebenezer Bryce. Mr. Bryce built a road from his canyon-floor ranch to the bottom of these cliffs for the purpose of transporting wood. Folks took to calling the area "Bryce's Canyon," and the name stuck.

The Indians Call It **River Muddy**

If you've been around during spring run-off, you'll agree the Paria River gets its name honestly.

The Paiutes called the Paria "the big river muddy." The water starts humbly in the region we now call the Dixie National Forest and Bryce Canyon National Park and feeds into the Colorado River by Lee's Ferry.

Along the way, the river has carved out some incredible scenery, including canyons 1,500 feet deep. Of special note, look for a 200-foot arch in Paria Canyon.

Farview Viewpoint is aptly, though not exactly inspirationally, named. Look for **Molly's Nipple,** a most interesting formation for the grade-schoolers in your family, and look more closely for the big natural bridge down below. **Natural Bridge, Agua Canyon, Ponderosa Canyon,** and **Yovimpa Point** follow, in full splendor.

And then the last stop, **Rainbow Point.** Here is a world-class view, and also a world-famous pine tree. The pine is a bristlecone, and when you look at this old, gnarled thing you may wonder why it's noteworthy. It is because this tree and its relatives are thought to be the longest living things on the planet. This particular specimen is about 1,800 years old, and it has survived by being tough and frugal with its resources. During drought years these pines actually kill off parts of themselves in order to save other parts. During years of heavy rainfall they soak up moisture and keep it in their secret places. The needles on the tree remain for decades.

The turnoff viewpoints are wonderful, but to really get the feel of Bryce, take a hike down into the canyon and surround yourself with rock formations. There are about twenty-three self-guided walking trails in the park, and more than a dozen are well managed by children. Bring water and snacks along in a day pack, and take it easy. Bryce's elevation is about 8,000 feet, and the thin air can leave you breathless. One more word of caution: The trails are carved from the surrounding rock, and they often are sprinkled by tiny stones that can act as ball bearings for human feet. The drop-offs from many of the trails are sheer cliffs, so be careful.

If you don't have all day, two good hikes to choose are Navajo Loop and Queen's Garden Trail. **Navajo Loop** travels 1¼ miles past some of Bryce's more famous landmarks. You've probably seen pictures of **Thor's Hammer** (next to Delicate Arch in Arches National Park, perhaps the most photographed piece of stone in Utah), and if so, you'll recognize it on this trail. Look for the **Pope, Two Bridges,** and the wedded pine trees that, together, have managed to find their place in the sun. Near its end (or beginning, depending on which direction you choose), this trail takes you up a steep set of switchbacks. A short side trail leads to a view of Silent City, which is described above.

Queen's Garden Trail is 1½ miles or so down and back up the canyon, courtesy of a self-guided, signpost-marked tour. This trail begins at Sunrise Point and ends at Queen's Garden, named after the big stone face of Queen Victoria that peers from on high. There are rest benches here, which you may want to use before you turn around and head back out and up this nonloop trail.

If you do have all day and your children are feeling adventurous, you might want to try the **Rim Trail,** which travels 11 miles (yes, 11, but the trail is fairly level and this hike is rated easy-to-moderate) from Fairyland Point to Bryce Point. Take a lot of food and water and prepare for much picture taking on this most-scenic hike. If you get tired along the way, you can always veer off at any of the car park viewpoints, and figure out a way to get back to your own automobile.

Another suggestion is tackling a section of the **Under-the-Rim Trail,** which travels the entire length of the canyon for 22.5 miles. Consider coming back for another visit and backpacking the entire rim trail, which takes two to three days to complete and requires a heavy backpack and a lot of steep up-and-downs. Information on permits, water, and campsites is found at the visitor center.

A good rule of thumb is to hike in the park early in the morning. One reason is that Bryce is a south-facing canyon and the morning light is spectacular. If you have the wherewithal to get to Sunrise Point at sunrise, clouds permitting, you'll have an unforgettable experience. Another reason for early morning hikes is the heat and crowds at Bryce in the summer months. (Bryce's high elevation makes for snowy and cold winters and fewer visitors, so attendance is down.) A workable plan is to get up early, hike a few miles, then have breakfast at beautiful **Bryce Canyon Lodge,** which is located inside the park, and then take the loop drive and stop and ogle at every one of the pullouts.

For younger kids, the **Mossy Cave** trail is a treat, because it is short and mostly level. To get there, retrace the park road to rejoin Utah Highway 12, which runs across the northern edge of the park. Follow it east into Water Canyon. The trailhead for this 0.4-mile walk is marked by a small parking lot. Hikers are surrounded by the red rock that Bryce Canyon is famous for, and kids find the trail easy and fun. At the end of the trail is a waterfall and a small mossy cave.

Canyon Trail Rides (all ages)
The sign-up counter for the rides is located inside Bryce Canyon Lodge; however, advance reservations are strongly recommended. Call (435) 679–8665 or write P.O. Box 128, Tropic 84776 for more information. $$$$.

Another fun way to see the park from April to October is on horseback. Canyon Trail Rides offers two-hour and half-day trips into the canyon. Children five and older are allowed on the shorter ride, and ages eight and older are allowed on the longer ride.

Bring Infant Supplies from Home When Heading to the Wilds of Utah

Don't plan on getting what you need in rural areas.

If you have young children and are traveling by car, bring diapers, formula, baby food, medicines, and other related items from home. In rural areas, retail stores are few and far between (most are gas/convenience stops). And, if you can find what you want, it will be very expensive.

If you are flying into Utah and renting a car, plan on stopping at a store in one of the more populated areas before heading out to the wilds.

Cannonville

Kodachrome Basin State Park (all ages)
Travel 9 miles south of Cannonville on a partially paved road. For reservations and general information, call (435) 679–8562. Vehicles $.

Just south of this small ranching town is one of the weirder configurations of rock formations you will ever see, and that's a promise. A unique geologic history has fashioned the rock here into free-standing petrified sand pipes and petrified geysers, which jut up all over a valley known as Kodachrome Basin State Park. The name reflects the colors of the rock, which glow surrealistically at sunrise and sunset, and change shades throughout the day. Several marked hiking trails weave throughout the basin, and offer a closer look at this natural oddity. Biking on these trails is another good way to see the park. The campground here has hot showers and rest rooms. A concessionaire provides horseback and stagecoach rides. A short side trip from the park leads to **Grosvenor Arch,** a huge double arch that is well worth the effort of finding it. This road is passable only in good weather.

Escalante

The isolated area surrounding Escalante, east of Cannonville on Utah Highway 12, is one of the last frontiers to be explored in the United States. It was not mapped until the mid-1800s, and the Pony Express carried mail here through the first part of the twentieth century. Today Escalante offers all of the modern amenities—lodging, restaurants, gas, and a great park for kids.

Beautiful Calf Creek Falls (all ages)

Twelve miles east of Escalante on Utah Highway 12; (435) 826–4291.
Campsites are available on a first-come, first-served basis; per night, $.

If you haven't been impressed by the overwhelming beauty of Utah yet, you're definitely in trouble. But if you do think that a little more persuasion would be nice, Calf Creek is the place for you and your family.

When you arrive at the small campground be sure to find a spot quickly. The sites are offered only on a first-come, first-served basis and you could be left without a place to stay if you wait too long. If you only plan on spending a day, there is plenty of room for a picnic along the trail or in the campground.

The 2½-mile hike to the falls at Calf Creek—in Calf Creek National Recreation Area—is very level, and even younger children should handle it without any difficulty. One warning: Be sure to carry water, especially in late spring or summer. The area is very dry and the heat can be suffocating.

At the spectacular waterfall, which plunges from atop a sandstone cliff, you will be tempted to jump right in. The water is beautiful, but extremely cold; be prepared for a shock if you dare take the plunge. It's a good place to take off your shoes and wade on a hot day.

Be sure to pick up a brochure at the start of the trail. It is full of wonderful tips and interesting facts about the area. The trail even has numbered stopping points, which coincide with information in the brochure. This gives you a chance to catch your breath and enjoy various wildflowers, pioneer farming artifacts, trees, Anasazi ruins, and even petroglyphs along the way.

Escalante State Park (all ages)

Advance reservations for a campsite can be made by calling (800) 322–3770 during business hours. For more information on the park, call (435) 826–4466 or write to 710 North Reservoir Road, Escalante 84726. Vehicles $, camping $$$.

Escalante State Park is a vast storehouse of petrified wood—huge pieces; tiny; twisted pieces; and everything in between. The park's two trails wind past fallen forests that have turned to rock, the bones of ancient dinosaurs, and petroglyphs and remnants of ancient Indian dwellings. Amazingly, there is a wetland bird-viewing site in the park—one of the few in southern Utah. Wide Hollow Reservoir rims the park, and trout fishing is popular here. Escalante State Park is found just west of town. It has a visitor center and campground.

Hell's Backbone (all ages)
Utah Highway 12, east of Calf Creek Falls.

From Calf Creek Falls, keep heading east on Highway 12, for one of the most thrilling car rides anywhere. When you approach Hell's Backbone, you'll know it. This twisty section of the road falls away dramatically on either side, leaving no room for error on the part of the driver. What you see spread out below is called Box Death Hollow, and it is a favorite primitive area for backpackers.

Utah's Newest **National Monument**

Grand Staircase–Escalante National Monument is Utah's newest addition to the national park system.

In September 1996, by presidential decree, 1.7 million rugged acres of cliffs, canyons, rocks, badlands, plateaus, rivers, and desert became the people's. In case you wondered, sections of the newest national monument were some of the last bits of real estate left to be explored.

The Grand Staircase is a splendid collection of sandstone cliffs ranging from the Grand Canyon to Bryce Canyon. The other part of this newest monument is formed by the Escalante River—there are wonderful side canyons and tall, many-colored bluffs.

Boulder

Just getting to this town, northeast of Escalante on Utah Highway 12, is an adventure. To the north the road leads through the Dixie National Forest, with myriad hiking and camping possibilities. To the south is some of the most dramatic desert country in the world. Due east is the Burr Trail, a partly paved road that twists and careens all the way to Lake Powell. Smack in the midst of it all is little Boulder, for years a quiet ranching community, and just now beginning to take on the look of a tourist destination.

Anasazi Indian Village State Park (all ages)
Utah Highway 12 in Boulder. For information call (435) 335–7308. Admission $.

A park in town pays tribute to the area's ancient inhabitants. Anasazi Indian Village State Park preserves the site of one of the largest Anasazi communities west of the Colorado River, occupied by "the ancients" from A.D. 1050 to 1200. The visitor center here does an excellent job of interpreting ancient life, and just beyond it are real artifacts and ruins that are accessed on self-guided trails.

Kanab

Countless Western movies have been filmed in and around this "authentic" looking town, on U.S. Highway 89, south of Panguitch. Sometimes Kanab is known as "Little Hollywood."

Old Paria and the Johnson Canyon Set (all ages)
Old Paria is located just a few miles off U.S. Highway 89 between Kanab and Lake Powell. The Johnson Canyon set is 9 miles from Kanab on U.S. Highway 89. Admission $.

Several old movie sets in this region are now tourist attractions. Old Paria was built in 1963 for the movie *Sergeants Three,* and it still stands. Only ten minutes from Kanab is the Johnson Canyon set, where all of the outdoor scenes from the TV series *Gunsmoke* were filmed. It is open for tours during the summer, and visitors may walk down the streets and peer inside the vacant buildings of Dodge.

Coral Pink Sand Dunes State Park (all ages)
Twelve miles west of U.S. Highway 89. Call (435) 648–2800 for park information and (800) 322–3770 for camping reservations. Vehicles $, camping $$$.

Picture fine sand the color of the inside of an exotic sea shell. Then picture tall hills of this sand stretching for as far as your eyes can see. You will now have an idea of what Coral Pink Sand Dunes State Park looks like. This mind-blowing place is just a few miles from U.S. Highway 89, but several planets from Earth in terms of scenery. For several thousand years the surrounding colorful rock has been evolving into these dunes, and the result is a huge playground of bright pink sand. Needless to say, photographic opportunities are many. Children will enjoy hiking on the nature trail and the short boardwalk trail that leads to an overlook. Drivers of off-highway vehicles love this park, too. The park is open year-round, and has a campground with rest rooms and showers.

Almost a Ghost Town . . . **and a Real One**

Take a side trip into the past—and the not-so-recent past. Tell your kids they are going to a ghost town!

As you drive into Paria, pay attention to the many-colored strata: the purple, the white, the red, the steel-blue. It's lovely.

As you drive into the generous parking lot, what you'll see looks like a ghost town—the weathered boards, sun bleached, sandblasted. The dusty appearance. What you are looking at is an abandoned movie set for Westerns from Hollywood's heydays in the 1930s. It's interesting to explore the set, still in pretty good, ghost-town shape.

After this adventure, if you want to explore a real ghost town, you can. If you have a four-wheel-drive vehicle, follow the dirt road, or take a nice walk. It's about a mile. The site you'll find is a real ghost town first settled in 1865.

How to get there: On U.S. Highway 89, look for milepost 31. Then it's a lovely 5-mile trip down a dirt road, and you're nearly there. The dirt road is in pretty good shape, but it can be rutted. (There is also a camping spot near the parking lot if you want to throw up a tent.)

Where to Eat

Escobar's Mexican Restaurant. 373 East 300 South; (435) 644–3739. $

Nedra's Too. 310 South 100 East; (435) 644–2030. Mexican. $

Wok Inn. 86 South 200 West; (435) 644–5400. Chinese. $$

Where to Stay

Holiday Inn Express. 815 East Highway 89; (435) 644–8888. $$

Kanab Mission Inn. 386 East 300 South; (435) 644–5373. $

Quail Park Lodge. 125 Highway 89 North; (435) 644–5094. $

Color Country Inn. 1550 South Highway 89A; (435) 644–2164. $$

A Rutter Family Adventure: **Four-Wheeling the Coral Pink Sand Dunes**

It might not be "PC," but I'll admit it anyway.

Sometimes I love to four-wheel drive. (In fact, I don't own a vehicle that isn't a four-wheel drive.) I enjoy locking it in low range, rolling down the windows, blasting the stereo, and pounding the off-road with a vengeance. We're all belted in, of course.

I suppose at best, I'm only a cultured redneck. I never played with trucks as a boy—so maybe I'm making up for it now. I love driving around the dunes in my Trooper, grinding the gears. If you like four-wheeling, motorcycling, or quading, this is a great place to do it. There's a lot of open space to tear across. My kids love the "grrr" of the engine and the fresh air.

This is also a good place to hike and look (which I also dearly love to do, too). But somehow, this park seems "machinery" oriented. It's a beautiful place that calls for horsepower (not too PC, is it?). I'll go for a long walk to try and self-correct this character flaw.

Springdale

The big deal around these parts is Zion National Park. The park literally surrounds the town of Springdale, and if you're driving from the direction of Kanab, you'll pay a fee at the park's eastern entrance and drive Utah Highway 9 through the park before reaching Springdale.

Zion National Park (all ages)

The visitor center in the park is located at the south entrance and is open daily year-round from 8:00 A.M. to 5:00 P.M., with longer hours in the summer. The congenial rangers here will help you plan a visit that fits the needs of your family; you'll also find books, topographic maps, and **free** brochures. A descriptive film is shown every half hour. For more information call (435) 772–3256, or write Zion National Park, Springdale 84767. Vehicles $$$$, people $$, camping $$.

Zion is a friendly, grand old national park, and one of the most family-oriented places in Utah. There are many small, fun hikes here, with stupendous scenery along the way and stunning scenic finales at trail's end. There are hundreds of flowers, animals, and rock formations to identify and make up names for, and even in the hottest summer weather, there is always a shady picnic spot to be found in Zion Canyon.

If Zion seems tame and orderly compared to Utah's other national parks, it could be because of its longevity and history. Zion is Utah's first park, and one of the oldest national parks in the nation. A section of the current park was set aside as a monument in 1909 by President Taft. In 1918 the monument was enlarged and given the name Zion. In 1919 it was made a national park by an act of Congress. Many of Zion's trails and viewpoints were marked and interpreted decades ago. Most of the trails are hard-packed, and some are even paved. There's a feeling here that the area is comfortable and safe.

The park's size may also be a factor in its homey feeling. While the actual boundaries are immense—147,000 acres—**Zion Canyon,** where most tourists congregate and the aforementioned small hikes are located, is relatively small. About 6 miles long, the canyon is as deep as it is wide until it terminates at the **Narrows,** a seasonably hikable section averaging 2,000-foot-high cliffs and a streambed 50 feet wide. The canyon's 6 miles contain about 60,000 miles worth of scenery. Anyone who has wandered in Zion's sandstone glow, or ventured into its cool grotto canyons, knows that words are not enough to explain its appeal. Visitors young and old alike are awestruck by its magnificent splendor. Famous natural stone landmarks such as the **Watchman,** the **Sentinel, Court of the Patriarchs,** and **Mountain of the Sun** must be viewed at least once in a lifetime. It is said that nonreligious explorers named many of the stone monuments here, but that none other than religious terms could be found to describe Zion's grandeur. You'll notice that temples, cathedrals, patriarchs, thrones, and angels are common.

The Virgin River **as Sculptor**

The Virgin River watershed is one of Utah's great sculptors, carving some of the state's most spectacular canyons. Below Zion, pay close attention to Hurricane Cliffs. This is artistry on a high level.

As you look at the tall mesas and ponder the deep canyons etched by the forces of erosion, think about what the land might have looked like one or two million years ago.

The Virgin is one of four main water systems (including Kanab Creek, Paria River, and Escalante River) that left its mark upon this part of the world.

The **Virgin River,** original architect of the landscape, runs a green, lazy course through the red rock, and still continues its canyon design, carrying the equivalent of 180 carloads of ground rock out of the park each day.

Some of the hikes best suited for children are the trails to **Weeping Rock,** a ½-mile, self-guided trail, ending at a rock alcove that features dripping springs and hanging gardens of wildflowers; **Emerald Pools,** a 1.2-mile round trip that leads past three waterfalls and the small pools they have created; and **Riverside Walk,** a paved 2-mile walk that follows the Virgin River upstream, past hanging gardens and marshy wetlands, to The Narrows. The trail to Angels Landing and the **West Rim** is a more challenging hike for young children, but it has sections along the way, such as **Walter's Wiggles** and **Refrigerator Canyon** (where early inhabitants once stored their perishables), that work as a hike terminus.

The **Canyon Overlook** hike requires a drive out of Zion Canyon along Mt. Carmel Highway to just east of a long tunnel. This 1-mile in-and-out trail passes under low-hanging rocks and by (but not too close to) steep drop-offs to end at a spectacular viewpoint of Zion and Pine Creek canyons. A good guidebook that interprets the plant and animal life along this trail is available at the visitor center. And speaking of Zion's long tunnel, you'll want to take a drive through this engineering marvel, constructed in 1930. It carves through rough terrain to connect lower Zion Canyon with the high plateaus to the east. Look around when you enter, because when you exit the landscape will look very different. On one side are the massive cliff walls of Zion Canyon, and on the other are fantastically eroded colorful sandstone formations. Be sure to notice **Checkerboard Mesa,** which is crisscrossed with cracks into a surprisingly geometric pattern. Between April and October, visitors need to use the free shuttle provided daily from 5:30 A.M. to 11:00 P.M.; it makes a continuous loop along the Zion Canyon Scenic Drive.

Watching nature is a favorite pastime at Zion, and the park is very obliging with its diversity and depth of "watchables." In spring, summer, and fall showy flowers can be seen. Look for the purple Zion daisy and the bright red cardinal monkeyflower, two of a family of 899 plant species found in the park. More than sixty species of birds are permanent residents, as well as sixty-eight species of mammals, thirty-six different reptiles, and seven amphibians. To help children ages six through twelve learn about the natural environment, Zion offers a Junior Ranger Program, held during the summer at the Zion Nature Center. The two campgrounds in this section of the park are open on a first-come basis. Both have fire grates, picnic tables, water, and modern rest rooms.

Zion Lodge (all ages) ⊝ ⊛ ⊕

Advance reservations are recommended; call (435) 772–3213 or go to www.zionlodge.com for lodging information and reservations.

Zion Lodge, located inside Zion Canyon, features motel units and rustic cabins as well as a restaurant and gift shop. Guided horseback rides are available from May through October. Make reservations at the lodge, or by calling in advance.

Zion Canyon Cinemax Theater (all ages)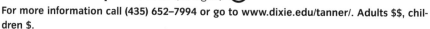
145 Zion Park Boulevard; (435) 772–2400 or (888) 256–3456; zioncanyontheater.com. Adults $$, children $.

When you've finished with Zion's natural wonders, head back into Springdale for a man-made adventure at the local Zion Canyon Cinemax Theater. The film shown here was made especially for Zion, and is known as *Treasure of the Gods*. It is thirty-seven minutes long, shown on the hour, and is designed "to enhance the visitor's Zion National Park experience by exploring Zion's hidden treasures and legends." The 500-seat theater is famous for having one of the world's largest screens (six stories high by 80 feet wide), and its effect is to draw you inside the action and make you feel one with the film. The theater complex includes a visitor center, gift shop, bookstore, art gallery, deli, and picnic areas.

The Kaibab Plateau: The Staircase

The Kaibab Plateau runs from the Grand Canyon country into Utah.

The northern part is a series of "terrace plateaus," according to the great explorer John Wesley Powell. They rise like a series of steps—a grand staircase. In many places, the plateau is 8,000 feet high and is forested—and haunted by many big game animals.

O. C. Tanner Amphitheater (all ages)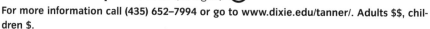
For more information call (435) 652–7994 or go to www.dixie.edu/tanner/. Adults $$, children $.

Another summer night's outing can be enjoyed outdoors at the O. C. Tanner Amphitheater. There, a rousing multimedia production called *The Grand Circle: A National Park Odyssey* spotlights the eight national parks and other scenic wonders that are within a day's drive of Springdale. The program is projected onto a large screen, with the cliffs of Zion acting as a dramatic backdrop.

Where to Eat

Bit & Spur Saloon. 1212 Zion Park Boulevard; (435) 772–3498. $$

Where to Stay

Harvest House Bed and Breakfast. 29 Canyon View Drive; (435) 772–3880. $$$

Under the Eaves. 980 Zion Park Boulevard; (435) 772–3457. $$$

Rockville

There are several lovely bed-and-breakfasts in this tiny burg that cater to visitors to Zion National Park. If you cross the river and head about 2 miles west of Rockville, you will see the signed turnoff for Grafton, one of the better preserved ghost towns in the West.

Grafton (all ages)
2 miles west of Rockville.

Grafton was originally settled by Mormon farmers in the 1860s, but disease, floods, and a war with the Blackhawk Indians caused the town to be abandoned early in the twentieth century. Several buildings here are still fairly intact—a brick church is the most notable. If you and your children have seen the movie *Butch Cassidy and the Sundance Kid*, you might recognize Grafton as the backdrop of the bicycle scene. A short distance north of town is its old cemetery, where the grave markers make an interesting historical record.

St. George

A decade or so ago St. George, just north of the Arizona border, was a sleepy desert town, known mostly as a gas stop on the way to Las Vegas. Much has changed since then. Because of its favorable climate, St. George's population has grown exponentially in the last ten years. Its main street is now a mile-long shopping, eating, and lodging opportunity. But there is one constant in St. George, and that is the beauty of its surrounding landscape. Wonderful hikes and biking trails for children, as well as beautiful canyons and vistas, rim the town.

Brigham Young's Winter Home (all ages)
67 West 200 North. Open daily from 9:00 A.M. to 7:00 P.M. Memorial Day to Labor Day; until 5:00 P.M. the rest of the year. Admission is free. Call (435) 673–2517 for more information.

The city's mild winter climate was not lost on the early pioneers. During Brigham Young's lifetime, St. George was winter headquarters for the LDS Church. Young spent much time here, especially during the last years of his life when he suffered from rheumatism. His century-old winter home and the surrounding grounds have been restored.

St. George Temple (all ages)

440 South 300 East. For more information call (435) 673–5181.

The temple is open only to Mormon faithful, but the grounds are available to everyone. Volunteers in the visitor center will give tours and explain local history.

Fiesta Family Fun Center (all ages)

171 East 1160 South; (435) 628–1818; www.fiestafuncenter.com. Open daily from 10:00 A.M. to 11:00 P.M.

For a more raucous outing, head for the Fiesta Family Fun Center. This huge entertainment complex has go-carts, bumper boats, batting cages, mini-golf, a video arcade and driving range, and, of course, pizza and snacks to appeal to every young appetite. All activities are paid for individually, although books of tickets may be purchased, and value packs are available.

Zion Factory Stores (all ages)

At St. George Boulevard's junction with I–15, at 250 North Red Cliffs Drive; (435) 674–9800. Open Monday through Saturday 10:00 A.M. to 8:00 P.M. and Sunday 10:00 A.M. to 5:00 P.M.

One of the state's better outlet-center malls is found on the eastern edge of town. Zion Factory Stores features high-end, name-brand merchandise at discount prices. The mall has food service and rest rooms. For more information call the number listed above.

Rosenbruch Wildlife Museum (all ages)

1835 Convention Center Drive; (435) 656–0033; www.rosenbruch.org. Adults $$, children $.

This museum allows you to travel the world without ever leaving St. George. Replicated habitats from every continent contain nearly every type of large mammal in the world. Visitors will see more than 200 species, many of which are posed as if in motion. Hand-held wands provide visitors with information about the animals they are seeing. This 25,000-square-foot building also contains a theater, an art gallery, and an extensive insect collection. Children will be pleased to explore the petting room.

Arts Festival (all ages)

On Main Street. The festival takes place on Friday and Saturday of Easter weekend from 10:00 A.M. to dusk. Call (435) 634–5850 for more information.

St. George is a favorite destination for spring vacationers because T-shirt weather arrives here much earlier than in the colder, northern part of the state. If you happen to be one of the flock of tourists who arrive here for Easter weekend, you'll want to check out the Arts Festival. Several blocks on Main Street are closed off to traffic for this event, which features hundreds of fine art booths, as well as food and entertainment. A special area is set aside for children, with games, crafts, and scheduled performances especially geared for a younger age group.

The Joshua Tree Forest: **A Different World**

Going into the Joshua Tree region, no water, no shade, strange-looking tree, is, according to my son, Jon-Michael, "like going into the TDZ" (True Desert Zone).

Welcome to the fringe of the great Mojave Desert—and you're still in Utah! This is one of the driest, harshest, hottest, most wonderful places on earth. You'll find Joshua Tree in the southwest tip of the state, off Highway 91. It's a unique desert and worth a visit. This is Bureau of Land Management country. The area is laced with dirt roads you can drive on and get up close to this heavenly hell. But don't just drive, hike a few miles through this unique desert.

We always look for one of the desert tortoises that roam the place, but we've never seen one (yet). Take along a lot of water, a hat, sunscreen, and a walking stick. March and April are very pleasant times of the year to hike about—it's even green and flowers bloom. If the weather is warm, do your hiking in the morning and evening. Keep an eye out for rattlesnakes (why I take the stick). Also, if you hike with kids, keep them hydrated—even if you have to insist. This land will suck the moisture right out of you.

Snow Canyon State Park (all ages)

Find Snow Canyon by following Utah Highway 18 northwest from St. George for 10 miles. A 36-unit campground with rest rooms and showers is open year-round, and reservations are accepted. Call (435) 628–2255 for park information. Admission $.

One of the canyons near town is so spectacular it has been preserved as a state park. Snow Canyon State Park is a relatively small area with a vast collection of geologic wonders. Volcanic cones, deep-red sandstone cliffs, twisted layers of rock, and sand dunes populate the narrow area between two steep cliff walls. An official scenic backway charts a paved path through the canyon, and it is possible to see its beauty without leaving your car. But, of course, a better experience is gained by hiking or biking in the canyon, or taking advantage of the guided horse trips that are available here. A surprising array of plants and animals thrive in this desert climate, including two endangered species: the desert tortoise and the gila monster. Petroglyphs and ruins are evidence that the area was occupied by the Anasazi Indians more than 800 years ago. The park is open year-round, but summer can be uncomfortably hot. Try to time your visit during the months of October through May for optimum weather—which brings up the subject of snow: Snow Canyon rarely receives any. It is named after a pair of pioneer settlers by the name of Snow (their first names were Lorenzo and Erastus).

Tuacahn/Heritage Arts Center (all ages) 🎵
Located just south of Snow Canyon on Utah Highway 18, at 1100 Tuacahn Drive, Ivins. The productions run June through early October of each year, Monday through Saturday nights. When you order your tickets, ask about the Western Dutch-oven dinner that can be included in the evening's activities. For ticket prices and other information, call (800) 746–9882 or go to www.tuacahn.com.

Tuacahn and its adjacent Heritage Arts Center host *UTAH!*, an epic musical drama that tells the story of this area's early pioneers and explorers. The backdrop for this production is the natural surround of a red-rock canyon. *UTAH!* is famous for its complicated special effects, which include lightning bolts, raging floods, cascading waterfalls, and howling coyotes. Tuacahn produces up to four musicals each year.

Where to Eat

China Palace. 195 South Bluff; (435) 673–0068. Chinese. $

2 Fat Guys Pizza. 144 West Brigham Road, #16; (435) 688–9775. Pizza. $

JB's Restaurant. 1245 South Main; (435) 628–3714. American. $

The Palms at the Holiday Inn. 850 South Bluff Street; (435) 628–4235. American. $$$

China King. 844 East St. George Boulevard; (435) 673–5656. Chinese. $$$

Where to Stay

Best Western Travel Inn. 316 East St. George Boulevard; (435) 673–3541. $$

Budget 8. 1230 South Bluff; (435) 628–5234. $

Green Gate Village. 76 West Tabernacle; (435) 628–6999. $$$

Seven Wives Inn. 217 North 100 West; (435) 628–3737. $$–$$$$

Hurricane

This thriving small town a few miles north of St. George was supposedly named after a whirlwind, which snapped the top off a settler's buggy and caused him to exclaim, "Well, that was a hurricane!" These days Hurricane is known for its fishing, warm weather, and even an international manufacturing company.

Chums (all ages)

101 South Main; (435) 635–5200; www.chums.com. Open Monday through Friday 9:00 A.M. to 5:00 P.M. and Saturday 10:00 A.M. to 5:00 P.M.

Hurricane is world headquarters for a company called Chums, which is famous for the manufacture of an item called an eyeglass retainer. The retainers fit onto your glasses and around the back of your head, saving you from losing your spectacles. Chums also makes caps, T-shirts, and other cotton clothing, and everything comes in kid and adult sizes.

Trout Pond at Zion View Ranch (all ages)

Head left at Chums and go up the hill for 3 miles. At mile marker 19 turn right on a dirt road. You'll pass by a whole bunch of ostriches, and finally reach the pond. For more information call (435) 674–4080. Full day $$$$, adult half day $$$$, child half day $$$.

From the Chums store it is just a few minutes' drive to a really fun fishing pond. The pond is privately owned and you must follow some complicated directions before you can dip in your reel, but if your children love to fish it is well worth the effort. First, go to St. George to the Hurst Ben Franklin store and find the sporting goods section. Then ask about the trout pond at Zion View Ranch. A reservation will be made for you, and you will be issued a pass, which you must have when you go to the ranch.

Where to Stay

Travelodge. 280 West State; (435) 635–4647. $$

Kanarraville

Kolob Canyons (all ages)

Find the turnoff to Kolob at exit 40 on I–15. For more information call (435) 586–9548.

This northwestern section of Zion National Park is known as the Kolob Canyons. Here an ancient stream has carved spectacular canyons from the stone of Kolob Terrace. Pick up a road guide at the visitor center, and then choose between two paved roads to see this area. The Kolob Canyons Road will take you 5 miles and a millennium back in time through Finger Canyons and terminate at a wonderful viewpoint; the Kolob Terrace Road overlooks the colorful cliffs of North Creek. A visitor center at the canyon entrance has a bookstore and rangers who will help you decide which of several hikes will best suit the abilities of your family.

Top Annual Events in Southwestern Utah

EASTER WEEKEND
Arts Festival, St. George; (435) 634–5850

SUMMER
Junior Ranger Program, Zion National
Park; (801) 772–0169

MAY THROUGH SEPTEMBER
Rodeo, Ruby's Inn, Bryce Canyon; (801)
834–5341

JUNE THROUGH OCTOBER
Shakespeare Festival, Cedar City; (435)
586–7880 for info, (800) PLAYTIX for tickets

SEPTEMBER
Oktoberfest, Brian Head; (888) 677–3101

General Index

E

F

N

O

P

Activities Index